Also by William Lindesay

Wild Wall–The Jiankou Years
Great Wall, Beautiful Jade: My China Loves
The Great Wall in 50 Objects
The Great Wall Explained
The Great Wall Revisited
Images of Asia: The Great Wall
Marching with Mao: A Biographical Journey
Alone on the Great Wall

WILD WALL

THE FOUNDATION YEARS

WILLIAM LINDESAY

Wild Wall–The Foundation Years

By William Lindesay

ISBN-13: 978-988-8769-39-1

© 2022 William Lindesay

BIOGRAPHY & AUTOBIOGRAPHY

EB155

All rights reserved. No part of this book may be reproduced in material form, by any means, whether graphic, electronic, mechanical or other, including photocopying or information storage, in whole or in part. May not be used to prepare other publications without written permission from the publisher except in the case of brief quotations embodied in critical articles or reviews. For information contact info@earnshawbooks.com

Published by Earnshaw Books Ltd. (Hong Kong)

To the Lindesays, of the past, present and future

I should like to rise and go...
Where the Great Wall round China goes

Excerpt from *Travel* by Robert Louis Stevenson (1850-1894)

Contents

FOREWORD
by Dame Barbara Woodward DCMG OBE ... 1

AUTHOR'S INTRODUCTION
From Wallasey to the Great Wall ... 4

PROLOGUE
In Ancient Times, My Time, and Time Again ... 8

I – Stepping Stones (1956-1986) ... 19

    1 The Adventurer in Me ... 21
    2 My Discovery in Egypt ... 35
    3 On Hadrian's Wall ... 41
    4 'Wall Fever' ... 47
    5 'Viewing Flowers from Horseback' ... 56
    6 My China Apprenticeship ... 68
    7 To the Far End of the Wall ... 84

II – A Foot in the Open Door (1986-1990) ... 93

    8 Barriers to the Pleasant Valley ... 95
    9 My Philosophy of Trespass ... 105
    10 The Rice Bowl of Friendship ... 111
    11 My First Escape ... 116
    12 Blisters & Plague ... 124

13 Swirling Robes & Blinding Sand	132
14 Fugitive & Captive	137
15 Lovestruck & Deported	143
16 Deception & Bravery	150
17 Lovers in a Forbidden City	162
18 Back to the Wall	168
19 Vertical, Wonderful, Monstrous & Forbidden	175
20 From the Desert to the Sea	184
21 Press Blitz	191
22 Beautiful Jade	198
23 A Great Wall Love Story	207
24 Alone on the Great Wall	211
III — Following in Footsteps (1990-1991)	**219**
25 My Appointment with the Long March	221
26 Living Between Journeys	226
27 The Berlin Wall	231
28 Slow Trains to China	236
29 My Route of Badges	246
30 Marching with Mao	250
31 To the Golden Sands River	257
32 At Luding Bridge	266
33 The Highest Mountain	275
34 Meeting Point	287
35 Across Tibetan Marshes	293
36 Reaching the Great Wall	302

IV — Feet Under the Table (1991-1994)   307

    37 Old China Hand, New China Job   309
    38 Back to Class   314
    39 Foreign Affairs   319
    40 Xi'an Incidents   330
    41 Hypothetical Questions   338
    42 Historic Days Remembered   344
    43 Thoughts About Chairman Mao   350
    44 Centennial Timing   362
    45 Family Planning   369
    46 'Eighty-Three, Forty-One'   373
    47 Foreword and Forward   378
    48 Meeting Dr. William Geil   382
    49 Diplomats, Politicians and Journalists   388
    50 Wonderful Rice   394

ACKNOWLEDGEMENTS   398

MAPS

    Author's Journey along the Great Wall   174
    Author's Long March 'Route of Badges'   306

FOREWORD
By Dame Barbara Woodward DCMG OBE

CHINA. 1986. 'Back then' as William writes, 'almost everyone you met ... was a pioneer of some kind, planning on doing, in the process of doing or having done something either unusual or extraordinary ...'. Her Majesty Queen Elizabeth II and HRH Prince Philip make a state visit. Bertolucci is filming *The Last Emperor* in the Forbidden City. World Snooker Champion 'Hurricane' Higgins disembarks a British Airways flight in Peking with his cues. And in March 1986, William Lindesay arrived in China with a goal that was both unusual and extraordinary: to fulfil a childhood dream to travel the length of the Great Wall on foot.

This first part of William's autobiography traces the genesis of the ambition — the history and influence of his family, including brother Nicholas, who is credited with reviving the seed of the the Great Wall journey idea during a break in a marathon along Hadrian's Wall; the role of inspirational teacher 'Maccie', who instructed 10-year-old William to keep an atlas of the world at his bedside — through to his marriage and the realisation of his destiny on and around the Great Wall.

The odds were stacked against William, as pioneers and adventurers before him have found. China was opening up ... except for the parts that weren't. His eventual triumph is all the sweeter for being crowned with love — meeting Wu Qi, his wife

WILD WALL-THE FOUNDATION YEARS

of 35 years now — and punctuated by the kindness and curiosity of ordinary Chinese people, like the unforgettable Yin and Wang families, and many others who had never seen a foreigner before, all of whom helped William along his way. This truly is a story which proves, as William writes, that 'where there is a will, there is a way'.

While there are ostensibly two journeys in this book, the run along the Great Wall and the retracing of Mao's Long March, which William has told separately in *Alone on the Great Wall* and *Marching with Mao*, this is far more than a travel narrative. William blends history, autobiography and memoir in the context of a journey being a lifelong experience. Encounters — from uplifting to alarming and plain baffling — are vividly described, characters and events warmly drawn, including the peanut eating competition with one of his students, all set against the backdrop of China's history and geography clearly explained, and woven in to a fluent and entertaining narrative. William gives us his answers to the deceptively simple questions about life that Chinese people ask him, and that we ask ourselves: 'Where am I from?' and 'What do I do?'.

It was not until almost twenty years after William's run that I met him, Wu Qi and their sons Jimmy and Tommy on the first of many hiking trips to the Wild Wall that William has championed, cared for and documented during his career. But at that first meeting we rediscovered the pivotal year of 1986, when William served his 'China apprenticeship' and I was teaching English in Wuhan, Hubei Province. It has been a pleasure and privilege that our journeys through China and life have overlapped and intersected since.

As Han Suyin wrote in her foreword to *Alone on the Great Wall*: 'It was William's wonderful candour, that purity of mind and aim, which brought him success'. Those are the qualities

WILLIAM LINDESAY

which shine through his life story which is so eloquently told in this wonderful book.

Dame Barbara Woodward, DCMG, OBE
British Ambassador to China, 2015-2020
New York, February 2022

Author's Introduction

FROM WALLASEY TO THE GREAT WALL

For many years I've had difficulty answering two personal questions. The first question is 'Where are you from?' The second is 'What do you do?'

I'm in two minds dealing with the first, because I've divided my life equally between two worlds. Should I reply 'Wallasey', or 'Beijing'? Answering the second question is much easier because I have been dedicated to a truly monumental subject. I simply say 'I do various things concerned with the Great Wall of China'.

People are usually intrigued by this response. Whether they have ever been to the Great Wall or not, most want to find out more about this extraordinary wonder. How long is it? When was it built? Where does it start, and end? Did it work? These are the kinds of Great Wall questions that are certain to follow. But I've found that it's my own Great Wall story that people are most interested in — no matter where they are from. What led me to the Great Wall in the first place? How far did I travel along it? Did I have official permission? How did I negotiate China's red tape? Did I have a support crew? Why did I decide to stay on?

It's not a spoiler to disclose that from my beginning China appears to have been more than a one-off destination for me, inspired by an ambition. Rather it was the leap that I took towards my destined future. Once here (or there) depending on where you are, I enjoyed and endured a roller-coaster year full of heavenly and hellish experiences. The wonderful and pleasing ones then prompted me to make my life changing journey to live in China.

WILLIAM LINDESAY

I'm now in my fifth decade at the Great Wall. As I enter my sixty-fifth year of life, I feel it's about time to review my Great Wall experiences and achievements, particularly as my age is significant in terms of 'half-lives'. I have celebrated thirty-four birthdays in China! This timely decision has been encouraged in recent years by hearing the Lukas Graham song *Seven Years* that features the line: '*Remember life and your life becomes a better one*'.

There are other reasons for why now. My first book, *Alone on the Great Wall*, was published in 1989. It's been long out of print, and I have begun to buy second-hand copies on the internet. The dust jacket, featuring a faded colour photograph of me on the Wall, sporting a full head of brown hair, of course looks dated. But inside, it is not only the coarse-paper pages that have yellowed at the edges and become foxed. The contents have also aged quickly. Most of the China scenes that I saw, and situations that I experienced and the procedures I went through in the 1980s are long gone. I described the China of Deng Xiaoping's 'economic reform and opening up' era when the country was tentatively and awkwardly opening its door to the outside world after decades of isolation. I gained early insight into that little-known Chinese world, amidst its streams of cyclists, beneath its hand-painted billboards, among its uniformly dressed people, surrounded by throngs of curious onlookers, all the while being generously hosted by salt-of-the-earth rural families. Retrospectively, the timing of my journey was momentous! I didn't simply undertake a journey along the Great Wall, I saw a China way of life that was soon to become history itself.

The Great Wall's story goes back approximately 2,300 years. Presenting explanatory historical background that is essential for a fuller understanding of my narrative has presented a challenge. My guiding principle has been to remember just how ignorant

WILD WALL-THE FOUNDATION YEARS

I was of Chinese history when I first arrived in China in 1986. When I consulted dynastic chronologies, I was overwhelmed by the sheer sweep of time that they covered, notwithstanding the difficulty of pronouncing them. How do they go? Was it Ting or Tang, Sing or Song, Qin or Qing—or both? I concluded that I should drip-feed Chinese history to my readers. At the outset I present only a few pertinent snippets about say, the Ming Dynasty, but by the end of my story, which is divided between two volumes, readers will become better- and well-acquainted with this titan of Great Wall building periods. Having said that, and even though I've lived half my life 'in ruins' as it were, this is not a history book. It is a memoir, and a little more; it's a book of journeys, of autobiographical recollections and thoughts. I have included dialogues in many places which recount the gist of conversations at that time.

In the main, I write about events and happenings in chronological order. One problem I faced was how to present my acquisition of knowledge, which so often is a slow process, a journey in itself. Should I present it as I acquired it, little by little, keeping my readers (like me at the time) in the dark about the full context? Or should I jump to the future for the sake of their (your) fuller understanding, and tell my readers (you) what I came to know much later? I have decided, in most cases, to do the latter, to let the cat out of the bag. Consequently, from the outset, the reader will understand what took me much longer to appreciate. I only avoid divulging the outcome if there is a story-telling value in delaying an explanation.

Wild Wall divides into two books. *The Foundation Years* is the first of them, and it covers all that is interesting and pertinent that happened in my life before 1994, culminating with my Great Wall and Long March adventures. After my feet-on experiences

WILLIAM LINDESAY

of these icons of China's ancient and modern history, and the bonus of a lovely Chinese wife who is a history graduate, it was almost inevitable and natural that we should gravitate towards China and build our new life together there. That is told in the next part of *Wild Wall* subtitled *The Jiankou Years*, which covers the period from 1994 to 2022.

William Lindesay
Xizhazi Village, Beijing
June 2022

Prologue

IN ANCIENT TIMES, MY TIME AND TIME AGAIN

As IN LIFE, a good start to a daunting journey helps a lot. During the early stages of my journey along the Great Wall, I knew that I needed to gain momentum and confidence by finding what remained of it, following it and accruing mileage. I set out alone from Jiayuguan, a town on the edge of the Gobi Desert, heading for Shanhaiguan, a town on the edge of the Yellow Sea, 2,500 kilometres away to the east. My plan was to take it step by step, one day at a time, region by region. The first million or so steps in the opening weeks would be along the Hexi Corridor, which, as its name suggests, is a long and narrow artery that threads it way between the Qilian Mountains and Gobi Desert in today's Gansu Province. Throughout, I'd be either in the presence or absence—the omnipresence—of the Great Wall, and also of the myriad tracks that for the past century or so have been dubbed the Silk Road.

The network of high defensive walls called the Great Wall was built to prevent conquests of China by nomadic enemies to the north and west. Ruins of these border barriers built by various dynasties still remain, either barely or grandly, here and there. The most prominent and prevalent date from the latest and greatest system, that built during the Ming Dynasty (1368-1644). Like the fossilised vertebrae of some gargantuan monster, long sections of it lie strung out across China's ancient frontier—several hundred kilometres of it within the Hexi Corridor.

But while the Great Wall was built to repel and restrict the

Silk Road tracks represent movement and connection. These ancient paths created by the tread of humans and pack animals connected China's imperial capital to city states on the empire's western periphery, and far, far beyond. The original paths have largely been obliterated, buried under the wind-blown sands of time, but they live on, compacted as one alluring name coined by a German geographer, just as the trading caravans that created them live on in the huge trading networks that today bind China to the world.

Only in one place do the Silk Road and Great Wall converge — in the Hexi Corridor. They run parallel for 460 kilometres. Midway along the corridor, southeast of Zhangye, the Great Wall stands high, and stretches largely unbroken. It was there, in April 1987, that I passed by, from west to east, treading a stoney track right beside the Wall. Countless people had gone before me, going this way, going that way, but in modern times I very much doubted that anyone from so far away had come my way. I came from way beyond the western end of the Silk Road. My preferred way was on foot. And the way I had chosen was to follow the route of the Great Wall, all the way from the desert to sea. I was never one to choose the beaten track, and that is exactly why I was in China, for it was very much off the beaten track at the time, as it had been for most of the 20th Century.

Between two extraordinary political upheavals, the Republican Revolution in 1911 that overthrew the last emperor, and the death of Chairman Mao Zedong in 1976 which brought the Cultural Revolution to an end, the rumble of rebellion and war had for decades made China a dangerous and a closed part of the world to most outsiders. China began to change into the global superpower we see today when Deng Xiaoping became its paramount leader in 1978. He advocated and launched so-called 'Reform and Opening-up' (*gaige kaifang*). China's relationship

WILD WALL-THE FOUNDATION YEARS

with the outside world restarted. It was back on the map, a new horizon visible.

China's long period of closure and its decisive opening-up made my own dream feasible. The upheavals of the three decades from the Communist victory in 1949 until 1978 effectively preserved one of the greatest and most desirable journeys for me — traversing the entire length of the Great Wall. The reforms appeared to have opened a long-closed door. In theory, the Great Wall was now accessible. As far as I knew, remarkably, no foreigner had previously traversed its iconic ruins from end to end on foot. The chance was there for me to grab, if I dared. It seemed to be my time, so I seized it.

To offset the overpowering feelings of solitude I needed allies, ancient ones to inspire me with pioneering spirit, contemporary ones to support me with their hospitality, for I had no support crew. Among the ancients, of course, I chose the Wall builders. But unlike them, those who came to the frontier and stayed for the rest of their lives, my goal was to conquer by foot, from one end to the other. With a well-defined starting and finishing line, I planned to follow the Wall until it went no further, when we both reached the sea. From there I would return to the UK, take-up my old life, find a beautiful wife, and live happily ever after.

But even with make believe and hoped-for allies, the odds were heavily stacked against me. Most areas of apparently open China were actually closed to foreigners. Detailed maps were unobtainable. I had no language skills and faced health hazards. At the outset, I felt I was a fugitive, alone, a trespasser, on the run in a land of a billion people, with next to no hope of success. And there was nobody, anywhere in the vast land of China who could help me.

As a geographer, I hoped to be inspired by the landscape, and as a history buff, I expected the sight of the monumental

Great Wall to uplift me. But two weeks into my journey, it was far from great. The vast lengths of the Wall traverse several different landscapes and so it is not a uniformly built structure composed of rock and brick. Out west, it was made entirely of mud and much eroded. I found little of it left, or still standing—until Saturday April 18th, 1987. Early that morning, I reached a section of the Wall that deserved the adjective Great, and I followed it all day to a place where it was breached by a road, the G312, the main trunk route through the Hexi Corridor, effectively the *new* Silk Road. Wanting a photograph of this crossing point, I decided to wait for a vehicle to approach.

I had already covered around forty-five kilometres. As the sun began to sink in the west, I happily lay down, my head on my backpack, staring up at the sky, bridging the blue yonder to where all my loved ones lived, far away in the west. My reverie was interrupted by the sight of a hawk, out hunting, circling high above on the warm currents. I imagined its view, mine in reverse, looking down on the giant mud Wall cutting across the desert, emphasised by its wide dark shadow, meeting this narrow tarmac road.

I was brought back down to earth by the chugging sound and sight of an approaching 'Liberation' truck. Large enough to make an impression driving through the gap in the Wall it made the ideal photograph. Next, I wondered, should I play safe and follow the road to a wayside farmstead, or stay right beside this, the first really Great Wall I'd seen?

Upbeat about the Wall's condition, I decided to stay with it. All the Wall I had seen that day was pockmarked with tiny dugouts, presumably shelters made by herders, to give them shade from the sun or protection from the wind. I could easily hole up in one of these dugouts, at any time, as late as I liked, for an overnight bivouac. Three hours later, I abandoned that plan. Two herders'

WILD WALL-THE FOUNDATION YEARS

dogs trailed me, their snarls and barking convincing me that I had little hope of a safe night's rest. Ahead in the twilight, the high Wall headed into low hills.

I crossed through a gap to the other side of the Wall and was relieved to see a few lights glimmering in the near distance. A silhouetted figure stood beside one farmstead, watching me approach. I expect it was my height, gait and posture that alerted his attention. I uttered my humble greeting "*ni hao, wo shi yingguo ren*" (hello, I'm British) as I neared, managed to beam a smile despite my exhaustion and mimed my foot-in-the-door request, cupped hands for a drink of water.

He beckoned me into his yard, and then into the tiny building. Inside, a woman was cooking while two young children were doing their homework. All stopped, jaws dropped, and they gazed at me. The woman smiled warmly and gestured for me to sit on the brick platform (*kang*) where her little boy and girl were seated below a single lightbulb hanging on the end of a long flex. I had arrived in the nick of time. Dinner was about to be served. I was ravenous and parched.

The five of us sat cross-legged around a small, low table on the *kang* as the mother ladled noodles into bowls. Plumes of steam billowed up in the dim light. I copied the actions of the father, adding vinegar, soy sauce and chilli, lifting my bowl to my mouth to scoop and slurp. It was perfection to my starch-starved body, the heat, the salt and spice taste and the just-as-I-liked stickiness between my teeth. I had several bowls-full.

After dinner the children had to resume their homework, but clearly they found their visitor with big feet, hairy legs and sharp-clicking backpack clips to be far more interesting. To set a good example, I pulled out my diary and began to write, describing the small room, about six by six metres, and the family of four whose home I'd found refuge within.

WILLIAM LINDESAY

By way of what I later dubbed the 'Chinese inquisition' — a quick-fire sequence of predictable, privacy-breaching questions about my age, marital status, occupation and salary — I saw how the Chinese were, without fail, surprised that at the age of thirty I was still single. To make encounters easier for me, I used a family group photograph taken at a Sunday lunch gathering to gain kudos in their eyes. "She's my wife and he's my son," I would say, borrowing a sister-in-law and nephew. There was a good 'character' reason for this white lie. The Chinese character for good is 好, *hao*, which is made up of 女, *nü*, which means woman, and 子, *zi* which means child. If a man has them both, he's regarded as having good virtue and character himself.

Before sleeping, we took turns in going to the outhouse. Icy air was blowing down from the mountain range rimming the southern edge of the corridor, and the sound of the howling wind buffeting the tiny house and outside clutter kept me awake at first. I felt so pleased that I'd been forced to change my mind about holing-up in a Great Wall dugout.

At dawn, returning to the outhouse, my 'right decision' feeling was reinforced as I opened the door. Snow was swirling around and already lay crisp and shin-deep in the yard. Back under my quilt on the *kang*, the blizzard presented me with a dilemma: to leave or stay? I'd made a rule not to linger in any habitation within closed areas, for fear of arousing interest, allowing time for the news of my presence to spread and eventually reaching the police. Go or stay, either way I would be taking a chance.

The storm forced me to stay put, but happily kept other people away. I ended up staying the whole day with the family, getting to know them by name. After completing their writing chores, I joined the children Yin Lanlan and Yin Jianxi, playing with their only toys — bottle tops, which they used in a shove-halfpenny fashion on the table. To entertain them, I then patched up my

WILD WALL–THE FOUNDATION YEARS

blistered feet. The little boy also managed to find a graze on his hand for me to treat, and seemed happy with the application of a dab of antiseptic cream and an adhesive plaster.

Saved from bad weather, enjoying such a fortuitous stay, I broke the second of my rules. To preserve my limited film supplies, I usually concealed my camera when in the company of farmers. But this family was exceptional. I definitely wanted a photograph of them. Mother and father insisted that I just photograph their children. I agreed, but the light in the room was too dim, so I stood them at the doorway with their rice-bowls and chopsticks in hand. Now that I had a photo to remember them by, I invited their father Yin to write a message in my diary.

Next morning, all was calm and clear under blue sky. Waving goodbye to the 'Yins', I headed off through deep, crunchy snow back towards the Wall. I turned around intermittently, seeing them all standing by their tiny house, until the beacon-like crimson jacket of the little girl Lanlan could no longer be seen. They were out of sight, gone forever. I would miss them.

I was alone on the Great Wall again. As I reached the tall earthen rampart, I looked along it from where I'd come, and then ahead, into the unknown, where I was going. I felt a surge of positive energy, a favourable wind, regenerated. A sensation of sheer exhilaration tingled down my spine. For the first time since setting off, I was confident in myself and inspired by the location. I felt privileged to cast my eyes on such a remote object of antiquity and beauty. With outstretched arms, I yelled at the top of my voice: "China! The middle of China!" In reality I was geographically towards the northwestern edge, and journey-wise just at the beginning, but I felt I had turned a corner. I was upbeat, no longer teetering, rather gravitating towards my goal.

I set off again, energized and enthused. My reception at the Yin's had reinforced my philosophy of trespass. If ordinary people helped me, what wrong could I be doing? It was clear in my eyes and in their minds that I wasn't a trespasser at all. The Yins had shown me that China's open door was for real. In their household, the people's policy was way ahead of the government's policy in terms of grass roots implementation. It was two-way cultural exchange, mutual friendship, good for East and for West, for them and for me, in the time-honoured Silk Road tradition. Although we would probably never see each other again, I knew that we wouldn't forget one another either. A tear of thankfulness moistened the corner of my eye as I glanced back, for one last look.

Sixteen years later, I returned to the mid-point of the Hexi Corridor. Only then did I begin to realize that my keeping a diary was more than just an *aide de memoire*, useful as a guide for writing my book, *Alone on the Great Wall*. Well-kept, those sweat-stained and soiled diaries, a record of where I'd been, what I'd seen, who I'd met and where I'd stayed, have since become field records and personal treasures. And in 2003, for the first time, one of them served as an address book, valid or out of date, I was about to find out. Without family names to ask for and village names recorded, most of my first Great Wall encounters would have remained one-offs.

I could easily recall that April weekend in 1987 that turned wintery. Back then the Great Wall landscape here had been blanketed with snow. I remembered the rampart's rare height and its impressive continuity. I recognised the great curvature of its line and the white skyline of the Qilian Mountains against the deep blue sky, but how the land between the Wall and 'my' village had been transformed, not just by a change of season. The bare desert scrub on which goats once grazed had been reclaimed as farmland by the extraction of groundwater. There

WILD WALL-THE FOUNDATION YEARS

were large fields of sunflowers, facing the sun, as if worshipping, and maize, just a head shorter. I sensed that I was very close to where I'd stayed, but I was disoriented by the curtains of highrise crops blocking the view.

From the 1990s, a new Chinese migration phenomenon had manifested itself. Seeking a share of the economic reforms, farmers began leaving their countryside homes to seek work and wages in factory towns and cities. Would the Yin family still be here, somewhere nearby? I hoped that the better farming conditions might have helped keep them here, rooted to the land. I wanted to find them so much, for it was through their hospitality on that wild weekend sixteen years before that I had felt the heart-warming glow of the rice bowl of China friendship in my hands.

I heard farmers talking loudly to one another and headed for them in what was a field of watermelons. They fell silent on seeing me approach. I guess the Chinese reaction to my height and gait have never changed. Even after living in China for almost fifteen years I was still a foreigner to the billion or more who'd never seen me.

"I've been here before back in 1987," I shouted at their volume, "alone, following the Wall ... I stayed in the home of a family surnamed Yin in Fengcheng village, Laojun Township ...."

"Haah! You're famous here!" exclaimed one of the farmers. "We all know your story! The first foreigner to come and stay in our village ... Lizhong is a relative of mine ... they've moved ... but I'll call him now." He pulled a mobile phone from his pocket, a telling indication of how society had changed since my first visit. I had left more than footprints in the snow here. I'd become a local legend.

He talked on the phone as we walked towards the Yin's new home. Within minutes, we were there. Who would have ever thought it! Yin Lizhong and his wife, Liu Huiming. I recognised them straight away and gave them each a heartfelt hug of thanks.

"Ay-yah! You're back! ... How many years has it been? Welcome back, welcome," they chorused.

"Your family's kindness over that snowy weekend marked a definite turning point in my journey," I told them, thrusting a copy of my book into their hands, opened at the page which showed their children's photograph.

"After leaving your home, many amazing things happened. The Great Wall not only brought me to your country, it has kept me here. And now I live in Beijing, beside the Wall myself. It's a long story!"

I

Stepping Stones
1956-1986

1

The Adventurer in Me

It's late on a Friday afternoon, and we have just arrived at the Barracks, our family home beside a section of wilderness Great Wall, north of Beijing. There's just enough light remaining, so Tommy, my youngest son, and I hit the ground running. We quickly change into our trail running shoes and start jogging up the stoney path in the forest that heads towards Xidaqiang, 'The Big Wall in the West'.

As we snake through the woods, snatching distant glimpses of the Wall here and there I, as usual, pinch myself, asking 'What on earth is *usual* about this?!' The sun is setting. A horizontal strip of the Wall running along a ridge, backlit, comes clearly into view, at the perfect time. Its silhouetted merlons and crenels, black against orange, remind me of my very first view of the Great Wall, marked as a battlement symbol on the map of China in my school atlas. Even though I've experienced many of these flashback moments over the decades, I cherish each one. They are always extraordinary.

We press on. After a sharp turn we stride out on a smoother, clearer, packed earth stretch of the path towards our destination and turnaround point, a glade on a ridge from where a magnificent view of Nandalou, 'The Big Watchtower in the South' standing at 1,010 metres is revealed. I ask Tommy what he thinks—about coming out from school in the centre of Beijing, driving for two

WILD WALL–THE FOUNDATION YEARS

hours, and racing the light to this personal place, named by me, bearing his name, 'Tommy's Viewpoint'.

"I'm luckier than you, Dad" he replied, "when you were a schoolboy you could only see the Wall on your map, but for me the Great Wall is something that's right outside my own door."

Although I'm now 'from' Beijing, I am originally from Wallasey, near Liverpool, so I can at least claim to have started life at a wall of sorts. I usually help pinpoint the town with the musical direction of 'Gerry and The Pacemakers' whose song *Ferry Cross the Mersey*, a global hit in 1964, mentions the ferries that take Merseysiders and tourists 'across the water' as Liverpudlians say, between Liverpool and terminals on the Wirral Peninsula to the west. Wallasey occupies the northeastern corner of the peninsula, and that's where I was born in 1956, and where I grew up.

When I was a boy, you needed a lot more than slow boats to travel to China and its Great Wall. It was well nigh impossible, neither by hook nor by crook. China was off the world map politically, but at the age of eleven I had an exceptional view of it, privately. I had what is tantamount to nothing less than a geographical vision of my future. I spotted a battlement-like symbol zigzagging across the map of China in my *Oxford School Atlas*, underscored with the magical name 'The Great Wall'! I became utterly transfixed by this Wall: It was love at first sight. I envisioned its height, it being made of rock, for I had surely seen a photograph of it, somewhere. While that showed the Great Wall in one place, the map showed it all, telling me how great it truly was! I followed each segment of the picturesque symbol from end to end, piece by piece. Some stretches were longer, others shorter. It crossed the ochres and browns of North China's deserts, plateaus and mountains, and met the snaking Yellow River in two places. I used my thumb and forefinger outstretched as a makeshift ruler, trying to work out this Great Wall's overall length. Above the many other mysteries that it contained, it was the distance it covered that was of utmost importance to me, but not to decipher merely as a geographical fact. For I had decided, there and then, that I was going to see it, all of it, from one end to the other, on foot, crossing those deserts and mountains, following the Great Wall. At the age of eleven, I had already planned an expedition, no less! And for this dream I have my first headmaster, the Reverend John Patrick Macmillan, to thank. We called him 'Maccie', and it is he who told us, the pupils of St. Aidan's Preparatory School in Wallasey, that "By your bedside you should have a Bible, a prayer book and an atlas."

How young William would stay true to his grand childhood ambition was a question for the future. A more immediate one was, 'Are adventurers made, or born?' What did my past, my family history, predict on the chances of me becoming an explorer and settling so far away from my place of birth?

In actual fact, both my immediate and distant ancestors did have a very early and varied history of travelling. Up until the 20th Century, most people around the world pretty much stayed were they were born, but my family did not. They were exceptional globetrotters. Later ones crossed the Indian Ocean several times and the North Atlantic many times. Earlier ones invaded, colonised, emigrated, traded and travelled, evangelised and served. If I take my three closest ancestors, my father, grandfather and great grandfather who stand right above me on our family tree, and map the geography of their lives, a world map is needed to show them, astonishingly, dividing decades of their lives among five of the seven continents: Europe, North America, South America, Asia and Australasia.

I start from my hometown, Wallasey. My parents, newly married, settled there in 1947 just after the Second World War.

WILD WALL—THE FOUNDATION YEARS

Having served as a radio operator in North Africa with the Royal Signals, my father, John Hamilton Lindesay, married my mother, Dorothy Lucas, in 1946. I would be their fourth child, born in 1956. From as young as I can remember, my mother, said to be very 'Lindesay-fied'—a proud promoter of family history—stressed that we were 'special'. But every family is special in the eyes of their mother, so what did the Lindesays of Wallasey have to make themselves so?

For one, it was impressed upon me that we had a very rare family name. Was it this rarity, I wondered, that made us special? Did it make us any better than the Smiths' or Joneses? Mother and Father explained to me that people must always spell our name, Lindesay, correctly, with the 'e'. Our surname was a variant of Lindsay, the more usual spelling. The problem was that 'our' Lindesay was pronounced in exactly the same way as 'their' Lindsay. Therefore, unless it was clearly pointed out, our name was always written down incorrectly, omitting the important 'e'. 'Make sure it's spelt correctly!' became a family mantra and mission.

I only started to realise how special we were when 'The Lindesay Book' was pulled out of a drawer. This was such a precious book, a thoroughly researched genealogy covering 'just' the last five centuries of our family history, that we children of the family had to wash our hands before touching it. I was impressed, and jealous, because, published in 1949, it included the names of my mother and father and my eldest brother, David. Once I saw their names on the printed page, and a chain of other pairings and products of marriages before them, I began to believe the specialness of our story. We went back into the mists of time.

As I grew up, I began to learn about how my ancestors played their parts in events that became history. The formal title of the

WILLIAM LINDESAY

family book is *The Lindesays of Loughry, County Tyrone*. In 1969, I was taken to Northern Ireland by my parents, together with my second brother Nicholas, who has now become our family historian. The grand manor house at Loughry, set amidst 1,000 acres, was certainly impressive, but I was utterly confused by its location. For years, during summer holidays spent touring Scotland by car, my mother had bought me various items that featured our clan tartan (used by all Lindsays and the variants). I had thus come to believe that we were an ancient Scottish family, not an Irish one. At the time, their explanation was too complex for an eleven-year-old to grasp, and perhaps too politically sensitive. Sectarian conflict in Northern Ireland, between Republicans calling for Britain to withdraw, and Unionists loyal to the United Kingdom, was beginning to erupt. It turns out that the root cause of those troubles were partly of my own family's making.

I returned home to Wallasey eager to know more. I wrote to the author of 'The Lindesay Book', a man surnamed Godfrey, who had married a Lindesay lady. He had passed away, but his son, the Canon Lindesay Godfrey, continued to live at the same address. He replied saying 'The Lindesay Book' enclosed was the last of his father's stock and he was very happy for me to have it after my recent pilgrimage to Loughry.

From the book, I learned that on June 24th, 1610, my great grandfather, eight generations back, Robert Lindesay, then Chief Harbinger to King James VI of Scotland (James I of England), left the borough of Leith in Edinburgh and travelled to Ayr on the coast of southwest Scotland to cross the narrowest part of the Irish Sea for Ireland. He had been appointed a Scottish Tenant by Royal Charter to command 66 armed men and their families to migrate to Ireland under the monarch's Plantation of Ulster scheme. This programme empowered Scottish noblemen to

WILD WALL-THE FOUNDATION YEARS

settle and consolidate Irish land in the name of the king. Robert Lindesay carried out his orders. He built a wooden fortification on a hilltop at Tullyhogue. In 1632, his son, another Robert, built a large manor house nearby, calling it Loughry, which means 'King's Gift'. For 280 years, the pendulum of life for nine generations of the Lindesays at Loughry swung from settling, surviving manor house fires, quelling local rebellions and fleeing to safety behind Londonderry's city wall, to reaping harvests and putting on social gatherings for 'the good and the great'. The estate remained in the family until 1895 when debt forced its sale. It became the Ulster Dairy School, renamed Loughry College of Agriculture, Food Technology and Rural Enterprise, which I have revisited twice in recent years with my own family, the Lindesays of Beijing.

More recently, and most relevant in explaining my own penchant for travelling and settling in a distant land, are the lives of three of my most immediate forebears, three Johns. My father lived his life on two continents: North America and Europe. My grandfather lived on three: Australasia, Europe and North America. My great grandfather lived on four: Asia, Europe, South America and North America. When I say 'lived' I mean settled, for they landed and intended, presumably, to stay for good — until they moved on. It is from their intercontinental life stories that I've realised where I have inherited an ability to adapt and a determination to survive and prosper in a distant place.

My father, John Hamilton Lindesay was born in Brooklyn, New York in 1915. His father, my grandfather John Middleton Lindesay, was born in Christchurch, New Zealand in 1879. His parents had migrated from England in 1869 to begin a new life down under starting with a voyage of more than two months. They opened a bookshop on Columbus Street, Christchurch, but indicative of the market for books in NZ during the 1870s it failed, and they returned to England in 1886. In 1893, my grandfather, having endured and perhaps enjoyed a long voyage from NZ to London at the age of seven, was enrolled at the age of fourteen as a cadet on *HMS Conway*, a 'school ship' run by the Mercantile Marine Serviceman's Association that was moored in the River Mersey at Rock Ferry, between Liverpool and Birkenhead. Naval training there was designed to produce men who could satisfy the growing demand for officers to man the empire's trading ships.

An oil painting of my grandfather's first vessel, the *SS Falkland*, a four-masted sailing ship with an iron hull, hung above our piano in Wallasey. Mother told us that it was painted by a Chinese artist, a crew member of the ship. For most of his forty-two years at sea, my grandfather was in the employ of the Lamport & Holt (Liverpool), serving as captain or first mate on more than twenty ships. The shipping line's fleet plied a lucrative triangle, taking British manufactures to South America, Brazilian coffee to New York and American wheat and corn to Liverpool. At the beginning of 1917 during the First World War, Germany waged unrestricted U-boat warfare in the North Atlantic. In August 1917, my grandfather's cargo ship the *SS Verdi* was sunk by U-boat 53, 175 km off the coast of Ireland. Six crew were lost, but my grandfather and thirty-three others survived.

Chivied along by an 'alligator pear' (an avocado) to jog his memory, my father would sometimes recall summer voyages out of New York with his seafaring father. Dad had acquired a nostalgic liking for avocados during a voyage to São Paolo, Brazil (I have my grandfather's copy of *The South American Handbook* in the bookcase of my Beijing study). He often mentioned the heartbreak of losing his baby monkey overboard. Two objects that did survive the journey captured my imagination at home in Wallasey. One was the pelt of a jaguar from the Amazon jungle, the other a large cream-coloured whale's tooth (also now in my study).

Capt. Lindesay circulated in English society when in port, and it was in New York City that he met his future English wife-to-be, Etheldreda Maria Theresa Cross, born in São Paolo and educated in England. They had much in common, and married in 1914, making their home in Brooklyn, where my father was born. In 1928, the Captain (as he was called by our family) decided to 'return' to the Liverpool area. He had a house built for his family in Sandy Lane, Wallasey — just a few miles from where he had been trained on the *HMS Conway*. Grandpa, the Captain passed away in 1955, so I just missed him by one year, but I do remember Grandma Lindesay very well, and it is her father's history, the story of the third and oldest of the three Johns, my great grandfather Dr. John Cross, that is the most international, and in my own eyes, the most interesting of all my ancestors. I would have loved to meet him because of our common ground: China.

The potential of my family having a China connection first emerged in 2009 as my brother Nicholas was researching the New York period of our family history. He obtained the death certificate of our great grandfather and was surprised to see 'China' recorded as his place of birth.

Dr. John Cross had been baptised Johannes Crescentius dos Remédios in Macau, the Portuguese settlement on Chinese territory, in 1846, where he was born into a wealthy merchant family living in the mansion *Bella Vista*. According to genealogical researcher Tereza Sena, formerly of the Ricci Institute, Macau, his grandfather was a Chinese, António dos Remédios (circa 1770-1841) who married a Portuguese woman, Rita Antónia de Sousa Peres, and in converting to her faith of Catholicism adopted the popular baptismal name Remédios. They had sixteen children.

This means that I am part Chinese myself.

Johannes excelled in his studies at St. Joseph's Seminary, Macau, and in 1864 at the age of eighteen he was recommended as a potential candidate of 'honourable parents' for study in Rome, to enter the Society of Jesus, the Roman Catholic Jesuit order. Then in 1879, after fourteen years as a Jesuit, he quit the order, citing 'great immorality witnessed within the Catholic clergy' and 'differences on religious matters'. He travelled to London, where he took the English translation Cross of his mother's name Cruz. As Dr. John Cross, he explained his reasons for leaving the Jesuit order and desire to join the Church of England through interviews and a long correspondence with the Bishop of London and Archbishop of Canterbury. He was eventually admitted after six months, and as a multi-lingual minister was posted to Brazil in 1882 with his new English wife. They produced two daughters and two sons there. By 1902, at the age of 56, Dr. John was sadly widowed, and he moved to New York City to retire, accompanied by his daughter Etheldreda. It was there that the seafaring John Middleton Lindesay would meet her and marry, with my father being their eldest son.

So, Johannes Crescentius dos Remédios was born and grew up in Asia, for eighteen years. He trained and worked as a Jesuit in Europe for fifteen years. He became Dr. John Cross, serving the Church of England in South America for twenty-one years. He spent his last eleven years in North America, the fourth continent of a truly intercontinental life.

This finding means that six generations ago I had a Chinese great x 4 grandfather. I have 1.56% Chinese blood! Was I thus pre-destined to have more than an inorganic fascination with the Great Wall of China, but gravitated towards it through an organic affection rooted in being part-Chinese myself?

Reminding me of the great journeys that my ancestors had

made, how the adventurer in me came to be, and how I received my few drops of Chinese blood, is the oil painting of my grandfather's first ship, the *SS Falkland*, in full sail, now anchored to the wall above my family's piano in Beijing.

In 1962, I faced my first test of endurance and determination. My parents decided that paying St. Aidan's private-school fees was too much of a burden. My father wrote to Miss Violet Walker, the headmistress, to announce that after my first year's education I would be transferring to St. George's, the local state school, which offered free tuition. Miss Walker replied saying 'everyone will miss William's lively little personality'. Likewise, I would miss St. Aidan's. I was determined to protest.

St. George's was the 'arch enemy' school around the corner from St. Aidan's, about 400 metres away. My brothers David and Nicholas, and sister Dorothy-Jane had all been schooled at St.Aidan's, so I thought it unacceptable that I should be short-changed.

During the middle of my first morning at St. George's I decided to leave, immediately. I asked to go to the toilet, but instead ran out through the gates and sped down the hill like greased lightning, covering about a mile at flat-out pace to my home.

The next morning my father took me back to the school. But I was determined not to give up my protest. When I asked to go the toilet the teacher said "yes" — but assigned another boy to go with me as chaperone. I remember us approaching the boys' urinal trough together. But this dim boy didn't understand that his job was to watch me, and not have a pee himself. He stood there, unzipping his fly, while I feigned to do the same. I waited until he was 'midstream' before bolting out of the toilet, leaving him fumbling to rearrange his shorts, by which time I had a head start. And that was the last I saw of him that day.

On the third morning, my father took me back the school once again. I asked to go to the toilet, but the teacher said "no". I had to wait until playtime for my next escape effort, only to find the main gates locked. But having gained much tree climbing practice back at St. Aidan's, I was an accomplished climber. A few seconds' clambering saw me up and over, down the hill and far away, back home once more.

For some reason, my sister Dolly was at home and surprised me beyond belief with the best of news. "Mummy said if you ran away again today then she'd let you stay at St. Aidan's for rest of your prep school years." I had notched up my first, and perhaps most significant, running victory.

Little did I know how useful the nerve to escape, an ability to outrun chasers when being pursued, a talent to give watchers the slip, and the skill to climb over fences and gates would turn out to be—nearly twenty years later in China. Yet the greatest reward of my determined efforts to stay at St Aidan's was that for my most important formative years, between the age of ten and thirteen, Maccie was there at the helm as headmaster. Maccie was a preacher, not a teacher. He was humorous, kind, learned, strong and strict, a tall and slightly rotund man with an imposing presence and stance, upright posture and commanding attire. He always wore a black suit, highly polished black shoes, a white dog collar and professorial round-rimmed spectacles. He taught us mostly about what he liked best, history and geography combined, as it should be, because all human development, all human stories, are linked to the lie of the land. In Maccie's mind, the 'Three Ps' — places, peoples and their pasts — were the fundamentals after mastering the 'Three Rs' (reading, 'riting and 'rithmatic). Essay titles were a weekly staple. Maccie's method would now be called 'project-based learning'. During class time,

WILD WALL–THE FOUNDATION YEARS

we were often left on our own to get on with work. For when the cloth called, Maccie would don his vestment and slip away for an hour or so to conduct a wedding or a funeral. Everyone worked studiously in his absence. Maccie's deterrent stood prominently on his desk at the front of the class; a bottle of embalming fluid. The threat of a mere squirt on the hands was enough to keep all in order when he was away.

School trips and sports are the most glorious memories of my prep-school years. Maccie took us to churches, cathedrals and castles, museums and mansions, farms and factories, beaches, forests and hills. We spent whole afternoons playing football, cricket or running in nearby Harrison Park. I displayed my athletic talent by making a clean sweep of all events on offer at sports day, an achievement famously preserved with a photograph of me holding five silver trophies.

A wise man once said the age of ten is the age of discovery, when children are most influenced by their teachers and travels. That was precisely the time when Maccie, through a book recommendation, ignited my imagination for the Great Wall, while his teaching methods instilled in me a fascination for the past. At one of those 'What do you want to do when you grow up?' discussions in class, one day in 1968, I announced that I was going to China, for an expedition along the Great Wall. Maccie reacted quite favourably. He didn't put me off, he put me on hold. He said something about there being 'a revolution in China, and nobody goes there'. At the time, I didn't understand what a revolution was, and besides, I felt sure that I would do it regardless. I didn't reveal my plan to my parents, because I feared they would try to put me off. It remained my secret, and before long it was forgotten, until the time was right and I was ready. Meanwhile, a place much further away than China was making big news.

I was enthralled by the Gemini missions approaching closer and closer to the surface of the moon, and the Apollo missions preparing to land. The Lindesays of Wallasey stayed up all night watching Neil Armstrong's moonwalk, at 3.56 a.m. GMT on July 21st 1969, and I spent the rest of the historic day buying the nation's newspapers with their commemorative supplements. I was captivated by the bravery of the astronauts who sat cramped-up within a tiny capsule, located at the tip of a rocket that dwarfed most buildings, ready to make a journey out of our world. Within the century of my birth, the two Earth poles had been reached, the summit of Everest conquered, and now footprints left in moon dust in the Sea of Tranquility.

My transfer in September to grammar school, called The Henry Meoles School, came as quite a culture shock, but one that I just had to accept as part of growing up. Gone were classes of ten pupils; they were now crowded with thirty adolescents. Gone, too, were un-timed periods that melded one subject organically into another, replaced with rigid subject periods of forty minutes. Understanding by discussion had come to an abrupt end, and the only thing that seemed to count was the passing of examinations.

Within the family, although I was one of four children, the gap between me and my sister Dolly was more than six years, so it was rather like being the only child. I developed independence, individuality, and felt quite happy and comfortable being alone, or at least within a small group. Looking back on my teenage years, some personal traits developed that in hindsight prepared me well for my adventuring challenges ahead. I accepted the loneliness of the long-distance runner, was not too much interested in the latest bands, but was more of a traditionalist. I ran alone. I played golf with my best friend Simon Brown, I holidayed with Mum and Dad, usually in Scotland, sitting beside Dad and helping with the route-finding. Yet probably the most memorable and influential holiday of my youth was in the summer of 1972 when we went to London. The reason for our trip was to see an exhibition at the British Museum: *The Treasures of Tutankhamen*.

It was the fiftieth anniversary of the discovery of the pharaoh's tomb by archaeologist Howard Carter and his patron, the Earl of Carnarvon. The occasion was being marked by Cairo loaning fifty prized antiquities found in the tomb, including the magnificent gold funerary mask. We stayed at a public house in High Barnett and went into town on the Underground, alighting at Russell Square. The queue within the grounds of the imposing museum snaked back and forth, but the wait of several hours only enhanced my sense of anticipation at seeing the treasures. I had read avidly Carter's classic account of the discovery and was inspired by his years of focus, trying again and again, season after season with his methodical excavations in each quadrant of the Valley of the Kings. This nurtured a nascent wish to study Egyptology, and so I joined the Egyptian Exploration Society. However, my love of geography eventually tilted me towards earth sciences, especially after the discovery of a more local kind of gold, North Sea oil, and the lure of the legendary high wages that one could earn there. When I told this story of how I might have become an Egyptologist to my son Tommy when we visited Luxor in 2008, he said, "So Dad, if you'd studied Egyptology, then maybe you'd have come to Egypt, and so I'd have an Egyptian mummy." We laughed hysterically.

2

My Discovery in Egypt

My choice of Liverpool University, just across the water from Wallasey, to study geology and geography gave no hint whatsoever of the overseas life that awaited me. Moreover, I was completely unaware of the events in China of the mid-late 1970s that had make-or-break implications on whether my childhood ambition might ever be realised.

In England, it is said that bad news comes in threes, but in China four creates the most apprehension. The sound of the word 'four' in Chinese is close to the word for 'death'.

In January 1976, China's premier Zhou Enlai died. Then in July, China's top marshal, Zhu De died, followed the same month by a massive earthquake, the Tangshan tremor, that killed an estimated 275,000 people. Then, on September 9th, the news finally came.

'*Mao-Tse-Tung, 82, is Dead in Peking, Choice of Successor Uncertain*' reported the *New York Times*. The People's Republic founded by Mao stopped, mourned, wept and waited. All Chinese and China watchers, wondered who, for better or worse, was going to replace the Chairman.

Mao had once said: "The Chinese peasantry are a blank sheet of paper on which any message can be written." The world was concerned about who would now be writing the message, and what it might say. For several years it had not been Mao himself at the helm, but a group of radicals whom he had empowered, including his wife Jiang Qing. They were later dubbed the 'Gang of Four'.

In the struggle for power, Hua Guofeng, chosen by Mao as premier to replace Zhou Enlai, and key military leaders decided to stage what amounted to a coup d'etat, and arrested Jiang and other members of the radical group. Hua was named as the Chairman of the Communist Party to replace Mao, and the radicals were put on trial and blamed for the excesses of the Cultural Revolution. The Gang of Four were given suspended death sentences. Chinese people rejoiced on the streets at the news. 'Madame Mao' ended up committing suicide in prison, in 1991.

In the late 1970s with Mao gone, Chinese life began to return to normal. People worked instead of just talking about politics and revolution. Children started going to school again. After a ten-year suspension, the national university entrance exam system was reintroduced. In Xi'an, unknown to me at the time, a cute nineteen-year-old girl with pigtails was studying hard, especially the subject that she liked the most, English. She was destined to enter my life a few short years later.

Within the ruling Chinese Communist Party (CCP), there were demands for even more decisive and faster reforms. Leading this call, Deng Xiaoping effectively became China's paramount leader in December 1978, and his pragmatic approach would usher in an economic and social renaissance, 'Reform and Opening-up'. Very shortly afterwards, this policy would theoretically permit, but in practice severely restrict, my future travels in China.

But for this very unworldly British university student, recent events in the People's Republic of China, tumultuous as they were, went virtually unnoticed. China remained far away. I only knew England, Northern Ireland, Scotland and Wales. Eager to travel 'on the Continent' I saved for and planned my own 'Grand Tour', which in the 1970s meant 'Inter Rail'. A thirty-day railway pass, permitting travel throughout most of Western Europe and Scandinavia, had become a rite of passage for 1970s students, a way of showing initiative, independence and adulthood. On my return, I excitedly wrote my first travel story, illustrated with photographs taken on my first Olympus camera, the 35RC, and submitted it to *The Geographical Magazine*. I was disappointed beyond belief that my piece was rejected, of course with good reason. It was the worst kind of travel writing, telling readers that I had gone from A to B to C and so on, and how marvellous things were all along the way.

It was at university that I became a dedicated, disciplined runner, an asset that would turn out to be my ace card when later I tackled the Great Wall on foot. I had always done well at school in athletics and chose cross-country as my winter sport. I enjoyed running long and slow, the worse the weather the better. My Wallasey home on Sandy Lane offered a number of doorstep long-distance runs along the coast, on the beach itself, through sand dunes, sometimes on the cast-concrete promenade. Much of the time, the weather was very windy and gales produced waves so high and crashing that even a five-mile run was a major physical effort. By this time, my eldest brother David was an accomplished Cheshire County champion in his late twenties, and during our thousands of miles of training together he imparted much of his running sense to me. When my second brother, Nicholas, took up running we had what was, for most purposes, our own Lindesay athletic club. From his home, Windy Ridge, beside Thursaston Hill at the north-western end of the Wirral Peninsula, we set out on our long Sunday training runs, enjoying sweeping views across the River Dee to North Wales. The best came last: gathering around Nick and Elizabeth's small kitchen table, drinking coffee and satisfying our raging hunger with jam-filled croissants.

In 1978-79, the British economy was suffering its infamous 'winter of discontent' but I hit the jackpot by obtaining employment relevant to my geology and geography degree with an oilfield-services company called Exploration Logging. Before being sent to an exploration rig on any continent, I attended a month-long training course in Windsor, along with fifteen or so other new recruits. I was thrilled to be offered what was considered at the time to be a very glamorous job. Working in the oilfield was synonymous with extensive travel, lots of time off, good money, and it had a macho image, all very appealing to a young man. At the end of the course, each recruit was summoned to the boss's office to discuss a first posting. I chose the Gulf of Suez. My reason was Egypt, the civilisation that I had almost studied. It proved to be a vital choice, because I met people there who absolutely loved what they did for a living.

After a hair-raising late-night drive into Cairo from the airport, I was dropped off at our company's apartment in Zamalek where I grabbed a few hours rest before catching an early-morning flight to the Gulf of Suez, the left 'finger' of the V-shaped top of the Red Sea. There was no chance of oversleeping here. Cairo had around 4,000 mosques, and each used an imam (rather than synchronized tape recordings as it does nowadays) to call worshippers to dawn prayer from the minarets. It was a memorable wake-up call for me, too, a newcomer to the Arab world.

From Cairo it was a short, low-altitude flight across the Eastern Desert in what I would describe as a small 'war-type' plane, with a very draughty door and un-pressurised cabin to a small service port by the name of Ras Gharib. The desert below was a graveyard of tanks, large guns and crashed planes, debris from the 1973 Middle-East War. The onward journey continued with a short hop of about twenty minutes in a James Bond-style Alouette helicopter that shuttled crew members to and from the oil rig. The view from the air over the sunlit, shallow sea was magnificent. Two of us sat beside the pilot, who would shout above the rotor-noise and point downwards to things of interest. "Coral reef"... "sharks" ... "shipwreck" and "Mount Sinai" and then as our rig came into view, "Suez Hilton, ha ha!" And so my international life in the oilfield began on *Discovery II*.

Any oilfield drilling operation brings together about a hundred men from all around the world who, from their training, speak an international oilfield language. They work hard for long hours, suffer a lot, earn a lot, moan a lot, look forward to their onshore time, dread their offshore time, but for various reasons, just do it. My first lunch aboard *Discovery II* provided a hint to the temporary nature of my oilfield life. A Canadian sitting next to me told me to leave at the earliest opportunity.

Frustratingly, floating in the Gulf of Suez, I was within a short radius of so much history, culture and archaeology, but it was out of reach. Everyone watched the calendar, counting down to their time onshore. When our crew change came around after twenty-eight days at sea, we headed back to Cairo, but instead of flying back to the UK, I stayed on to explore what I had really come to Egypt for — the ancient monuments.

Without assistance, and with much persistence, I managed to somehow procure a rail ticket from the chaotic Ramses Railway Station in Cairo to Luxor. On the train I met two women, a German archaeologist and her American student, who kindly adopted me. Immediately on arriving at Luxor, site of the former capital of ancient Egypt known as Thebes, we crossed the Nile on a tiny ferry and hired a donkey cart to travel past the fields spread over the flood plain towards Sheik Ali Abdul Rassoul's

WILD WALL–THE FOUNDATION YEARS

Inn (now called the Marsam Hotel). The Sheik, then in his early eighties, was descended from a family renowned for its tomb-robbing activities and shady dealings in antiquities. I was given a mud-walled room on the top floor with a view across fields of emerald green dotted with white egrets. The next morning, the women planned to walk to the Valley of the Kings, and they invited me to join them.

We set off at dawn, passing by the ruins of Deir-el-Bahri, known as the village of the tomb builders. From thereon, we were following in the footsteps of diggers and decoraters as they made their way to their place of work, as did my female guides. Incessantly they discussed ancient Egypt and, even though I could understand little, I was both moved by and admired their enthusiasm for Egypt's past. How different these dedicated professionals were from my oilfield colleagues—they lived, breathed, thought and loved their subject, Egyptology. On the far side, remote from the river, we descended to a point from where I immediately recognised the outline of a legendary peak, Babel el Malouk that looks down on the Valley. The first tomb of many that I visited there was KV 62: the tomb of Tutankhamen.

A few days later, alone, I retraced the route along the cliff-top path to the Valley, arriving in the late afternoon and finding myself the only person in its most famous tomb. All the time, I was thinking how marvellous it would be to become expert in some aspect of the ancient world's history, to be intensely interested—to be in love with—one's subject and to live it, and if possible, earn a living from it.

3

On Hadrian's Wall

It took me more than two years to leave the oilfield, return to terra firma, and the UK. I landed a two-year contract as a project manager overseeing a team of graduates working on environmental issues under the Manpower Services Commission, a government body set up to give people who had never worked before a chance to obtain work experience. The programme was based at Manchester Polytechnic, so I moved to the suburb of Chorlton, close to Manchester United's stadium, Old Trafford, taking a room in the same house as my best friend from grammar school, Simon Brown.

In and around Manchester, I immersed myself in training. Tow paths beside canals, built during the Industrial Revolution, provided opportunities for 'countryside' running within the city. I conscientiously followed a training regime that I dubbed 'morning, noon and night' involving three runs per day. This featured running to the polytechnic in the morning, a lunchtime run with one of the other staff, and an evening run back home, usually by way of an expanded loop. On Fridays, I would go home to Wallasey, usually running down to New Brighton to do hill training up and down Atherton Street, a steep road that climbed about 150 metres from sea level within a distance of 400 metres, from the promenade up to St. Peter & St. Paul's Church on a summit. Six repeats of that hill was an epic workout! On

WILD WALL—THE FOUNDATION YEARS

Saturdays, I would run long and slow, while Sundays were reserved for the brotherly twenty milers.

During a run with Nicholas in the springtime of 1984, he first suggested a 'real cross country run' — by running Hadrian's Wall, following the line of Roman fortifications which lie strewn in segmented fashion from coast to coast across northern England. The route appealed mainly because it had a definite start and finish, plus the challenge of self-sufficient running while looking for the ruins of the Wall in between. My first task was to plot a route on an Ordnance Survey map. The starting point was the Swan Hunter shipyard on the banks of the River Tyne at Wallsend in the eastern suburbs of Newcastle. The finish would be at the Wall's most westerly remains, on the coast of the Solway Firth to the west of Carlisle – a distance of about 120 kilometres.

We decided on a long weekend traverse, which required taking only one day's holiday, and set off by train from Liverpool late on a Friday. Like me, Nicholas never had any difficulty getting up early. We took the first bus from Newcastle out to Wallsend, before most Geordies were stirring. From there we U-turned to begin our run, westward, back through the city and out through its suburbs to Heddon, where we saw our first stretch of the Roman Wall, ruins of a small temple (in someone's front garden), and the long, straight B6318 road crossing the Northumbrian countryside beyond. Our afternoon incentive was to reach the Roman fort of Chesters beside the River North Tyne before closing time. We did, and celebrated nearby with a pint of beer in a pub called 'The Hadrian', in a village called 'Wall'.

Next day, we entered Hadrian's Wall country *par excellence*. Beyond Shield-on-the-Wall the so-called Military Road and the Roman *Vallum*, a ditch, diverge. We followed the ditch headed due west towards a prominent area of dark trees in an otherwise treeless landscape. Emerging from the woodland, perched on

Sewingshields Crags, were stretches of the Wall forming a broken line along the edge of an escarpment known as the Great Whin Sill. Sewingshields also marked the beginning of the real cross-country run, beside the Wall on soft turf and gravelly paths. We were near the Wall-side fort of Housesteads, sitting on rocks, doing what chiropody 'footwork' was necessary, enjoying the magnificent view, when Nicholas remarked: "Will, d'you know what, you should do the same thing on the Great Wall of China."

"Mars, Snickers or Kit Kat?" I replied.

"Honestly," he persisted. "Now's your time. The papers are reporting that the new leader Deng is opening China up to the West."

I don't recall what I said in return, but I do know his comments moved something deep in my subconsciousness, stirring a memory from my distant past.

We ran on, but for less than a mile, before it was absolutely necessary to make another stop, to photograph what is the most admired of all Hadrian's Wall views. Using my Olympus XA2 camera, said to be the world's first compact camera with a sliding front to reveal the lens, there and then, Nicholas took 'the photograph'. Over the years, it has featured in scores of newspapers and magazines and on television — mostly in the country that has the greatest of all Walls. It is a photograph of me running beside the Wall at Cuddy's Crags with it snaking away into the background along Housesteads Crags.

A little further along, we passed a signpost indicating the intersection of Hadrian's Wall with the Pennine Way that follows the mountain spine of northern England. Virtually everyone walking Britain's most famous long-distance footpath carries the definitive pocket-size guidebook written and beautifully illustrated by Alfred Wainwright. On the page describing the Wall Wainwright proclaims: 'There is an affliction known as

WILD WALL—THE FOUNDATION YEARS

Wall Fever, which besets many visitors to these fortifications and results from enthusiasm and imagination, and a passionate urge to discover more. This is a healthy and rewarding pursuit'.

Gradually we edged our way towards the village of Bowness-on-Solway, the western extremity of the Wall. We went directly into the King's Arms pub, and I downed a welcome pint of beer before thinking that I should look for some kind of memento.

There were few other facilities in the village, except a tiny post office cum general store, which I entered. Sadly, it had little of interest, not even a postcard of Bowness itself. It should be remembered that, in those days, this remote village was just an unknown dot at the end of Hadrian's Wall. Today, in contrast, it is the place where a waymarked national trail ends. As I heard the postmistress stamping an envelope, I thought of the best possible souvenir. My Hadrian's Wall OS map was tucked in the waist of my grey sweatpants. I took it out, and unfolded it to show the western end, where we were.

"Would you mind franking my map, just here, at Bowness?" I asked the postmistress.

She thudded the franker on her ink-pad, franked a piece of scrap paper as a test, before asking, "What are you going to do next? Land's End to John O'Groats?"

"No," I replied, pausing. "I'm going to … the Great Wall of China."

The stamp landed on the map, she smiled, folded it, handed it back across the counter and chuckled "Good luck to you … now, that is something isn't it? From Hadrian's Wall to the Great Wall …."

Running along the Great Wall of China would, of course, be an entirely different proposition. It had received its Great name in English and other European languages for good reason, and I'd later learn that the Chinese actually call their Wall by a name that directly reflects its enormous length by acknowledging it to be simply 'immeasurable'. The various sections denoted on available Western maps appeared to show it traversing a route that is twenty or more times longer than Hadrian's Wall. They crossed terrain which, by relief colour codes at least translated into images of uninhabited desert and mountain ranges. I didn't expect detailed maps, the Chinese equivalent of Ordnance Survey standard maps, to be available to the likes of foreigners who had for so long been prohibited from entering China. And I wasn't wrong. Later I'd learn that throughout Chinese history the circulation of detailed maps has always been within a very privileged circle, during many dynasties under the administration of the Board of War, the equivalent of a modern day ministry of defence. Hadrian's Wall was just a toy compared to the greatest of man's walls, and the Great Wall was in one of the most mysterious lands on the planet at that time.

But, like the length of the Great Wall I had a confidence-boosting accumulation of miles in my legs that convinced me that I could match it distance-wise. My meticulously-kept training diary of 1984 recorded every run I had undertaken. Ten weeks before Hadrian's Wall I had run the London Marathon in 2 hours 40 minutes, finishing in the top percentile. Two weeks before, I had run the Great North Run, a half-marathon in Newcastle, in 74 minutes, only 10 minutes slower than the winner. Two days later, I ran a 10 km in Manchester in a brisk 33:40 as part of my 'recovery' for the Tour of Tameside—a muscle-busting six races in the same week—when I finished 20th overall in a very high class field of 600 competitors, sometimes beating or just getting beaten by European internationals. By year's end I'd clocked up a total distance of 3,205 miles (5,156 km), and missed only thirty days' training through injury. I felt confident that this consistent training would pay dividends on my China adventure. My athleticism was a resource I could depend upon in exploration, to fulfil a childhood dream that had fortuitously reappeared on my radar after a fifteen-year-long absence.

Aged 27, I had no loves, little ones or loans to hold me back. My employment certainly wasn't a job for life — running, at that point, was my life. I could easily leave everything behind and go to China in pursuit of my goal.

4

'Wall Fever'

As Nicholas had mentioned, the political winds in China were somewhat warmer. Mao had been a recluse behind China's closed doors. Deng Xiaoping was outgoing. He had become China's friendly face on the world stage. I remembered him from the news, visiting the US in 1979 and sporting a Stetson at a rodeo, and at meetings with our own Iron Lady, Margaret Thatcher, brokering the return of Hong Kong to Chinese sovereignty. While he differed not at all from Mao on the Communist Party's dominant role, he ushered in bold economic reforms and promoted an open-door policy to the West. Like Mao, he promulgated his own maxims, that would become well known and liked way beyond the confines of China. "To get rich is glorious", "It doesn't matter if the cat is black or white, as long as it catches mice" and "Communists don't need to be poor" are among the most popular. I would never, ever have considered visiting Mao's China. Deng's China was visibly different. His open-door policy was a timely invitation that I could not let slip by. I would try to find my way, alone, along the Great Wall.

I returned home and eagerly consulted my 'current' atlas, *The Times Atlas of the World*. Its depiction of the Great Wall seemed more detailed than that in my *Oxford School Atlas* of years ago. The Wall ran from desert to sea across northern China, crossing the Yellow River at two places because of a huge bend that great waterway describes. It did not appear to be continuous along its course—it was shown with a few breaks in it, for reasons I did not know at the time.

As well as feeling excited at the sight of the Wall's symbol meandering across the map, I also felt suspicious. In spite of its enticing and commanding presence, I could find no record of anyone having ever traversed the Great Wall from one end to the other by the purest of means, on foot. I could only assume that Chinese had made such journeys; I announced my intention to become the first foreigner to do so.

While having a post-run pint of Guinness in the Horse and Jockey pub at Chorlton with Simon Brown I announced what I intended to do.

"Next year, in the spring, I'm going to China to run the Great Wall."

"Fantastic, Will!" said Simon. "If anyone can do it, you can." Then he added some words of warning. "I can't see the distance being any problem for you, but I think China's bureaucracy might be a hassle ...."

"Well, I guess it's not called 'red tape' for nothing, hey?"

That evening, Simon bombarded me with a variety of logistical questions, unknowns that I needed to confront, not least of all because I was about to begin the search for sponsors. To that aim I wrote a brochure to market my adventure, which I dubbed my 'prospectus'. It summarised the who, what, where, when, why and 'if' of the journey. Who was I, and why was I planning this stunt? What is 'the Great Wall', and where does it go? Why is the 'when' now? And if I am successful, how will the sponsor benefit?

An office colleague typed up my prospectus, and the reprographics office produced thirty spiral-bound copies. For the front cover, I designed a logo myself. It was an outline map of China with the normally castellated symbol for the Great Wall replaced by the sentence: '1986 – *The Year of the Great Wall Run*'.

Actually, the 'length of the Great Wall' that I aimed to cover, should be qualified with 'as it appeared on my map at the time, and as it was known and understood by me at the time'. Maps at that time, and as they still do today, mark the Great Wall of the Ming Dynasty, which ruled China between 1368 and 1644 AD. This was the last of many border defence systems built intermittently, by various dynasties over a 2,000-year period. Great Wall building began circa 300 BC and was eventually abandoned as a defence strategy after 1644 because 'the barbarians' came through the Wall to seize power.

The Ming Great Wall is what I now refer to as 'The Great Wall as the world knows it'. The western end is at Jiayuguan in Gansu Province, where Gobi Desert meets the Qilian Mountains., while the eastern end is vaunted to be at the coastal town of Shanhaiguan on the Bohai Gulf, part of the Yellow Sea. During the more than three and a half centuries since the Wall was abandoned, many forces have conspired to change it. Contemporary maps of China only show the principal remains of the structure, or what is clearly visible on the landscape and omit any barely discernible stretches. For this reason, it was necessary to explain my traverse strategy, my rules of engagement with the Wall, to potential sponsors. I intended to begin my journey at one end and follow the remains of the Wall, wherever visible, to the other end. Where there were no traces of Wall I would proceed along the shortest connecting route, to find the next section.

In reality, as I looked at my small-scale map, detailed route planning was out of the question at this stage. I hoped that once I found one end of the Wall then following it for fairly long distances would be fairly easy. But when remains of the Wall disappeared I had no idea how I would align myself with the

WILD WALL–THE FOUNDATION YEARS

next surviving section. The scale of the main map I was using was analogous to using a map of all Europe for the popular 'end to end' walk from Land's End in England to John O'Groats in Scotland. If lost on my home patch then I could ask the way, but in China I'd surely be struggling even if I manged to master some 'survival Chinese'.

I desperately needed better maps. I expected to find them in Peking, but in the meantime I grew impatient to know the scale of the navigational challenge facing me. Advertised on the jacket-flap of my *Times Atlas of the World* was *The Times Atlas of China*. I couldn't find a copy of this in any of my local libraries, so optimistically, I wrote to Times Books, the Edinburgh publishers enquiring if they might have copies to sell. One week later, early one morning, there was a knock on the door and the postman handed over a large padded envelope bearing a Times Books label. Inside was a scrawled note: 'Last copy, apologies it's damaged, good luck!'

I was thrilled to achieve my first 'sponsorship' success, with such a pathfinding object, an atlas dedicated to China and featuring a classic image of the Great Wall on the dust jacket. The maps therein, being larger, gave me a better sense of the Wall's route but for the journey proper I was still banking on finding not just larger maps, but geographically more detailed ones in Peking.

Deciding it was time to announce my expedition in the newspapers, I contacted the news-desks of the *Liverpool Daily Post* and *Liverpool Echo*. Geoff Barnes, based in New Brighton, part of Wallasey, was assigned to interview me by telephone. After ten minutes he said, "I'll send a photographer around and we'll try and run a report on New Year's Eve."

Within the hour, Wallasey's most famous press photographer Bob Bird was at the door. Wearing a baggy jacket sagging with the weight of lenses, he rushed in, glancing here and there around the room as if he'd lost something. He soon found what he was looking for, the perfect visual. "Sit down here ... and hold it like this," he said, placing the *Times Atlas of China* in my hands. "Click ... click." He was in and out of the house in less than three minutes.

The Christmas to New Year period was always a tense time for we running brothers. January was the busiest and most important month in the cross-country calendar for championship races, but in the winter of 1985-86, the talk on our training runs was different. The Great Wall dominated. Keen to conclude the year memorably, we set off early on New Year's Eve to drive into North Wales and parked at the foot of Moel Famau to run a circular route across the Clwydian Hills in light snow. On the afternoon drive back, we stopped at a newsagent's in Mold to pick up a few copies of the *Liverpool Echo*, and there I was, clutching my prized atlas, poised to go to China, edging closer to the great adventure. That evening, I completed my 1985 Training Log, writing 'Not a day's training missed! Year's total = 3,188 miles (5,130 km)'.

Once the holiday was over, there was a tremendous response to my prospectus mail-out. Several shoe manufacturers offered their footwear. How things change! One week I was in two minds about spending £50 on a pair of training shoes, opting instead to squeeze another hundred miles or so out of my current pair by using shoe glue on the heels, while by the end of January, we had more deliveries of shoe boxes than we received letters. I had approached all the major shoemakers, who were obvious sponsors for what would be a feat of ground-pounding endurance. Nike, Adidas, Le Coq, Asics and Reebok all responded promisingly with complimentary test shoes.

Remarkably, the founder of Reebok, the only British

WILD WALL–THE FOUNDATION YEARS

manufacturer (which I favoured, being a patriot), Sir Chris Brasher, invited me to discuss my project, not at their office in Bolton, Lancashire, but at his Lake District cottage! It was an honour and I was thrilled not only at the prospect of being given shoes and perhaps some vital money, but also encouragement by an Olympic gold medallist and founder of the London Marathon.

As a rank outsider, looking far more academic than athletic, Brasher had snatched a gold medal in the gruelling 3,000 metres steeplechase in the 1956 Melbourne Olympics. I felt confident that he would be understanding and supportive of me in my audacious task. I was completely wrong.

Brasher asked me about my personal best (PB) times, and then dismissed my achievements as those of an 'ordinary club runner', telling me that I would have little chance of succeeding in such a gruelling expedition, especially in a country as bureaucratic as China.

"As a goodwill gesture," he said, "Reebok would be willing to take a gamble and give you a few pairs of training shoes."

I left Brasher's home deeply disappointed and utterly flabbergasted. On television, he appeared such a big motivator, but I found him pompous and condescending with an offensive superiority complex. I knew that succeeding on the Great Wall was going to be a test of endurance, grit and persistence, living off my wits. Brasher's attitude irritated me immensely, but also served to fire me up and made me even more determined to succeed.

Back on the Wirral, I angrily crossed-out Reebok from my list before heading out for a long run to gather my thoughts. I wore Asics Tiger shoes, my preferred brand, bought with my own money. Tom Haddley, their UK boss, had informally indicated his willingness to support my adventure. A phone call confirmed his enthusiasm and the news that the latest Asics models would be featuring a new shock absorbing material called Gel. "We can at least provide all your shoes," he assured.

Getting well shod was a great start, getting cash was the next hurdle.

One lunchtime, the telephone rang and it was the financial controller of Thomas Cook Travellers Cheques, Mr. Neil Pirie. He expressed great interest in my prospectus, saying that I could not have timed it better. 'TCTC', as they called themselves, was marketing a purpose-designed traveller's cheque to cater to the predicted rise in travel to open-door China for both tourism and trade.

"And lucky for you that the cheque has an etching of the Great Wall on it," said Pirie.

A few days later, he invited me to Thomas Cook's HQ in Peterborough, to discuss my plan and join him for a lunchtime run. I went with Nick.

At the start of our meeting, I was immediately made aware of the great unknown that I was heading towards. Pirie said he had been to China forty-three times to negotiate with Bank of China officials, and that he had found the Chinese 'devilishly difficult to deal with'. Although Thomas Cook was the world's oldest established travel agency, it didn't have an office in, or any tours to, China. But the company had recently been acquired by Midland Bank, one of the so-called 'big four' British banks at the time, and they had opened a representative office in Beijing 'that may be able to offer some practical help,' Pirie said.

I felt terribly ignorant of China in Pirie's presence, but in one respect we were equal: he had never visited the Great Wall.

"Airport, Bank of China, airport, that's always been my China itinerary," he said. "Never any time for sightseeing ...."

Pirie then explained that he would have to make some telephone calls during lunch. "So I've asked a colleague, Ian

Thomson, to take you for a run," he said.

Nick and I looked at one another, obviously wondering the same.

"D'you mean ... the Ian Thompson?" asked Nick.

"Oh yes," said Pirie, smirking.

Ian Thomson was Britain's faster marathon runner. His 2:09 PB was just 40 seconds off the world record. He held both European and Commonwealth Games gold medals, and his 'steady five' (miles) was a gut-buster trial for Nick and, I suspect, a test to see if I was indeed the runner I claimed to be. Nick hung on by the skin of his teeth while I managed to stay right behind Ian and give short answers to his questions. The purgatory lasted for about 25 minutes. But all's well that ends well, I must have passed the test. Neil Pirie and I shook hands on a financial sponsorship "subject to getting a few okays, just formalities."

Our day trip to Peterborough had taken me a giant stride closer to China.

Geoff Barnes, the reporter, telephoned the next day asking for a progress report. I confidently told of my planned late-March departure for Peking (as Beijing was then known in English). He suggested a new story in the daytime *Post* and a follow-up feature in the evening *Echo* for the forthcoming Chinese New Year. The idea was perfectly timed. I had just signed my deal with Asics Tiger. Tom Haddley, anticipating the favourable outcome was producing a limited-edition '1986 Year of the Tiger' sweatshirt in my honour. I was eager to express my gratitude for the generous 'whatever shoes and kit I wanted' Asics deal that he had negotiated with his Japanese boss, Mr. Kitimura, so I readily agreed to wear the shirt.

Barnes proposed a novel scheme to show readers how I was preparing for my Great Wall expedition: I would master the two survival essentials of how to use chopsticks and how to speak

Chinese. On-the-spot tuition was to be given at Mr. Chow's restaurant, the best in Liverpool's Chinatown, the oldest Chinese community in Europe.

Photographer Tony Kenwright captured the decisive moment of me confidently placing a king prawn into my mouth on the end of perfectly-pinched chopsticks, an accomplishment overseen by Chef Luk Shan Lau, smiling broadly. Meanwhile, the chef's daughter who spoke passable English drilled me with what would be my key phrase of self-introduction: '*nei hou, ngo hai ying gwok yan*', translating as 'hello, I'm British'. Unfortunately, however, it was taught to me in the southern Chinese language of Cantonese, incomprehensible to people in the Wall country of China's northern provinces. This, I hoped, would be my icebreaker to open farmyard doors before miming my requests for water, food and shelter that I'd need along the way, and I expected to expand my repertoire of stock survival phrases as I went.

5

'Viewing Flowers From Horseback'

I HAD WRITTEN to the Chinese Embassy in London asking for advice about my expedition, and they told me to contact a company called the China Sports Services Company, which sent me a reply appearing to state that for a service fee of US$85,000 they would arrange support services for me. However, I only wanted permission, not a road show. Whatever 'support services' meant, I did not precisely know. However, the term came up more and more, and seemed to be an essential component of a foreigner doing anything in China. The UK Foreign and Commonwealth Office, meanwhile, sent a curt response to my letter, stating that travel in China was solely a matter for the Chinese authorities.

Fearful of getting bogged down in a quagmire of bureaucracy, I decided to apply for an ordinary tourist visa and travel to China. Once there, I would make my way to one end of the Wall, set off along it, and would see what happened.

Beside the door of the Chinese Embassy in London was a small brass plate stating, 'Visa Section – Open Monday, Wednesday, Friday 9-12 a.m.'.

At opening time I was the only person in the queue. The door remained closed. I knocked. I heard movement inside: the door was being unbolted. It opened by a few inches and a bemused face appeared.

"Hello, I want to apply for a visa," I said.

"Wait moment," the man said. He closed the door.

Several minutes later, the door reopened, the man reappeared and handed me a visa application form, but I could barely make sense of it. There were many ambiguities. If this first experience at the door of the Chinese embassy was an indication of China's open-door policy, then it was not as wide open and foreigner-friendly as I had hoped. This turned out to be the first of four visits to the embassy before the visa was finally issued.

As my travel date approached, I was involved in hectic last minute press appearances that became distractions from my essential preparations, including the actual issue of my visa. But in fulfilling one of these obligations for my sponsor, I ended up benefitting far more than I expected.

I was invited to appear on *Pebble Mill at One,* a popular lunchtime chat show, beamed live from the foyer of BBCs Birmingham studio, and presented by former newsreader, Pamela Armstrong. They had designed the show as a China special, and my co-guest was Dr. Han Suyin, a renowned author and China watcher. She was surprised that I had not prepared a letter of introduction for use in China. She offered to compose a letter for me in Chinese which she said I could use to 'impress officials'.

Two days before my flight to Peking, I was in London with my brother David who was giving me moral support during nerve-wracking pre-departure press contacts. Thomas Cook had engaged a PR company to arouse interest, first in London, and then in Hong Kong, where I planned to stay for several days overcoming jetlag before setting off on the final leg of the approach journey to Peking, and there was huge interest.

From the photographs of the Wall that I had seen, I realised that falling off it was a realistic danger. It was apparent in many places that its edging battlements and parapets were no longer

WILD WALL—THE FOUNDATION YEARS

standing. I was coaxed into a dress rehearsal to test my head for heights during a photo shoot with a few press photographers. Those from the *Daily Mail* and *Daily Express* suggested a shot of me running along the Albert Embankment, across the river from Big Ben. The location seemed perfect, and rekindled fond memories of my London Marathons. But the man from *The Times* wanted a different angle, once the other photographers had left. He asked me to actually climb up onto the embankment wall. It was a cold and damp day, and the stones on top of the wall were wet, mossy and greasy. On my left, ten metres below, the River Thames churned menacingly, while on my right was the hard pavement, and a sizable crowd of bemused onlookers. My concerned expression, clearly evident in the photograph published in *The Times* the next morning, on March 8th, said it all.

My father delivered my passport to me at Heathrow Airport and I was then ready, with thirty minutes remaining before check-in, to travel to China.

The existence of the autocratic Soviet Union and its satellite countries made a great circle direct flight route to China impossible, so the routing was London-Rome-Bahrain-Hong Kong-Peking. There were some Chinese people on board—I would estimate about ten percent—but they would all get off in Hong Kong, where I would too in order to perform more PR obligations. A large group of Italians boarded in Rome.

"May I ask why you are going to China?" asked an Italian woman who sat beside me.

"For rather an unusual reason," I replied, "Although I think anyone who goes to China is quite unusual, hey?"

"We too have an unusual plan," she said.

"Okay, tell me you plan first."

"After many years of negotiating for permission, we're going to make a movie, in the Forbidden City, we're a film crew."

"Sounds like quite a project. I'm going to make a journey along the whole length of the Great Wall ... on foot."

"On foot? That must be thousands of kilometres. More difficult than our project," she laughed. "I'll keep an eye open for your news in the newspapers."

"It'll be a while. I'll look for your movie when I go back home. Any idea what it will be called?"

"*The Last Emperor*," she replied.

Hong Kong was my first view of Asia, the Far East and China, and my second experience of PR. To the Fleet Street reporters I had explained that I was running because I was a runner, and it was the quickest way of travelling on foot. Editors pitched my news as an inspirational, human-interest story to a readership that was largely ignorant, but very curious, about China. It was all about a Briton's eccentric fascination with a wonder of the world. In Hong Kong it was difficult for people to comprehend why anyone would want to go to mainland China in the first place, let alone to attempt something so demanding there, when everything in China was difficult enough anyway. Besides, to most Hong Kongers, anyone who ran was simply stupid. People did not run anywhere, full stop.

I discovered precisely why, when I foolishly agreed to a midday photo-shoot for the *South China Morning Post* (*SCMP*) and the *Hong Kong Standard* on the Kowloon waterfront. It was a classic 'mad dogs and Englishmen' mistake to leave air conditioning in such humidity that made the physical effort feel as more like a swim than a run. Heavy legged, I plodded back to my hotel, pouring with sweat, frustrated at having to dodge through the churning tide of people milling around during their lunch breaks. I cringed to think how the Hong Kong press would frame my story, but thought I probably wouldn't have the opportunity to see the resulting newspaper articles at least for a couple of months, for I'd be on my way up to Peking first thing next morning.

I was relieved to leave overcrowded Hong Kong and to put the seemingly endless PR behind me. With an overwhelming sense of anticipation, and a feeling that it had all turned out well in the end, I made my way to Kai Tak Airport to 're-join' a British Airways flight that had originated in London.

As I was about to board, out of the corner of my eye I noticed the words 'Great Wall' in large print on newspapers stacked on a rack by the passenger entrance. For a brief moment I thought, 'Fantastic, my story has already made the front page'. But as I picked up copies of the *SCMP* and the *Standard* I saw the headlines, '*Griffiths May be Beaten to the Great Wall*' and '*Griffiths' Great Wall Plans Shattered*'.

"Who on earth is Griffiths?" I wondered.

The reports stated that another Briton, based in Hong Kong, David Griffiths, had planned a Great Wall run beginning in August 1986 and was paying around US$300,000 to the China Sports Services Company to organise and authorise it. The writer explained that my sudden appearance on the scene and my plan, if successful, would deprive Griffiths of a first. My achievement would thus negate the PR value of his own expedition, thereby making it less attractive to sponsors. Who remembers the second expedition up Everest?

Griffiths branded my attempt as 'illegal' and called for 'Lindesay to be stopped'. The newspapers appeared to side with the local boy, accusing me of being the bad lad, who knew nothing about China, who was going to the Wall without official permission.

Years later, while introducing myself over cocktails at a casual gathering at the British Embassy in Beijing I mentioned the 'political aspects of my adventure back in the 1980s'. The comment stirred the memory of a diplomat who was at the UK's Foreign and Commonwealth Office at the time. He recalled receiving messages from 'someone in Hong Kong' insisting that 'Lindsay must be prevented from making his journey.'

Distracted by the distasteful press hullabaloo, I don't think that I even looked out of the window during the whole flight, missing all those landscape views of China. And as we landed in a yellowish haze at Peking's Capital Airport I wondered if what had been published in the Hong Kong newspapers might not be the only surprise in store for me. Would I be prohibited from entering the country? I really didn't know what to expect.

As we taxied towards the terminal building, a cyclist wearing a huge overcoat passed under the wing tip. Everything was monotone — whitish, grimy, grey, dusty, dull — with the occasional red splash of the Chinese flag. The plane parked directly outside the small terminal building. As I descended the stairway I was immediately hit in the nostrils by the strong smell of coal, smoke and metal combined. It would become familiar to me, known as 'the smell of Peking in winter'.

Peking Airport in March 1986 was the last place I expected to see someone I knew, or knew of. But striding briskly ahead of me as we made our way to passport control was a short man, smoking, sandwiched between two burly bodyguards who carried long thin tubes. It was none other than World Snooker Champion, Alex 'Hurricane' Higgins. In the 1980s, if you wanted to hit the headlines, to attract massive crowds, and to be truly world famous, you had to take what you did and do it in the People's Republic of China. The pop duo 'Wham', consisting of George Michael and Andrew Ridgeley, had led the way in 1985, I had encountered Bertolucci's film crew just days before, and now Hurricane Higgins and myself had landed to claim our own big prizes in the Middle Kingdom. If they let me in.

They did.

My one and only contact in the country of more than a billion people was an Englishman named Lance Browne. He was chief representative of Midland Bank, owner of my main sponsor, Thomas Cook. Kindly, Browne sent his driver to the airport to pick me up. As I entered the arrivals hall, I spotted the familiar yellow-and-black rampant griffin logo of the bank, just as it appeared on British high streets, and beside it were chalked the words 'William Lindesay — The Great Wall.' The driver took one of my bags and led me to the car, a bright orange Mercedes 240SE that looked as if it had been made for the Dutch Ambassador.

We drove along a narrow, straight road into the city. The whole route was lined with tall leafless poplars, planted at regular intervals, each with its lower trunk whitewashed. (The most quoted explanations were that it was a pesticide to fend of insects or a means to catch the lights of vehicles at night). I didn't even know whether Chinese traffic drove on the left or right of the road, but on this chauffeur-driven trip the driver stayed in the middle, presumably to give the cyclists plenty of space. There were few other vehicles, but when one approached another there was a mutual slowing down and much honking of horns.

The driver took me directly to the Midland office in what was really Beijing's first modern office tower, the CITIC Building. The office was open-plan, on the 11th floor, and there I met Jennifer, Stephanie, Linda, and Jimmy, who in spite of their English names were all Chinese. A foreigner, slim, short and almost bald, strode out from behind a screened-off section of the office, holding a wad of newspapers.

"William Lindesay, I presume? ... Lance Browne." He frowned, thrusting the papers towards me. "You're causing quite the stir already," he added, rolling his eyes.

Browne broke into Chinese and asked one of the staff, the petite Stephanie, to show me around. From then on, this office was the nearest thing I had to an expedition headquarters, a haven to retreat to, sometimes for a cup of coffee, or to pick up a letter, a fax, to make a phone call, read the papers, or just to talk to the staff.

That afternoon, I ventured alone onto the streets of Peking for the first time. The boulevard leading west, Stephanie told me, could be followed all the way to Tian'anmen Square. It was the widest thoroughfare I had ever seen, an astonishing ten lanes across from kerb to kerb, and called 'Chang'an Jie', which translates as the 'Avenue of Eternal Peace'. But the trickle of snail-paced motor traffic made the road look planned for a motor age that hadn't yet arrived. Peking was still a city of cyclists. The bikes looked all the same—black, dusty, rusty, cranky and bell-ringing. The people too all looked the same, most wearing shabby dark-blue or field-green cotton jackets and matching baggy trousers, like boiler suits. When they saw me, they looked, even stopped, and stared.

I saw my first bike parking lots, where hundreds, sometimes more than a thousand almost identical black machines were lined up outside a subway station. I took my first photographs from a foot bridge across one of the wide intersections, called Dongdan.

Thirty years on, although China, and Beijing especially, have changed almost beyond recognition, the features of this particular location remain largely the same. Only the people and vehicles passing through have changed. Chang'an Avenue remains ultra-wide, Dongdan's footbridge, though new, is still there. Back then, Peking's eight million residents pedalled along at a snail's pace, mudguard to mudguard. Now ten million cars grind, also at a snail's pace, bumper to bumper. In 1986, only government ministers and foreign diplomats—and Mr.

WILD WALL–THE FOUNDATION YEARS

Browne – were in the Mercedes class. Now, it is one of the most common brands on Beijing's roads. The red billboards with their white characters that were Chairman Mao's quotations are no longer there; they have been replaced by Chairman Xi Jinping's quotes on 'Communist Core Values' or his 'One Belt One Road' project.

A good hour's walking and gawking up the widest avenue led me to the largest square in the world, Tian'anmen, which is actually a rectangle. Everyone congregates there to have their photograph taken. Few Chinese had their own cameras in 1986, so photographic-vendors did a roaring souvenir-snapshot business. After the click, the photograph inscribed with golden placename characters would be mailed in a self-addressed envelope to the furthest corners of the country (I saw one or two examples in the homes of my future farmer hosts.)

I made my way directly to beneath the enormous portrait of Mao that hangs above the tunnel-entrance into the ancient vermillion-walled building on the northern edge of the Square: Tian'anmen or 'The Gate of Heavenly Peace'. Behind him was ancient China, the so-called Forbidden City, the Imperial Palace that was used by the last twenty-three emperors of China for some five hundred years between the early 1400s and the early 1900s, and where the Italian crew would presumably be filming the story of number twenty-three, the very last emperor.

Mao's portrait was strategically placed. He looked forward, away from imperial China and its old ways towards the New China that he founded. Directly above his portrait was a rostrum, the place where on October 1st 1949 he stood to announce the founding of the People's Republic of China.

As I turned around to witness his view, unbeknown to me a huge audience had gathered quietly around me. There were at least two hundred people, silent with stone-faced expressions, an encircling wall of staring faces. For a few seconds, I felt intimidated. I could feel their steely gazes, examining my height and foreignness, from my brown-haired head to my size 14 training shoes. I had large feet by any standards, and in China they were the feet of giants. I needed to break the ice and escape from this uncomfortable siege. Now was the time to use my introductory line learned in Liverpool, perfected through repetition on the plane, which had worked so well in Hong Kong, 2,500 kilometres to the south – where they speak Cantonese.

"*Nei hou, ngo hai ying gwok yan.*" I expected smiles, but their faces remained expressionless. I repeated myself, louder. Then there was a little giggling and smiling, but nobody seemed to reply. Southerners warm, northerners cold, I thought. I edged forward, parted the waves and started my long walk back to 'the office' ready for a dinner appointment with the Brownes, which I was dreading.

Given the furore in the Hong Kong newspapers, I feared that I was about to be admonished about causing trouble for Thomas Cook, my sponsor, and for Midland Bank, its owner. Mr. Browne surprised me completely. He told me not to even think about 'getting permission' but to 'just do it' and ask for forgiveness, if necessary, later on. It was the first time that I was given this advice, which I would often hear repeated.

Browne had studied the Chinese language in Taiwan and his wife was from Taipei. I recounted my afternoon walk to Tian'anmen, and described 'the encirclement'.

"They laughed because they couldn't understand you. Here in the north they speak *Mandarin*, not *Cantonese*."

At noon, next day I visited the office again, to check out the newspapers coming in on the first flight up from Hong Kong. Overnight telexes from Thomas Cook in Peterborough also awaited me, ominously requesting that I 'get in touch immediately to discuss implications'. The furore had escalated, not subsided.

I had no idea what would happen if I simply continued to travel to the end of the Wall as planned, and began my journey. Would I be stopped, questioned, detained, deported? I was new to China and cautious of the authorities. In hindsight, I realise that absolutely nothing would have happened. China has no interest in a squabble between two foreigners. However, I was forced to step back, with Thomas Cook explaining that they had backed me for a Great Wall story, not a slinging match. I was in a conundrum as to whom I should listen to. Lance Browne of the Bank advised me to have a go while TC were asking me to step back. Although the former owned the latter, it was Thomas Cook that was funding me to the tune of £2,500 in traveller's cheques.

It is often quoted 'there's no such thing as bad PR', but this was not the kind of coverage that my sponsor had hoped for, and my appetite for having a go under such intense press glare was shaken. We agreed to let the dust settle and I was to rest and wait for a while, assured that I could rely on Thomas Cook's continued support when the time was right.

I'd come to China to see all the Great Wall, from one end to the other. But in the end I had become embroiled in a press furore and, as yet, seen nothing. I felt a failure. Mr. Browne convinced me, with a rebellious tone of voice, that I might as well just go and have a look at the terrain 'for future reference'. He readied his driver to take me there, to the place that everyone - from state leaders to businessman, from tourists to non-starters — are taken to when they first visit China: the Great Wall at Badaling.

Over the decades, I've had the pleasure of taking thousands of travellers to the Great Wall for the first time. I've seen the delight in their eyes as we approached it, the wonder on their faces as they follow it snaking from behind to disappearing beyond, and heard their regrets at not having the time to see more of it. I just wanted to go through the motion of seeing it for the first time, the worst time, and leave as soon as possible, with no regret whatsoever, for I was determined that I would indeed be back when the time was right. Next, I was obliged to stopover in Hong Kong to tell the press there about my decision. They thought that I had been defeated. Griffiths was quoted in one report as saying, "I think William Lindesay is naive, just going to China and thinking he could run the Great Wall."

Back in Britain, April was a critical time for the future of my adventure. I came perilously close to getting cold feet, abandoning my goal because it seemed bureaucratically impossible. I was utterly dejected, but somehow I managed, by the skin of my teeth, to hang on to my dream objective. My daily routine of running helped to a small degree, but indecision was the main cause of pain. The problem was that I did not know who I was waiting for to make a decision, until the realisation dawned that I was the sole decision maker. Phrases like 'under cover' and words like 'clandestine' started to come to mind. As I ran, I thought more and more about doing the unexpected.

Nobody thought that William Lindesay would be naive for a second time, returning to China believing that he could run the Wall without permission. So that is exactly what I decided to do. I booked my ticket, a one-way ticket, from Manchester to Beijing, for the middle of August 1986. I had told Neil Pirie of TCTC of this return trip and he agreed to keep it hush-hush and only he and the Midland office staff would know about it.

6

MY CHINA APPRENTICESHIP

JUST A FEW months before, I had been in Peking for a week. This second time was very different, both in circumstances and season. I was not exhausted by any PR. There was no Peking smell of coal. People had cast away their cold glares, there was a relaxing warmth, and the hum of cicadas. Fur hats were replaced by sun-hats, face-masks by sunglasses, piles of cabbages by mounds of watermelons, women in trouser suits by women in dresses. It hardly seemed to be the same place.

Since the 16th Century, the city had been known in European tongues as Peking, or slight variations thereof. This name had been reported by the first Jesuit missionaries who landed and lived in Macau from the 1550s. They had heard the name of the distant imperial capital spoken by local Cantonese, who pronounced the two characters 北京 as *bak ging*. But the city's own residents (and all northerners speaking Mandarin) pronounced the same characters quite differently, as *bei jing*. Aware of my own mistake, I had abandoned my 'incorrect' introductory line 'hello, I'm British' in Cantonese, and replaced it with the appropriate Mandarin form *'ni hao, wo shi yinguoren'*. The city in summer seemed so much more agreeable than the one I'd seen in spring that I decided to mark this change in my mood by adopting the use of Beijing as the city's name from then on.

Strictly speaking, all foreign independent travellers were

obliged on arrival in every Chinese city, to report to the local China International Tourist Service office to be assigned a hotel that was authorised to accommodate foreign guests. I requested a hotel in the cheapest category, and was instructed to take bus No. 42 to the Longtan Hotel, which was located beside a park of the same name in the city's southeastern quadrant. It was quite handy for Beijing Railway Station, from where my real China journey would begin—if I was successful in buying a ticket to my starting point, the seaside end of the Great Wall.

The station concourse was jammed with people milling around islands consisting of piled-up baggage and sleeping bodies. Not just suitcases, but makeshift bundles and bamboo poles (the roller case was yet to be invented) for carrying, and large supplies of food ranging from sacks of melons to neatly-tied packets of convenient instant noodles.

Alongside the station facade were rows of ticket kiosks with mousehole-sized windows, and it was here that I first came shoulder-to-shoulder with Chinese ways. It was immediately clear that they did not queue for tickets, they barged for them, so I had to also. Within a metre of the mousehole, I thrust out my hand, along with three or four other hands clutching crumpled-up banknotes. Mine was a different hand, yes, clearly that of a foreigner, but mine also held a paper on which I had meticulously copied out the three characters 山海关, *shan hai guan*, along with the numerals for the month and day I wished to travel. These were the first Chinese characters that I ever wrote, so I held my breath in anticipation as the ticket seller's hand snatched the items from me. I tried to see their face, but the hole was too small and the crush too great. A minute or so later, the hand reappeared and I grabbed its mass of a smaller number of screwed-up bank notes and a small thick card. I now had a one-way ticket to Shanhaiguan, the day after tomorrow.

WILD WALL–THE FOUNDATION YEARS

The long string of military-green carriages trundled along with their windows wide open and ceiling fans whirling. The luckiest passengers were sitting on bench-like seats, while many others sat on their baggage in the aisles, between each carriage, beside the hot water boiler, and outside the filthy toilet. Amid this mass of humanity, a trolley bearing mysterious snack foods was constantly pushed back and forth, interspersed with the passage of individual vendors selling magazines or books. Every half hour or so the train pulled into a station where passengers would lean out of the windows, shouting and dangling grubby banknotes to buy food ranging from greasy fritters and chunks of watermelon to 'tea eggs' piled high in washbasins from vendors on the platform. Within an hour, the carriage floor had, like the bottom of a bird cage, become thickly carpeted with inedible parts of what has just been purchased, debris that included sunflower seeds, peanut and egg shells, chicken bones, melon pips, rind and juice, cigarette butts and phlegm. The latter was a common pairing because almost all Chinese men chain-smoked, and hawked continuously. I was immensely relieved to reach Shanhaiguan and escape from this seven-hour-long travelling nightmare.

Leaving the station, I walked through the large waiting room cum ticket hall where a huge 3-D style map of Shanhaiguan was painted on tiles. This diorama extended from the coastline where the Great Wall meets the Bohai Gulf to the mountain front, with the wide coastal plain and the walled-town in between. It was the kind of detailed map that I needed, and it certainly gave me a sense of the local layout and scale of the Wall. It was rather fuzzy on its western edge, seemingly leaping amidst precipitous peaks, and disappearing behind clouds and pine trees, which I assumed was artistic license at play.

A massive thunderstorm raged from late afternoon confining

me and my neighbours to our hot, clammy and mosquito infested hotel rooms. With no air cons, doors were left open to assist the buzzing electric fans create a draught-through jet stream, a turbulent air corridor that was at least mosquito free. But the open plan of it, and childrens' use of the corridor as a playground amplified every shouted word, turning the whole floor and those above and below into a vast communal cavern. If Beijing was the place where I realised Mandarin, not Cantonese was spoken, it was in my Shanhaiguan hotel that I discovered that Mandarin was not spoken at all, it was shouted. Barely able to get any sleep before my big departure day I felt relieved to leave the hotel, emerging into the clammy, grey sauna outside at first light. It was 4 a.m. and I was anxious to get going.

Muddy pools covered the roads and a brigade of sweepers armed with brooms had already begun to deal with the aftermath of the deluge. I passed through a small opening in the town wall and took a long straight road down towards the sea. A Wall buttress stood obstinately on the edge of the beach, its bricks pocked-marked by sand-laden winds, their fired clay dissolved by the salty water of crashing storm waves. About 200 metres away, large angular blocks of granite lay in disarray on the beach, extending into the shallow water for a short distance. For a feature with such an imposing name, Old Dragon's Head, that is vaunted as the eastern terminus of the Great Wall, I was expecting something more impressive. But this was all that was left, and it was not very much at all. Rather than being an Old Dragon's Head, it was more like a headless old dragon. The Chinese have, since the 16th Century, likened the course of the Great Wall to the writhing body of a dragon coiling its way across the northern edge of their empire. I speculated on who had done the slaying, nature or man?

I stepped from block to block, until I was a few metres from

WILD WALL-THE FOUNDATION YEARS

the shoreline and, feeling I should be performing some sort of ceremony, I took off my shoes and socks and let the waves lap at my feet. Rather than savouring the significance of this moment for me personally, I pondered the fate of the Wall. How must it have looked during its heyday, in the early 1600s, I wondered?

This was the first of countless times that I would stop, sit, sometimes lie down and wonder what if I could see all that is missing put back in place. What if I could learn the story behind the changes that had clearly—though unclearly as to precisely how—occurred? Surely even the greatest ocean storm could never have destroyed the original head structure founded on such massive granite blocks. A more catastrophic event must surely have been to blame. Perhaps an earthquake, or a ferocious battle, but not one fought with the cold weapons of old, like bows and arrows, or spears and lances, but with hot weapons, those containing gunpowder, such as cannon or bombs. The Japanese had invaded China in the 1930s, so perhaps it was their evil doing? Years later, embarrassingly, I discovered that the British Navy bombarded Old Dragon's Head in 1900 during the Boxer Rebellion, prior to landing soldiers nearby on a mission to relieve the siege of the British Legation in Peking. I also found photographs taken in the 1890s that showed it really had been a head, extending out into the sea for about twenty metres like a stone pier.

And while I thought of times past, people around me got on with ordinary things. A man, also on the rocks, fished, another walked along the shoreline, collecting seaweed. A few couples strolled. One couple, hand in hand, smiled and in perfect English said a larger-than-life "Hello! Where are you from?"

Here, I met my first of many Great Wall friends-to-be. Shi Hong was a tall, skinny young man with his lovely new wife, Han Rong. They were Peking University postgraduates (which explained their more than reasonable English) honeymooning on the coast for a few days. And they were both surprised and delighted to meet me, although I was reluctant to tell them why I was there. They wrote their names and department telephone number in my diary, and insisted that I should contact them if I needed any help. Then we said goodbye.

I brushed the sand off my feet, gave them a few minutes to dry off, pulled on my socks and shoes and without ceremony set off, destination the western end of the Great Wall.

For such an immense journey I was shockingly, perhaps inadequately prepared, yet very happy to feel the ridiculous lightness of my backpack. It contained less than just the essentials. Despite having been inundated with enough athletic kit for an Olympic team, apart from the the T-shirt, shorts, underpants and socks that I wore I carried just two changes, plus an 'ultrafleece' pullover and trousers (yet another latest-material innovation) that was warm, windproof and low volume when compressed in my backpack. I'd assembled a tiny first aid cum footcare kit and opted for my familiar Olympus OM2 camera with a 35-105 mm zoom lens and 16 rolls of Fuji slide film.

To introduce myself and my purpose I had the letter provided by Han Suyin, to show my family I had a lunch gathering photo, and to pinpoint my country I had a postcard of HM the Queen. But it wasn't where I'd come from that was important, it was where I was going. To Jiayuguan, at the west end of this Wall. It hit me there and then how far away it was, far, far beyond to the west. Immediately I experienced a crushing feeling of uncertainty, only hopeful of one thing, that by following this Wall hour after hour, day after day, week after week and month after month, with a lot of luck, I might reach that far end, and that would be the end, and enough for me.

I began pondering the strange nuances of the word 'end'. Rather

WILD WALL-THE FOUNDATION YEARS

like a piece of string, the Wall had two ends — the 'eastern end' and 'western end'. This appeared to be the case on any map, whether my *Oxford Atlas*, *Times Atlas*, or *Map of the People's Republic of China*. While these maps and most others do show the Wall ending at Shanhaiguan on the Bohai coast, I would come to realise that the Ming Great Wall does in fact continue further east, reaching the outskirts of Dandong city, located on the north bank of the Yalu River in the northeastern province of Liaoning. Being of poorer quality construction this 'continuation' has decayed faster than the rest, and no longer remains as such a visible landscape feature. In reality, Shanhaiguan is not the eastern end as is claimed. Later I would refer to it as the 'seaside terminus' of the Great Wall.

I had at first naturally become acquainted with the Great Wall's geography. I knew virtually nothing of the Great Wall's or even China's daunting history, apart from a vague notion that it stretched back thousands of years and was sub-divided into many dynasties. I'd delved into an encyclopaedia to scavenge a few historical facts as background to drop into my marketing prospectus. That, I'm ashamed to say, was my only Chinese history 'class', for when I was educated in Britain during the late 20th Century, China was far away and irrelevant, as absent from the school curriculum as it was from world affairs. This journey promised to be a history lesson on foot, taught at every place, by everything and everyone, past and present. The only dynasties that I was confident about so far were the Qin, whose symbol is the memorable terracotta warriors, the Ming, for both its cobalt blue and white porcelain and the Great Wall, and now, thanks to Bertolucci's film crew, the Qing, whose Last Emperor story featured on the final page of many volumes that detailed 2,200 years of Chinese dynastic history. But from these first three familiar dynasties I learned a lot that was immediately relevant. Simply by spacing them out across eighteen centuries, they record when the first Great Wall began in the Qin, when it reached it height of development in the Ming, and when it came to its sudden end in the Qing. The Qin, Ming and Qing are pillars of the Great Wall story.

Since the First Emperor had founded the Qin Dynasty in 221 BC, a surprising total of sixty-six dynasties had risen and fallen. This is because between the dynasties that ruled large territorial areas for long periods of time there were frequent intervening periods of division during which rule was contested among many smaller states. The final dynasty, the Qing or Manchu Dynasty, fell to the Kuomintang, or Chinese Nationalists under Sun Yatsen in 1911. It was here at Shanhaiguan that the Manchus made a decisive military move to establish their own piece of Great Wall history. In 1644, an 80,000 strong cavalry army rode out from their homeland in the northeast to attack Shanhaiguan. The timing of their approach was perfect. The Ming capital of Beijing had just been ransacked by a peasant rebel army, and the last Ming ruler, Emperor Chongzhen (r. 1628-1644) had committed suicide. This placed the Ming commander of the Shanhaiguan garrison, Wu Sangui, in a critical predicament. His army was caught between a peasant army to the southwest and the Manchu army to the northeast. In a desperate bid to avoid annihilation and perhaps create a future role for himself, Wu decided to offer the Manchus a deal. He would open the gates of Shanhaiguan to allow their army to pass through the Wall to join his own forces, to form an alliance that would together face the peasant rebel army. The Manchu accepted, and the alliance won. This led to the founding of the Qing Dynasty.

With their innate knowledge of nomadic politics and skilled cavalry warfare the Manchus went on to subjugate the tribes beyond the Great Wall and incorporate vast swathes of northern desert, mountain ranges and steppeland into their expanding realm, pushing the Qing frontier far to the north. The Ming Great Wall, an object of their ridicule, redundant in their aggressive defence policy, was now not only useless but no longer in the border region. An entirely new era of Great Wall history had dawned, its retirement period.

Working at his height, the Wall had been manned and maintained by an army of approximately 750,000 soldiers, but was now abandoned and left to the ravages of nature, to those pillaging its stones and bricks, and to future explorers of the monumental ruins – until the next invasion to originate from the northeast. Remarkably, the Wall came out of retirement to play a brief operational role in the face of the advance of the Japanese Imperial Army out of Manchuria which they had annexed in 1931. In an attempt to face them off, Chinese forces chose the line of the ancient Wall as their strategic high ground to stand upon, using its towers as garrisons for troops once again. I envisaged I'd use them too as places to spend the night. I carried a ground mat, sleeping bag and bivouac bag for that purpose.

From the coast I followed a barely perceptible, overgrown path on top of the Wall, a high mound that struck inland without any remaining battlements. In the distance on the other side of the town, I could see it climbing the dramatic break of slope that marked the rim of the coastal plain and the rise of the mountains, and then disappearing amidst peaks that continued into a hazy distance, the fuzzy edge. In front of me at regular intervals, I encountered a squarish platform of earth, remains of watchtowers, that had long since been razed to the ground. Every now and then a track cut its way obliquely through the Wall, forcing me to descend as well. Flanks of the Wall sometimes retained their brick-facing, while in many places the clay interior was laid bare, either slumped away or dug away. I became aware of just how much the Wall had aged, had become decrepit, during its long retirement.

After several kilometres I reached a temporary end to the Wall, at a place where a dozen or so railway tracks cut through its line. All towns and cities in north China once had their own enclosing walls, but while most have been demolished, Shanhaiguan's wall still stood proud, and most of the town was crammed within it. The high structure was pierced by numerous arched tunnel-like openings, both large and small. I headed for its famous gateway called 'The First Pass Under Heaven' (*tianxia diyiguan*), a name that was intended to convey the impregnable status of the defensive position, once all the gates had been closed.

I filled up my two large water bottles and ate a bowl of noodles and headed for the far side of the town where the Great Wall reappeared, linked to the town wall. It continued, like a large grass snake for several kilometres through more fields of maize to reach the foot of the mountains. The first two-hundred metres of Wall ahead located at the break of slope at the edge of the coastal plain appeared to have been recently rebuilt. This reconstruction presumably presented a view of the Wall as it might have appeared during its period of operation. As the light began to fade, I selected a large platform below a handsome watchtower for my first overnight on the Great Wall of China, stuffing my down sleeping bag inside my bivi bag and laying it on my foil-covered ground mat. I watched the landscape fade to black, the town of Shanhaiguan light up, and bright specks ply their courses across the Bohai Gulf.

A wide variety of nocturnal animal life kept me alert throughout the night. The night air was refreshingly chilly for a while, then dew laden, before I felt cold and began to long for dawn. Confident of a clear sunrise, I climbed higher up the Wall, leaving the rebuilt stretch and reaching its crumbing parts, to obtain an even better view. I sat down, waiting and watching, with my tried and tested Olympus OM2 in hand.

WILD WALL-THE FOUNDATION YEARS

Although I have been privileged to enjoy hundreds of clear sunrises along the Great Wall over the last three decades, seeing its stone or brick or earthen ramparts highlighted in dawn gold, the first Great Wall sunrise that I was about to witness over Shanhaiguan stands out as one of the very best. The photograph I took that morning has been published widely and admired many times over the years.

I took just two exposures, one portrait and one landscape format. Back in the good old days of film photography, each shot was more considered, carefully setting the aperture, shutter speed and making any necessary compensations to let in more or less light, to over-ride the exposure meter, before finally 'making' the photograph. It was analogous to one shot at the target, performed sparingly, that of a sniper, in stark contrast to the modern age of digital 'machine-gun' photography.

The portrait format photograph of the two proved to be my first great Great Wall landscape photograph, what I would later call a 'Wallscape'. I recounted the experience in my 1989 book *Alone on the Great Wall*, and I am unable to better what I wrote back then:

> 'Looking to the Yellow Sea coast, I watched the sun's disc edge above the horizon and the slow trading of colour between the fading orange sky and the brightening green and yellow hues of the plain. Gradually my route of the previous day clarified, from the sea to the town, over which now hung a patch of dawn smog, caused by the coal-burning stoves of the townsfolk. Between town and mountains, the low angle of sunlight gave the Wall a shadowed edge, underlining the strategic importance of Shanhaiguan – 'mountain-sea-pass'. I thought of soldiers from centuries ago, waking up and pausing to watch this morning ritual of the sun'.

The higher I climbed, the more broken-down, indistinct and less-continuous the remains of the Wall became. Suddenly, the risks of entering such a remote area without a detailed map began to worry me. I looked around, heard my own heavy breathing and felt my heart throbbing. I realised that my two guiding beacons had both disappeared from view. The coastline behind me was no longer visible. The Wall ahead of me was gone too. I stood amidst scattered rocks, surrounded by thick bush, no longer sure of the way ahead. How could the Great Wall disappear? A few minutes before, I had been standing on it. Now it was gone from under my feet.

I wrestled my way through thick bush until I realised that I was going deeper into trouble. To my relief, at least my bushwhacking had left a trail of destruction that would be possible to retrace. Backwards or forwards transformed into a tormenting 'should I?' or 'shouldn't I?' moment. Stop or go? Then wider questions. Those who give up never win, winners never give up. Sensible or foolishness? Up or down or contouring? Forwards or backwards? Now or never? Naivety or bravery? First is first and second is nowhere. Griffiths or Lindesay?

I rummaged in my backpack for my water flask. It was already frighteningly light in weight, containing little more than a mugful at most. Two litres was nowhere near enough for an afternoon and overnight and an uncertain day ahead. There was just enough room on the ground to lie on my back. Looking up, it was if I was on an island seeing just a tiny patch of sky above. If only I was up there instead of being down here, the terrain would be so easy to appreciate.

I had genuinely believed that 'where there is the Great Wall there is a way' — because the Great Wall made its own way. And I desperately wanted to become living proof that where there is a will there is a way.

WILD WALL-THE FOUNDATION YEARS

Oddly, if I had benefitted at the time from a bird's eye view, the likes of which I would only enjoy thirty summers later in 2016, I would not have seen any Wall close by, or found the answer I hoped for, to see the way ahead. I would surely have been overwhelmed and intimidated. Only an advanced understanding of Wall-building strategy in high mountain areas, that I would learn much later, could explain the navigational predicament that I had encountered.

The break in the Wall's continuity had occurred due to a strategic 'borrowing of the landscape'. From 2007-08 the State Administration of Cultural Heritage organised surveyors in the nine provincial-level administrative regions traversed by the Ming Dynasty Great Wall to locate and measure the system of fortifications. They discovered that the Ming Wall is 8,851 km long and they subdivided this length into three categories. Built fortifications measured 6,259 km; trenches dug in areas of soft sediments (constructed to slow the charge of attacking cavalry who would flounder when their horses encountered the wind-blown sand of the ditch) measured 359 km; while 'natural features' incorporated into the defensive line measured a significant 2,232 km. This latter category, comprising cliffs, narrow ridges and river gorges, became part of the overall defensive system when connected by built fortifications. I didn't know this back in 1986, although it had been a subtle detail illustrated in antiquity.

The first maps of China produced in Europe from as early as 1584 show strips of Great Wall amid mountains, which reflected the rampart-mountain-rampart makeup of the defence. Further, the most prominent Jesuit in China, Matteo Ricci (1552-1610), wrote in his memoir, published in modern times as *China in the Sixteenth Century*, that '(The Empire) is quite well protected on all sides by defences supplied by nature and science.' He continues: *'To the north the country is defended against hostile Tartar raids by precipitous* hills, which are joined together into an unbroken line of defence with a tremendous wall four hundred and five leagues long'.

If only I had known all this back then. During afternoon the humidity rose, the visibility diminished, and my confidence and morale plummeted. I spent one of the most uncomfortable nights of my life huddled among the bushes. The night sky was cloudy and starless and the howl of wolves echoed eerily in the valley.

Next morning, severely dehydrated and weak, I began my retreat to Shanhaiguan. Within two hours I had thankfully regained the Wall and followed it in reverse until I came over the crest of Jiaoshan from where the view of the coastal plain opened up before me. This foray into the mountains from Shanhaiguan seemed foolish, desperate and reckless, although retrospectively I would see it as a necessary baptism of fire. Without maps I'd learned the hard way, that the Wall is discontinuous, and a gap could easily throw me off-course. I had to work out a proper route. But at that point, I didn't see a way from Shanhaiguan so continued my retreat, to Beijing, to regroup.

The slow train ride back to Beijing gave me time to think. It was late August and while I was sure that I needed to wait for temperate weather, when it came, the autumn season wouldn't be long enough for me to complete an end to end traverse — in either direction, for the distance was not only too long, but the North China winter would bring its own barrage of survival challenges. But I wanted to get out again, on the Wall somewhere, to scout out the terrain, regain confidence and overcome my fears. Besides, I needed to show my sponsors that the year was a valuable period of preparation, while the following one would be the year of the full-length journey.

"This is an essential reconnaissance — this is a necessary China apprenticeship," I told myself.

A good and cheap basecamp was necessary in Beijing to

WILD WALL–THE FOUNDATION YEARS

take stock of my situation. I went back to the CITS office, and specifically requested and obtained lodging in the Longtan Hotel. I was happy to be back there. It was clean, efficient and friendly, and as soon as I arrived, I looked forward to next morning's homely Western breakfast of toast, jam and butter, as well as fried eggs and Nescafé with creamer. Ten yuan per night got me a bed in a three-person dorm with other male travellers, all foreigners, while Chinese guests appeared to always be lodged in separate rooms.

I'd passed on the opportunity of showering in Shanhaiguan as the hotel's facility was 'open plan', and while I was okay with mass showers after running races back in the UK, as a hairy foreigner, I preferred to avoid being stared-at in the nude. Washing in the Longtan's cubicle shower was top of my list of several housekeeping and communicating chores.

As an illiterate foreigner I was getting used to finding my way to toilets by smell, and likewise I made my way to the shower room, the source of running water. But as I pulled my T-shirt off, I heard a loud shrill from behind. I turned quickly to see a young woman stark naked in the steam! I grabbed my clothing, she covered her scenic spots with arm and palm and I ran out shirtless, swiftly returning to my room. That night, I made sure to learn the characters for 'male' and 'female', and fortunately there were no repercussions – well, at least not until the following year.

After some encouraging talks on the phone with my brother Nick, who was always pragmatic and positive, we decided my next move. I'd travel by train to the western end of the Wall at Jiayuguan, to see how far I could get along the 'mud' Wall in Gansu Province. The terrain was higher out west, sandwiched between high mountains and desert, far away from the coast and the summer humidity of the east. It would be autumn, so my original plan of bivouacking out might be challenging in the cold. Nick suggested staying with farmers. That seemed like a good idea, but would there be anyone eking out a living in those remoter areas?

I learned from Stephanie at the Midland office that my friends Shi Hong and Han Rong had telephoned. I called them back and we set a time to meet at the Friendship Store right beside the CITIC building, where there was a small cafe that served Nescafé and slices of 'sponge cake'.

When I divulged exactly what I was planning to do, they were horrified. They warned me how dangerous and dirty the countryside was, and they seemed to genuinely fear for my safety and health. To allay their fears and give them a task to make them feel helpful, I asked them to write an introductory note at the front of my diary. I spoke and Shi Hong wrote the following in Chinese for me to use when I got to Gansu:

> *Hello Chinese Friends! I'm William, from Liverpool in England, travelling on foot along the Great Wall from Jiayuguan to Shanhaiguan. I am alone, so I will need water, food and a place to sleep. Thank you for helping me. And please write your name, village name and anything you know about the Great Wall in your locality. Long live the friendship between China and Great Britain!*

7

To The End Of The Wall

BEIJING RAILWAY STATION is an impressively large building, one of a group of ten designed and financed by the Soviet Union to mark the tenth anniversary of the founding of the People's Republic of China in 1949. Its two clock towers showed Beijing time, which all China officially adheres to, even though at its furthest flung western edge, there is, longitudinally speaking, a three-hour plus time difference. The clock chimed melodically, not in any ordinary ding-dong ding-dong rhythm, but offering ever-longer snippets as each hour progressed of the 'The East is Red', the hymn to Chairman Mao Zedong, describing him as being 'The Red Sun of the East'.

On the wall of the cavernous station concourse, my purpose loomed before me: the largest painting of the Great Wall one could possibly imagine. Over the ensuing years, I would see this iconic image time and time again in different forms, but never as large as this giant presentation. Flanking it on both sides were the departure boards, and despite their alien Chinese characters, finding my train was surprisingly easy, because each train route had an individual number. The lowest numbered trains were the most important. Number 1 ran between Beijing and Changsha, the capital of Hunan, Mao's home province. My train was No. 69, to Urumchi, in the northwest corner of the country. The very thought of a long, hot, filthy, smokey train journey of fifty-five hours duration to Jiayuguan was too much, so I decided to break it up into two stages. The first leg would be 'just' twenty hours to Xi'an where I would overnight. I wanted to take in a history lesson there, visiting the world-famous terracotta warriors.

I had procured a 'hard sleeper' ticket. There were six beds within each doorless recess, three stacked on each side with a small table between, beside the window. The train left on the dot. A station master saluting on the platform floated past the window. Lovely melodies were piped through the loudspeaker system.

Soon after we started moving, the carriage conductor began her rounds. She carried a large black PVC zippered file which contained rows of little pockets. Without any expression apart from pouting, she snapped "*huan piao!*", which meant 'exchange your ticket'. One by one, she proceeded to swap everyone's ticket for a plastic token which denoted their carriage number, berth number, and position, either lower, middle or upper. At the time, I had no absolutely no idea of the purpose of this procedure, but years later, I worked it out. Some passengers would reach their destinations in the middle of the night or while they were napping during the day, so by holding all the tickets, the conductor always knew which passengers in which berths needed to alight where — and so she could wake them up in advance of the train's arrival.

I had a middle bunk, and lay down to read about China's history, while watching the landscape go by. I was travelling among today's Chinese in the land of their ancestors. Everything was new to me. It was the perfect vantage point.

The first stage of our journey was southwest, across the North China Plain, through Anyang towards Zhengzhou on the Yellow River. During the second millennium BC these cities were centres of Shang Dynasty rule (circa 1700-1000 BC) which extended

WILD WALL-THE FOUNDATION YEARS

across and around the lower reaches of the river. This dynasty registered easily because of its handsome museum 'markers'. In the dusty and dark National Museum of Chinese History on one side of Tian'anmen Square, I had admired excavated treasures of the Shang, especially the first historical (written) records, pictographic characters etched on 'oracle' bones used in mysterious divination ceremonies, and inscriptions on large bronze cauldrons used in rituals. (Many of these first characters can still be recognised by literate Chinese today, and partly evidence China's claim to being the oldest and most continuous of the ancient civilisations with a longevity enduring to this day).

It was captivating to observe how the Chinese all did things in a very similar manner. They each pulled a very large enamel mug from their baggage along with a neatly rolled hand towel (face cloth), toothbrush and paste. Washrooms were placed at each end of the carriage and after waking up, the Chinese would go there to rinse hands and faces and return to neatly hang their towels to air from the luggage rack above the aisle. If any towel was placed untidily, or was not folded corner-to-corner, the conductor would put it right on one of her patrols to deal with such problems, as she would for dangling baggage straps. But among all of the locals' quirky habits, it was tooth-brushing that I found to be the most inexplicably regimented. This was performed—and it really was a performance—using only lukewarm water in their mugs. After vigorous brushing came a baritone gargle, then a puffing of cheeks to rinse thoroughly, terminating with an ejection of all the mouth contained with explosive gusto—spraying into the basin and beyond (the same routine persists nationwide to this day).

Our approach to the Yellow River was preluded by sophomoric melodies piped over the PA system, giving way to a solemn-sounding commentary on the Yellow River, which the

Chinese call Huang He. The change in tone of the piped delivery was clearly noticeable even to me. Passengers looked up from books and out of the windows. For a minute or so, iron girders of the bridge flashed past and I stared down into the muddy current below. I wondered where, when and how I would cross 'the River' in the two places where the Great Wall encountered it.

On north-south and east-west journeys by train over the coming decades I would cross the Yellow River many times and witness its seasonal moods. Sometimes a churning muddy torrent, sometimes flats of cracked and curled dried mud plates, sometimes solid ice. Despite these mood swings, it remained the respected Mother River of China, for control of it established a foundation for the evolution of Chinese culture. Contrary to common belief, in terms of quality land for farming, the Chinese weren't quite born with a silver spoon in their mouths. The farmers' life growing crops on the fertile flood plain was fraught with danger. The River flooded every summer due to heavy rains and during spring as the ice melted in its catchment areas to the west. Over the centuries these floods have taken many lives, and the River gained the epithet of being 'China's Sorrow'.

To unlock the farming potential of the River's wide and fertile floodplains and adjacent land, the Chinese had to make their fields and hamlets safe. This demanded an immense and sustained effort, to build and maintain dykes. These long earthen mounds may be considered forerunners of defensive walls, although they functioned as barriers against floodwaters. The large workforces raised to construct them needed organisation, and that could only be delivered by an hierarchical system in which an elite ruling class wielded absolute power to command. The long-term effect on Chinese society was profound and is still evident. People were forced to work together to prosper, and benefited equally from a reliable flood-control and crop-growing system. The Yellow River valley began to produce more than enough food, freeing up some of the population to do things other than work and worry about their next meals. Artisans made utility goods, and then crafted objects of beauty. Next came philosophy, science and art. Farming behind the protective river dykes brought together people who had once lived separately and in conflict, marking a step in the evolution of urbanisation and civilisation. For this reason the Yellow River gained a second epithet, 'The Cradle of Chinese Civilisation'.

The train now headed west, following one of the Yellow River's tributaries, the Wei, towards Xi'an, traditionally the most-favoured of geographic locations for siting a dynastic capital throughout Chinese history. For more than 1,200 years, thirteen dynasties, including the 'Golden Ages' of the Han and the Tang, favoured Xi'an. It was placed on the inside edge of the Central Plains, it stood at the eastern end of the Silk Road, and most importantly, it was far from the dangerous northern frontier.

When the train got to Xi'an, I was more than ready to get off. There had been overnight rain, and the French plane trees shading the city's roads fused the air with natural goodness. Vendors on the pavement sat beside their melon mounds and baskets of fruit as streams of cyclists glided along the washed roads with tyres purring like smooth zips on the wet surface. I more than noticed the women, who wore thin, loose dresses to catch the breeze and my eye. Some hand-held their hems as high as their handlebars to save them from entanglement in their wheels. I couldn't resist making eye contact with some of these lovely women, and got shy responses from a few. I wanted to go with the flow like them, to my destination. I rented a bike for the day, and knowing that maps were a no-no, I bought a set of postcards, selected one showing the terracotta warriors, and set off, pulling the postcard out at every intersection to ask for a pointer direction.

The method worked perfectly. Three hours later, I stood in a large dusty building resembling an aircraft hangar, facing a phalanx of hundreds of life-sized warriors standing in formation. The army of statues had originally been regimented in underground chambers. These were violated by rebels, just a few years after their closure and burial. They smashed the warriors, stole the weapons they were holding, and set fire to the chambers which were walled and roofed with wooden posts and beams. The subterranean structures then collapsed, crushing the warriors and compressing them under the weight of earth and ash. Thereafter they lay undisturbed, for nearly 2,200 years, until 1974. Now the Qin army had stood up!

In 1986, Chinese museums had no English language labelling, so I needed to decipher what clues there were. Here, beside the terracotta warriors' pit, were drawings of thin wooden strips (*mujian*) bearing ink characters. These, I suspected, were select 'pages' from one of China earliest history books, and certainly its most famous: Sima Qian's *Records of the Grand Historian*, a general history of China in 130 chapters, covering the period from the year dot to when the chronicler lived (circa 140-90 BC). *Records* is the most precious primary source of information on the Qin's unifying conquest and the First Emperor's underground palace tomb. Its half a million characters were written on tens of thousands wooden strips that were linked together, like pages being stitched together, represented by the Chinese character 冊 *ce*, meaning 'bound book'. I couldn't read any of it, but thankfully two large maps offered a geographical explanation.

The first, headed '230 BC', showed many small blocks of territory, states, about a dozen, most of them having 'Long Walls', denoted by that mesmerising battlement symbol, running

WILD WALL–THE FOUNDATION YEARS

between them, or along their northern edges. Within the territory of each state was a pictograph and a sketch of a coin. These all looked similar at first, but scrutiny revealed that they were not quite the same. Actually, some of the coins looked like paper knives.

My take at the time on what was being depicted proved to surprisingly correct. In 230 BC the land was divided among many states that were hostile to one another, and their northern nomadic neighbours, and they wrote slightly different characters and used metal coins of different shapes. Over the next decade, everything changed. The Qin State won victory after victory, year after year, one by one, as state after state was defeated, Qin territory grew in size, becoming the one and only by 221 BC: the Qin Empire. The second map, headed '215 BC', recorded the massive geopolitical change achieved by conquest, unification and standardisation. The many of everything—states, Walls, characters and coins—had been reduced to just one of each. One script. One currency. One empire. One Great Wall along the northern perimeter of the empire.

Emperor Qin Shihuang standardised the writing style and currency shape, virtually overnight. Making necessary changes to the 'Long Walls' took much longer. Armies of workers were dispatched to demolish 'interior' Walls—to literally wipe them off the map—in a bid to prevent them being reused by rebels aiming to split the empire apart. While the Qin had defeated other ethnic Hans, it could not expect to match the cavalry skills of the northern nomads. No Chinese army wanted to confront those superior mounted archers in open-field battle, so the Qin kept the three 'Long Walls' of the north for their strategic advantage, as advocated by Sun Zi's military treatise *The Art of War*: occupying the high ground and waiting for the enemy to approach. Put even more simply than the map, the 'formula' for the First Great

Wall was as follows: The Qin Long Wall + Zhao Long Wall + Yan Long Wall = Qin Great Wall. The + represents new building work to link up existing Walls. Much later, I found out that the '+ work' to join up the three Walls was quite considerable. Sima Qian recorded that *'General Meng Tian conscripted an army of 300,000 to march north'* and do this work.

Xi'an had been a vivid history lesson—I was now clear on the origin of the first Great Wall, and where it was—much further north than the Great Wall marked on China maps of today. But I was going to follow the latter-day Wall, the Ming Great Wall.

The next day, in possession of another sleeper ticket, I rejoined train No. 69 for the remaining 35-hour journey. From Xi'an we headed west to Lanzhou, to cross the Yellow River for the second time. It was slow-going, walking-pace at times, as we gained height, hauled by a steam engine at the front and 'banked' by a second steam engine at the rear. After several hours of grinding along, near Wuwei we entered a narrow strip of level, cultivated land wedged between the Gobi Desert to the north and the Qilian Mountains to the south—the Hexi Corridor.

I had pared all my gear down to the bare essentials, and even trimmed unnecessary portions of territory off my whole China map. What remained showed Gansu as a bone-shaped province with two bulbous ends, with fragments of the Great Wall, and the railway I was on, running in parallel along this narrow corridor route.

Hour after hour, I failed to spot any signs of the Great Wall, even though my map showed sections of it appearing to be right beside the railway. Then, between Wuwei and Zhangye, I saw it for the first time. It was a very different kind of Wall here in the west compared to its build on the mountains to the far east. That more familiar face was constructed in stone and fired-brick, what

WILD WALL–THE FOUNDATION YEARS

I would later call 'Classic Dragon Wall'. This less-familiar western form was made of rammed earth, now dried and crumbling mud, looking like a giant worm cast. It wasn't occupying any high ground, because the Wall itself here *was built to be the high ground*. Far east and far west, both were part of the same Great Wall, yet being so unlike one another in material, appearance, architecture and location they were more like counterparts.

My fellow passengers certainly noticed the attention I paid to the fragments of the Great Wall that kept appearing and disappearing close to the track. "The Great Wall" said one passenger in strained English, while the others mentioned "*wanli changcheng*". I pointed up the carriage, ahead, west and said "Jiayuguan" and then pointed the other way, back, saying "Shanhaiguan". I prodded my chest, looked ahead and back, and then pointed to my eyes, expressing my intention to see it all.

II

A Foot in the Open Door
1986-1989

'British friend travelling the Great Wall'; calligraphy by Feng Jinhai of Jingbian, Shaanxi, given to the author during his journey in May 1987.

8

Barriers To The Pleasant Valley

Arriving in Jiayuguan gave me a feeling of being on the edge: the edge of China, the edge of Central Asia, the edge of the Great Wall. I liked the frontier feel of the town compared to clammy Shanhaiguan, and checked into the only hotel open to foreigners, the Jiayuguan Binguan, a guesthouse beside a large traffic roundabout. Next morning, in pre-dawn darkness, I began to walk out to the Jiayuguan fortress, which marks the western terminus of the Wall, hoping that it would not turn out to be the anticlimax that I had experienced at the Old Dragon's Head.

Slowly, as dawn broke, the buff-coloured walls of the fortress and its various structures within grew larger. Jiayuguan is the most westerly of the many so-called strategic passes strung out along the whole length of the Ming Wall. My slow approach to it gave me the time to consider what the original strategy had been at this location. I sensed that the Hexi Corridor was narrowing at this point, with the Qilian Mountains closing in on my left and the Mazhong, or Horse Mane Mountains on my right. Jiayuguan seemed to guard the bottleneck at this end of the Hexi Corridor.

I was the first visitor of the day, and waited patiently for the gates of the mud-walled fortress to be unlocked. When they were pushed open by a rather tired-looking nightwatchman, a more impressive wall, higher and crenelated was revealed within, and a line of three high gate towers. I strode towards the first one, passing a small temple and entering a barbican immediately beneath the huge structure. Hundreds of swallows twittered and darted about its eaves. The building was pierced at ground level by a dark tunnel paved with large and well-worn rock slabs, plenty wide enough for the passage of carts, for they had come and gone this way with their nail-studded wheels for so many centuries that they had worn deep ruts, just the opposite of rails, in the rock. Beyond lay the large and almost-empty centre of the fortress, save for the yamen, a cluster of buildings within its own gated courtyard where the fortress commander had garrisoned.

My priority was to locate my starting point, the precise western end of the Great Wall. I made my way up to the gate tower via a ramp. From there, the magnificence of fort and mountain location could be fully appreciated in a wide vista that stretched from the intricate woodworked eaves above me to the snow-capped tops of the Qilian Mountains on the distant southern skyline. Eager to see what the lie of the land was like between this fortress and those mountains I walked the perimeter wall. From its battlement, I was surprised to see what was clearly a long section of the Great Wall extending far across the desert, at least to the foothills that rimmed the edge of the mountain range proper. I immediately decided to abandon any further exploration of the fortress interior, impatient to follow the Wall outside to wherever it went.

I made for the pair of gate towers ahead and descended to ground level by way of another ramp, via a tunnel, across another barbican, then out through another tunnel to exit the fortress and reach the open desert. Looking back, above the tunnel entrance I noticed a stone plaque set into the brickwork and inscribed with three large characters. Oddly, even though I was a complete illiterate I half-recognised them. No wonder! They were the three characters that I had diligently copied from my map onto a scrap of paper in order to buy my train ticket to Jiayuguan. I retrieved my ticket to check, and sure enough I was correct, more or less, and although there were some minor differences, it was easily readable. Chinese characters used to be written top-to-bottom and right-to-left, but the Chinese world has now moved to the Western standard of left-to-right. Also, since the Communist takeover China has simplified many of the most-used characters, partly in order to increase literacy rates by making writing simpler. Either way, simplified or standard, Jiayuguan translates as 'Pass to the Pleasant Valley', meaning the green lands inside the barrier being China.

I set off on my walk to the end. In some places, the Wall had a recognisable shape, in others it was shapeless. After crossing the main highway and several railway lines breaking the line of the Wall, I regained it. The only noise was the sound of my shoes scuffling in the sand, the occasional echoey klaxon horns of trucks driving along the road, and hoots and whistles from passing trains. As I plodded on, I wondered where that end would be—at the foot of the hills, or somewhere within them? Near or far? Today, or days away?

After an hour's walking the fortress behind me was far away while the foothills were just ahead. Partly sunlit and shadowed, their slopes stretched out like an apron of screwed-up brown paper along a mountain front of an altogether different scale, high enough to host glacial fields. Soon, the scene ahead seemed, or rather sounded, very different. I could hear the sound of running water. Surely there could not be a river nearby, on the edge of the Gobi Desert?

Only when I veered slightly left to go around the next tower did the lie of the land start to reveal itself. The hissing sound became amplified, and I could see a sharp edge up ahead and the ground disappearing and then reappearing far beyond. In front of me was a drop-off to a deep chasm below. I crouched down, then crawled on my hands and knees towards the edge. About as deep as it was wide, perhaps 70 metres, the gorge indeed contained a river, a wide grey torrent. I edged back, stood up and looked around, listening. My heart was thumping. On the far side of the canyon, there was no Wall. A shiver went down my spine, as I realised exactly where I was. At the very western end of the Great Wall of China.

A large mud tower stood perched on the cliff edge, but it had lost most of its shape, presumably because of its vulnerable location. There were some helpful footholds that aided me as I clambered up its friable face. From the top was the place for the perfect photo, of the last few metres of the Great Wall, the gorge and the river. To the southwest the chasm snaked away, clearly functioning as a giant sluice to take away summer meltwater from the high peaks.

Just as I'd unknowingly encountered the 'borrowed mountain' strategy outside Shanhaiguan in the far east, here the ancient Wall-builders had also incorporated a valuable landscape element. By building the Wall up to the edge of the Qilian Gorge they had included it as part of their defensive layout, effectively extending the length of the fortification by the addition of a natural barrier. Here, at the Qilian Gorge, they had also 'borrowed the landscape'.

At dawn, I had thought this would be a reconnaissance day, but now I thought 'no, this is the day, this is the starting point'.

I set off from the true western end of the Great Wall, first heading back to the fortress. Beyond, with my poor maps, lay terra incognita. I realised there and then that the greatness of this Wall was a tantalising combination of what can and what cannot be seen. Together, this added up to its all, all the Wall. I drew in deep breaths at the prospect of all the Wall that I was going to encounter, less or more, sooner or later, and to the innumerable challenges I was about to face. And I was very conscious of the need to take this journey one day and one night at a time, to settle down to the basics of travelling on my wits. It was time to shut out the far and think of the near. I told myself to focus purely on the primary needs of food, water and sleep.

I discovered that there was little or no convenience food to be found in Jiayuguan town, so I expected there would be none in tiny rural shops. My favourite finds were jars of various fruits in juices. And, because sugar was an expensive additive, it wasn't overly sweet. The choice was wide—apricots, pineapple, tangerines and pears. But there was an aggravating challenge: the lids were not twist-off, and my simplest and lightest two-bladed Swiss Army Knife wasn't strong enough to open these jars without the risk of some kind of deep cut. The quickest opening method was using a meat cleaver. Shopkeepers first made cross-shaped cuts across the lid of the jar, and then prised the four metal quadrants back to make an opening large enough to insert chopsticks. I resorted to using a single chopstick in a spear-like fashion, a method that led me to describe this rigmarole as 'spearing fruit'. Main courses were harder to come by though. Just about the only options were steamed bread (*mantou*) the size of very large buns, or little packets containing a sandwich-sized wedge of dried noodles.

After easy overnight hotel stays in the 'open' cities of Jiayuguan and Jiuquan ('Wine Spring') – open meaning that foreigners were allowed in them—I entered a tract of unpopulated and drier country. A couple of nights of desert bivouacs had proved to be cold, hungry, miserable and lonely experiences, so I tested out a new approach to sleeping near Qingshui ('Clear Water'), about 70 km from Jiuquan. It was the first large oasis, an area of richly cultivated ground with a water supply, that I'd come across after

WILD WALL-THE FOUNDATION YEARS

the miserable desert scrub of the previous days. I was tired, dusty, dehydrated and sore all over. The location I chose was a solitary farm in the shade of tall poplar trees where I tried out my *'ni hao, wo shi yingguo ren'* (hello, I'm British), my warmest smile and best sign language, accompanied by loud sound effects to denote drinking. Once I had my foot in the door, I introduced myself in detail using the front page of my dairy. Next morning they wrote a message in it, from which I'd learn they were surnamed Wang, the most common name in China.

The Wangs, mother and father, in their mid-thirties, their daughter, perhaps ten or eleven, and a grandmother in her late sixties, set a high standard for offering full board and lodging to a stranger. Here I found simple luxury. Clean, cool water to bathe blistered swollen feet, and sufficient water to rinse my hair, wash my face and wring-out my socks. The remoteness of the farm made for a peaceful stay: no one came near to look at me or ask questions. I sat on a tiny stool in the yard, watching the family go about what was for them not just another working day. I was likely to be the first foreigner they'd ever seen, let alone been up close to and accommodated.

When I woke up the next morning, the autumn sun was already splintering through the thinning poplars, a chilly breeze thinning them even more. A wok full of water was coming to boil in the yard, while the women kneaded dough to make noodles. I prepared my feet and packed my bag.

After breakfast it was time to say goodbye. The couple gave me a tiny photograph of themselves and I thought I might return the gesture by taking a photograph of us all together. I needed to improvise a tripod. Mr. Wang had a bicycle with a stand, which I tried, as the whole family watched on bemused. I placed my Olympus OM2 on the saddle, tilted the lens barrel upwards by wedging straw beneath it, and framed the family, using the zoom to pull in the now-visible Mount Qilian, map marked as being 5,547 metres. I was just about to trigger the self-timer when mother realised what was about to happen. She started shouting excitedly, ran inside, and came out holding a pink dress — which the little girl pulled over what she wore. I took just one frame of us all, and it turned out to be perfect.

Later on, I rarely took photographs of my farmer hosts, to avoid the inevitable slew of requests for family portraits and shots of the neighbours. My limited film stocks prohibited me from assuming the role of village photographer. Over the years, the photograph of the Wangs of Qingshui, with me alongside them, has been seen by thousands of viewers. When I'm speaking live, I usually ask the audience: "Can anybody spot me?" Just like Mt. Qilian, towering over the range it names, I'm head and shoulders taller than the Wangs, looking like someone from another planet.

Beyond Qingshui, I saw little of the Wall for days. But ten days east of Jiayuguan, near Zhangye, I did see my first sand dunes. And what dunes they were! Large 'barchan' dunes, shaped by wind into perfect crescents. Despite the heat of the afternoon sun I just couldn't resist crossing them. I had for several days felt a pain in the ball of my left foot, so thought that the softer surface might be more comfortable. That evening, I was exhausted, probably due to my rather rash waste of energy, and near midnight, I began to feel a little nauseous.

I got up to relieve myself but the door was bolted and two minutes' fiddling with it in the dark proved critical, as my stomach churned and I began to soil my pants. Out in the moonlit yard, I had a terrible time improvising for the absence of lavatory paper and removing my soiled clothing.

In the morning, I got up to find that one of the women had kindly washed my clothes which I'd left outside. I was weak and running a temperature, and couldn't stomach the thought of eating. I just lay on the *kang*. Around noon, there was some commotion and the family and a few neighbours came in and helped me to my feet, out of the yard and onto the back of a donkey cart.

The ride down a rutted mud road was cushioned by a quilt underneath me, so I lay looking up at the bright blue sky and avenue of tall poplars. Despite the noise and discomfort, I dozed off and a while later we reached a larger village. Our destination was a clinic. It looked newly-built, had the smell of paint, and a distinct lack of furniture and fitments. My first public medical examination followed. In attendance appeared to be a doctor, some other staff from the clinic, and spectators who'd heard there was a foreigner in their village. At the curtain-less windows, which extended the full length of the wall, dozens of people gazed in, their noses pressed against the glass.

One of the crowd spoke in some English. "I am teacher, she is doctor, she is nurse, they our leaders of this team," he said.

"Thank you," I murmured.

The doctor, actually 'he', prodded me here and there, looked in my mouth and eyes while the group around the bed chattered and smoked.

"The doctor says you the ill person,' said the teacher. "Our leaders are worried."

Gradually they went away. By my bed was a flask of hot water, a towel, a basin and pile of toilet paper. The crowd at the window had largely dispersed, but there was always someone on shift there, looking, peeping or giggling, even when I was defecating in my basin.

Next day I was woken by someone speaking better English. "I'm the interpreter from the Zhangye Public Security Bureau Office of Foreign Affairs — we heard that a foreign friend was ill in Linze," he said. Several suited men surrounded my bed. "We are taking you to the big hospital in Zhangye city."

There I received an even more public medical check up, drawing a large and attentive audience for a jab in the backside. "You have *la li*," said the interpreter. Some kind of gastroenteritis perhaps, I wondered? My worst symptom was diarrhoea. Even a cup of water set my intestines churning within minutes. I was taken to the Zhangye Hotel, the city's guesthouse, to be alone to contemplate my health, my journey and my future.

The next morning the teacher returned, I presumed to take me to the hospital for a check-up. But I was wrong: we went to the police headquarters. There I received a few words of sympathy before an interrogation.

"How did you reach Linze?"

"I came on foot, looking for the Great Wall."

"Where did you start from?"

"I started from Jiayuguan."

"Where did you stay, which hotels?"

"I stayed with farmers."

"Do you have an Alien's Travel Permit?"

"I have a visa for China."

"With a visa you are allowed to visit the open places, but not the closed places."

"All the way from Jiuquan to Linze is closed to foreigners without an Alien's Travel Permit," explained an officer through the interpreter.

"Can I get the permit, from you?" I asked.

"No. You must go to our Gansu Province capital, Lanzhou city, to apply the procedure. We can fine you money and other punishments, but our leader sees that you are ill, and your attitude is good, so we will not punish you this time."

The interpreter added his advisory postscript. "The Great Wall in Gansu has turned to sand. The best place to see the Great

WILD WALL–THE FOUNDATION YEARS

Wall in our country is at Badaling, close to Peking." he said.

With my severe stomach problem permit chasing in Lanzhou was out of the question. We went to the railway station, and procured a ticket for the fifty-hour journey to Beijing. It was 'hard seat' class (without any sleeper berth), and for the duration of the journey I dared not eat or drink beyond only a few mouthfuls of boiled water for fear of being caught short again. I arrived in Beijing feeling like death warmed up, and barely had the energy to go directly, without asking China International Travel Service which was the rule in Beijing, to 'my' hotel, the Longtan.

My room-mates adopted me. Graham Taylor, a nineteen-year-old lanky and bronzed Aussie was cycling around China, and had been doing so for months. He brought me fruit, yoghurt and a walking stick from an 'old folks' fair' in Longtan Park. Our threesome was completed by Millard Farmer, an American Vietnam War veteran, in his mid-thirties, who was taking a decade-long cycle ride around the world. They were entertaining room-mates, and we had one thing in common: trespassing in the closed areas of China.

I called up Shi Hong and Han Rong, my student friends at Peking University, to explain my problem, and they promptly decided to take me to Beijing Hospital to see a doctor. It turned out that *la li* was amoebic dysentery. A foot injury, which I'd almost forgotten about given the more serious ailment, happened to be what the doctor termed 'a Long March fracture'. I'd need months of medication and rest to fully recover. How unfit would I become during that convalescence, unready for another, third, and perhaps final, attempt?

9

MY PHILOSOPHY OF TRESPASS

I BOOKED MY ticket back to London with mixed feelings, and pretty much self-confined myself and my ailments to the Longtan Hotel, nursing my wounds and conducting post-mortems into why so much had gone wrong and so little had gone right over the year. Thankfully, my room-mate Graham Taylor came back one evening with a copy of the English-language newspaper *China Daily* reporting the upcoming state visit of Queen Elizabeth to China, beginning in Beijing. The news made it a must to somehow get to Tian'anmen Square to see Union Jacks flying there for the first time. I grabbed my new walking stick and gave it a go.

The Queen's visit was the first to China by a British monarch, and would surely auger well for the future of UK-China relations. I saw the flags and milled amongst the crowds, but only saw the motorcade of the royals from afar. An unexpected bonus, though, was there for all to see, close up—one of the Square's last displays of the images of revolutionary heroes.

National Day, October 1st, had just passed, and to mark the 37th birthday of the People's Republic, the Square was decorated with spectacular floral displays and graced with giant painted portraits of five 'guest revolutionaries' hauled out on this special occasion for an audience with Mao and the masses alike—Dr. Sun Yatsen (1866-1925), who had led the Republican Revolution of 1911 that overthrew the Qing Dynasty (1644-1911) and

WILD WALL-THE FOUNDATION YEARS

founded the Republic of China was flanked by four foreigners, communism's ideological mainstays, Lenin and Stalin on one side, and Marx and Engels on the other. They all faced north, towards the portrait of Mao over the entrance to the Forbidden City.

Like many foreigners new to China, I found it hard to understand why Mao's image remained there, especially given his calamitous Great Leap Forward and Cultural Revolution. In 1980, the Italian journalist Oriana Fallaci asked Deng Xiaoping: "Will Chairman Mao's portrait above the Tian'anmen Gate be kept there?" Deng answered, "It will, forever." He went on to assess Mao's policies as having been seventy percent correct and thirty percent mistaken, and that remains the official verdict. The days of the four foreigners, however, were numbered. They came back to the Square for a last time on National Day in 1988.

Tian'anmen had been my first Beijing experience back on day one in March, and my last Beijing excursion in October before heading home. As my taxi drove along the familiar narrow airport road, I considered how my 1986 had unfolded. My best achievement was 280 km following the Wall for ten days out of Jiayuguan, ten percent of the distance of a full-length traverse, hardly a pass with flying colours. But not everything important can be measured. By learning the hard way — getting lost, falling ill, being 'arrested' — I now appreciated what the 'barriers to the pleasant valley' really were. The makes or breaks of my comeback journey were sure to depend on finding my way without suitable maps, staying healthy, and passing undetected through areas closed to foreigners. I boarded the plane knowing that I'd return. But by doing so would I be sinking to the level of a blatant trespasser?

My 'case for the defence' might have called as witnesses the six families that had welcomed me so warmly as I passed through their tiny villages in the Hexi Corridor. They had played a pioneering part in an accelerated form of China's open door policy. When might rural homestays be officially permitted? While I expected that, in the future, more of China would be officially opened up to foreigners, I had a nagging feeling that it wasn't going to happen quickly. It might take ten years, and by then my legs wouldn't be as good. I had to do it next year, without question. Despite the steepness of my learning curve, my Wall fever had not abated, it had intensified. I'd done ten days and 280 km, so why couldn't I do a hundred days and 2,800 km next time?

Back in Wallasey, I set out on my road to recovery. I was prescribed Streptotriad for dysentery and electro-therapy for the stress fracture. I kept my expedition mind focussed by reading about early travellers in China, books that I found either as reprints or in my local libraries. Of particular interest was Cable and French's *The Gobi Desert*, Aurel Stein's *On Central Asian Tracks*, and Francis Younghusband's *Bayonets to Lhasa* and *The Heart of a Continent*. But what promised to be the most relevant title, *The Great Wall of China* by William Edgar Geil, an American, published in 1909, eluded me. References to it suggested that Dr. Geil may have been the first person to journey along the line of the Great Wall, travelling by conventional means at that time, a mule caravan. I contacted Probsthain's Oriental & African Bookseller, in Great Russell Street, opposite the British Museum and they responded saying they had a copy in fine condition, priced at £275, a hefty price tag for 1986. Although I had Neil Pirie's unofficial confirmation that TCTC would back me for a final attempt, nothing was certain until signed and delivered. As for general living expenses, I was supported by my mother and father, while my own savings were almost exhausted. All things considered, I couldn't indulge in purchasing Geil's book, and besides, it documented his journey along the Wall some eighty years or so ago. I told myself it was too old to be useful; my journey was through a different China. It would be eight years later, but certainly not too late, before I began to learn the great relevance — and practical value — of Dr. Geil's milestone book.

Convalescence gave me plenty of time for pondering how I might improve my chances of success in 1987. Surely it would be my last chance. I couldn't expect sponsors and my parents to support me beyond the two-year mark. I needed a victory. My China apprenticeship, after all, was merely a stepping stone, not an achievement.

Rudimentary Chinese language and literacy would also be a boon. I'd bought a Chinese textbook reader that I began to study and mastered a good few hundred Chinese characters over the long, hard winter, which was normally my peak time for mileage training. Instead, I guarded against my stress fracture becoming chronic. I cycled a few kilometres to the outpatient's department for my physio and played snooker with my father. I took consolation in the knowledge that my second-best London Marathon time of 2 hrs 40 minutes and 15 seconds was achieved not on my usual high-mileage regime, but just running for fun after a six-month rest enforced by serious injury. Rather than thinking that I'd lose a lot of fitness over the '86-87 winter, I thought the other way — that I'd be very well-rested. I told myself that the first few weeks of the journey itself would be my 'come back' in more ways than one — I'd get fit en route.

I had already passed through closed areas quite successfully, completely oblivious to the fact they were closed or that China even had such a restrictive policy. My enquiries revealed that there were 325 places, cities and counties, open to foreign visitors with tourist visas. Although this sounded a lot, when plotted on a map the imbalance soon materialised — more than 99% of China's territory was closed. Apparently there were also 'forbidden areas' too, along China's borders and around sites of strategic importance, such as military bases.

The policy of 'open' and 'closed' areas was introduced after the abandonment of China's decades-long policy of banning entry to most foreigners. A significant part of Deng Xiaoping's reform policies involved China normalising its relationships with the outside world by encouraging trade and initiating tourism. Deng himself led the way, travelling to the USA, allowing the signing of business deals that brought in American goods ranging from Boeing jets to bottles of Coca-Cola. As a result, in 1979, Deng was named *Time Magazine's* 'Man of the Year'. Ordinary people, too, could be part of this change-around, but how would foreigners be managed in a country that had remained isolated for so long?

Chinese authorities assumed that foreigners would be visiting the country for either business, tourism or language study — or spying. If a location had sights to see or goods to sell — tourism or business potential — then it could be designated as being 'open' to foreigners, provided that the city or county could provide reasonable transportation links, accommodation, communication facilities and basic medical services. If some of these practical boxes could not be ticked, the place remained closed, and the default setting was 'closed'. But what about the Great Wall?

Ever since the first foreigners saw a map of China the Great Wall had advertised its presence, and from then on it became a must-see monument. But wanting to see the Great Wall and wanting to see it all, from end to end, were completely different goals, as I had just started to find out. Only a few places on or near its line were on the 'open' list, namely Jiayuguan, Jiuquan, Wuwei, Zhongwei, Yinchuan, Datong, parts of Beijing, and Shanhaiguan. Everywhere in between was closed. But the Wall was my chosen way, and just as its builders were undeterred by any terrain in their path, neither would I be. I'd be a roving British ambassador, providing a view of the outside world in exchange for water, food and shelter from farmers along the way of the Wall. We had established some excellent bilateral relations already, and I would be making more. This was my philosophy of trespass.

For climatic reasons I decided to divide my journey into two stages, the spring and the autumn. Looking at my map, it appeared that the eastern meeting of the Great Wall and Yellow River in the region of Shenmu, on the Shaanxi-Shanxi provincial border, was a natural mid-way point. As for the intervening summer, I'd stay in Beijing, maintain my China momentum by learning more of its language, culture, and history. Not least, of course, this would save me the hefty expense of a return air ticket to England. I reckoned that I could live well on a subsistence allowance of £5 per day in 1987 Beijing.

It was mid-March when my mother gave me the Lindesay traditional Sunday-lunch roast party send-off. The whole family was in attendance, with their spouses and children. We took a photograph that I would use on my journey to introduce myself and my background.

My mother, then seventy years old, was understandably quite worried to see me go. It took weeks for a letter to be delivered to the UK from China, and while I was en route, it would be impossible for me to receive news from home. So we agreed to communicate by what we called 'British Telepathy'. There was an eight-hour time difference, so at midnight in the UK, when my night-owl mother was still watching television, it would 8 a.m. breakfast time in Beijing, while at midday in the UK it would be early evening in Beijing. At these preset times my mother and I vowed to 'talk' to one another.

10

THE RICE BOWL OF FRIENDSHIP

MY THIRD ARRIVAL in Beijing was a lot easier. My taxi drove down the now-familiar guard of honour, the poplar-lined airport road. I re-established base camp in the Midland Bank office, and all the staff looked happy to see me again. I was now skilled in ticket purchasing at Beijing Railway Station and bought a soft-sleeper railway ticket to Jiayuguan. It almost felt like going home as I checked into the Longtan Hotel.

Jet-lagged, I was up and ready for an early breakfast and entered the large dining hall at seven o'clock. It was empty except for a solitary young breakfaster, who I joined. Our meeting reminds me how, back then, almost every foreigner you met in China at that time was a pioneer of some kind, planning on doing, in the process of doing or having done something either unusual or extraordinary. Tom Broadbent was reading a rather old copy of Francis Younghusband's *The Heart of a Continent*. This was his guidebook. Tom explained that Younghusband was an ancestor on his mother's side, and he was about to retrace the illustrious man's footsteps. Nobody could claim a more revered forebear in Central Asian exploration. Treating the volume with reverence, Tom unfolded a route map of Younghusband's 1887 traverse from Peking, across North China and through the Mustagh Pass to Rawalpindi, now part of Islamabad in modern day's Pakistan. He planned to set out from the former site of the British Legation

WILD WALL–THE FOUNDATION YEARS

near Tian'anmen Square at 6.00 a.m. on April 4th, precisely one hundred years after Younghusband's departure. We exchanged concerns, theories and worst-case scenarios on negotiating closed areas, vowed to do our best to keep in touch and wished one another the best of British luck. We did keep in touch. About twenty years later, we met again to exchange books.

I decided to set off from the very western end of the Wall again, and not merely pick up my route near Zhangye, where I'd been forced to abandon it the previous autumn. The train took me on the same route, but this time in early spring North China was bare, brown and windswept. The Hexi Corridor was no longer a string of oases, it was more like a dust trench.

As I had done the previous year, I began by marching out to the Qilian Gorge. (The site is now well-known, and is on the tourist trail. It is named 'the First Tower' (*Diyi Dun*)). The first two days were straightforward, but I reached Jiuquan, an open town, completely exhausted. My loss of fitness was very apparent.

Supplementing my poor physical shape, I suffered a psychological setback near Qingshui via a strange encounter, an exchange of sorts, with a goat herder. As I approached he didn't react in any way. He sat huddled under his soiled sheepskin-fleece cape beside the remains of a mud watchtower. I can still see his weather-beaten and wrinkled face, unshaven and expressionless beneath a faded navy-blue cap. He was completely unmoved at seeing me, a foreigner, here, in the middle of nowhere. Typically, the opening question of the Chinese inquisition—"*Na guo ren?*" (What country are you from?)—would have been asked. Instead he said "*Qu nar?*" (To where?). I replied "East, to Shanhaiguan, I'm travelling the Great Wall on foot." He seemed to scoff. Then he said something that sounded like "*Wanli changcheng, zou bu wan, zou bu wan*" while shaking his head and waving his arm. My language study over the winter had been a worthwhile use of downtime. As we sat there, looking at his foraging goats, I mulled over the meaning behind his comment. *'Wanli changcheng'* was of course what the Chinese called 'The Great Wall'. *'Zou'* was the action word, the verb, meaning 'walk' or 'go'. I'd come across *'bu wan'* in the form of *'che bu wan'* which means 'can't finish eating', so did *'zou bu wan'* mean 'can't finish walking'? A chill rippled down my spine. I bade him farewell. He just grunted in response.

Though the herder was soon far behind me, and much as I wanted to forget him, I just couldn't stop thinking about what he had said and wondering what he meant. Whenever I met danger or difficulty in future that negative *'zou bu wan'* of his echoed in my mind.

I chivvied myself along at the welcome prospect of revisiting the Wangs of Qingshui who'd hosted me six months before. But the great difference in the seasonal appearance of the landscape left me puzzled as to exactly where they lived. Then, one morning, as I made my way along the lanes of an oasis, who did I see working in a field ahead of me but Mr. Wang! I was unable to explain in any detail what had occurred in the interim, so could only imagine the family's conversations that evening when he told them he'd seen 'that foreigner' again.

I worked hard on accumulating mileage and finally neared Linze, where I'd fallen ill the September before. Passing Zhangye would psychologically mark my full recovery from the illness and injury that had forced me to abort my last effort and return to Britain. I was about to advance onto new ground.

Between Zhangye and Shandan, I found the best preserved stretch of mud Wall so far, and it was continuous. The kindest of families, the Yins, fed, watered and sheltered me from a snow storm, which confined me, rather happily, to their home beside the rammed-earth Great Wall for a whole weekend. By Monday morning, the blizzard had given way to clear and calm conditions. Snow lay deep and crisp all around, and I set off once again, treasuring my hosts' warm-heartedness, inspired by the Wallscape's majesty. It was here that I hit my stride.

I met shepherds beside this fine section of Wall leading to Xiakou, after which the Wall deteriorated as it climbed into low hills. A tail wind helped me to fly along. I had never felt better, never felt more excited, nor more privileged. I turned around before reaching the top of the pass, to bid farewell to the most magnificent Wallscape of the Hexi Corridor, and to the hamlet where the Yin family lived.

The city of Wuwei, about 500 km into my route was an important target. To think of destinations too far away, of Shanhaiguan and the Yellow Sea, was intimidating. I needed to set my mind upon closer, more easily achievable targets, such as where would I end that day, and importantly, when might I have the luxury of a rest day, a day off in an open city. For that reason, Wuwei had been in my thoughts for several days.

Once in the town, for a few days, there would be no running, no walking, no looking over my shoulder for 'the boys in green' as I nicknamed the police, no need to constantly search for solutions to my primary needs. My most important job was to mail off my clutch of exposed film cartridges to Stephanie in the Midland Bank office in Beijing. Firstly, I didn't want to run the risk of having films confiscated if and when the police intercepted me, and secondly, I didn't want the films to be subjected to excessive and prolonged heat.

My post office excursion in Wuwei turned out to be an education in its own right. Post offices were always hives of activity occupied by crowds of people. There was stamp collecting mania, with much trading of sets on the street outside.

Nearby, sage-like elderly men sat with pen and paper offering scribe services to illiterate rural folk. Inside, the only way of working out what was going on, and how to post my films, was to watch and emulate. Items to be mailed had to be first shown to a clerk. Then a form had to be filled in. The items needed to be packaged, but there were no such things as padded envelopes or boxes. The procedure was that things needed to be 'bagged up' or literally 'sewed up' in cloth. This requirement explained why people were squatting around, busily stitching away. Many customers used pillow cases, but cotton cloth was sold at the counter, as were needle and cotton. After half an hour's cutting and stitching, and copying out the address in Chinese, I joined the scrum to have the clerk accept my package. She looked at it and shouted and shook it. It just wasn't good enough: too untidy, a big bag with a few films moving around, and the address was illegible, even though I had written it large, clear characters.

To solve the problem I resorted to wrapping the films in a T-shirt. I then asked a woman to do the stitching for me. Next I went outside to hire the service of a scribe to write the bank address on both the calico bag and the form. I paid about 1 yuan (less than 10 cents), received a franked chitty in return as proof of posting, and saw my small pillow being thrown in to what looked like a basket of laundry. *When will I see you again?*, a popular song by 'The Three Degrees', rolled off my tongue.

11

My First Escape

Departing Wuwei for Zhongwei meant leaving the Hexi Corridor and the Silk Road. From here, the ancient trading route veered southeastwards towards Xi'an, but I would be heading due east, following the Wall. From the map, the Wall appeared to remain fairly close to a railway line, the two features keeping each other company over an otherwise blank section of my map, skirting the Tengger Desert. I soon found them to be more than parallel lines. They are parallel stories.

The workers on the Wall had long gone, but teams of railway workers were busy maintaining and servicing the tracks. I met a group of workers, all men except for one woman. They downed their tools and crowded around me, offering me hot water from their flasks, and asking the usual questions that by now I was becoming proficient at answering. The woman began to unwrap her bright scarf, the Gansu version of the Muslim veil, that women wear to block-out the sun and dust, which burns, dries and wrinkles the skin savagely at this altitude. Simple communication was easy. I had come from 'that way — Wuwei' and was heading 'that way — Zhongwei'. I took out my notebook to let them know more about me. Then I was lost for words. As the woman completed her unwrapping and shook her long hair in the wind, I saw how gorgeous she was, the most beautiful girl I'd yet seen in China, truly a hidden beauty revealed.

As I followed the railway line, I began to suspect that I also was being followed. Quite a number of locals were walking beside the track, but I saw two men in green stop when I stopped, start when I started, slowed and speeded-up when I did. Close to a station in the middle of nowhere, they caught up with me and made various gestures and then escorted me to the station master's office where they tried making telephone calls. After a long wait, a car arrived, and an unlikeable man who spoke English with a squeaky voice introduced himself as being from the 'Wuwei Foreign Affairs Office'.

I was peeved about being carried off in the car, so I closely observed the driver's route. Within ten minutes or so, we reached a paved road that appeared to run parallel to the railway line to its north, back to Wuwei. What had taken me seven hours' jogging and fast walking—maybe 35 km—was undone by a 40-minute drive.

The police station, it turned out, was right next door to Wuwei Hotel, where I'd lodged earlier. There, I was told about Wuwei city being open, but the county around it being closed, and how I must pay attention to staying away from closed areas. It was suggested that I should go to Lanzhou if I wanted to enter closed areas. There, they said, was the place to apply for an 'alien's travel permit'. I agreed.

Adhering to the maxim of 'asking for forgiveness is better than asking for permission' I'd already decided on my next step. To return to the point where I'd been picked up. Next morning pre-dawn I was walking on the road leading out of Wuwei, looking to hitch a ride. Within minutes, a young truck driver and his two companions stopped, and I climbed into their dusty cab. After thirty minutes or so, I began to scour the landscape for a recognisable landmark where I could hop out. Worried about going too far, I alighted early and walked along the road, and was soon delighted to recognise the dirt road leading towards the railway. I was quickly back on track. I'd made my first escape.

Almost immediately, I received another bonus, thanks to the Wall. As it ran parallel to the railway, it could also serve as a screen to hide me from any suspicious train drivers who might report me. With adrenalin flowing, I marched well, hour after hour, well past the mid-afternoon point at which I habitually began looking out for a farm stay. Dusk was falling and soon there was no Wall, only the railway line.

The evening proved memorable, for it was my first stay at a railway station. The station master offered me a 'single room' — the workers' recreation room, with a table tennis table for my bed. And although passing trains seemed to shake the whole building throughout the night, at least it was a fairly safe haven, being a freight and not a passenger station. At the crack of dawn I literally made tracks.

I liked the down-to-earth railway workers. Their work was similar to that of the Wall builders. They worked on something linear, and were posted at stations along the structure. It was not a military frontier, as they were maintaining a transportation line, but it was a signalling route. Maintenance crews always had some laborious work to carry out along the line, no matter what the weather.

The Hexi Corridor has water, trees, cultivated fields, and tree-shaded lanes and roads. Here, the railway line was exposed, a hard slog. Underfoot were pebbles and gravel, but the work teams inspired me to keep me going. Every few hours I would see a gang, and because they were on site for the whole day they always had water and food. From them, I learned that Chinese people show compassion towards friendly, hungry and thirsty strangers.

With sixty km covered, I arrived at a small village and was

readily taken in by a farming family. They fed me well. All I had to do was to wait until the gathered crowd became tired of staring at me and then turn in for a good night's rest.

But after nightfall, a new wave of visitors included a police officer. He didn't seem to be on duty, but I sensed him observing me in a different kind of way to the others, the peasants. They were curious in a childish kind of way, here to see the difference between me and them, surprised by my height, shocked by my large shoes, my hairy limbs, my thick beard. I suspected the policeman thought otherwise, along the lines of, 'What is this foreigner doing here ... I've never seen a foreigner here before ... perhaps I should tell my superior?'

Soon he came forward and gestured to me, moving his hands to mimic the opening of a book, and using his fingers to outline a square. I gathered that he wanted to see my ID, passport or permit, so I feigned ignorance, and the assembled crowd helped by repeating *"ta ting bu dong"* (he can't understand). Finally, the policeman pointed to his watch and kept saying *"mingtian jiudian"*. I knew that meant 'tomorrow, nine o'clock', but again feigned confusion, responding by showing my fatigue.

I immediately decided on an escape plan. I'd get up and depart by midnight at the latest, to get out of Gansu and cross the provincial boundary into Ningxia. In the meantime I needed to put my feet up as soon as possible. To clear the crowd I mimicked sleep with sign language and began to strip off in front of them. The crude method worked perfectly. Five minutes later the yard was empty, and I, along with the family's other menfolk were lying in a row on the *kang*. By the door my bag was ready to go, while I clutched my torch.

I was worried about falling asleep, but in practice the chance of that was remote. The adrenalin was pumping; I was psychologically prepared for a night walk. The whole project was at stake.

The heavy snoring of my bed mates was my all-clear signal to begin the escape. I glanced at my watch, and although I'd only had an hour's rest, I was wide awake and simply itching to go. I slipped on my shoes, picked up my bag from beside the door and left. If anyone was awake they would just think that I was going out to relieve myself, and would be asleep again before I returned.

I was soon away from the dark, quiet village of Peijiaying, under a star-spangled sky with the light of a silvery moon. I could see the skyline of the low Wujiao hills with the Wall running along their foot, rather than along the ridge-line. It was bitterly cold and I was wearing everything I had with me, including my sleeping bag wrapped around my torso as a quilt jacket.

I managed to keep going for a couple of hours before I felt to be sleepwalking. My eyes were closing for several seconds at a time before a stumble woke me up. I had to stop, there and then. So I pulled out my mat and bivi bag and lay down on the spot. A shooting star streaked halfway across the sky. My lucky night, I hoped. I closed my eyes thinking, 'I've covered at least 80 km in less than 20 hours'.

I overslept. The sun had already risen and it was broad daylight. As I'd sleepwalked, I had veered a little off course. The Wall was about one kilometre away with bare farmland between, and I soon spotted a distinct path leading back to it. As I prepared to make the crossing I saw three people, probably children, making their way along the track towards me. It was a stunning landscape, with the morning sun almost reflecting off the hard-packed earthen track as if it were a curving and silvery stream. Despite my hunger and thirst, I took out my camera. Keeping my head down in a hollow I waited for the three to get closer, gauging the decisive moment to capture them silhouetted on the path. It was a memorable shot—children of the Wall making their way to school. As soon as they saw me they ran over excitedly, then suddenly fell silent when they saw what I was—a foreigner.

"*Wo shi yingguoren, wo e le,*" I said (hello, I'm British, I'm hungry). They pointed towards the Wall and mentioned the word *mantou*, meaning steamed bread. Fifteen minutes later, I entered a courtyard that was no ordinary family farm, but the local 'bakery'. Large baskets of freshly steamed *mantou* had just been prepared. Almost too hot to hold, they made the perfect breakfast. I wondered what story the three children might be telling their classmates and teachers—meeting a Briton beside the Great Wall on their way to school one bright sunny morning.

To deny my mind and body the opportunity to tell me that I was still exhausted, I got going again whispering the mantra 'Ningxia, Ningxia, Ningxia'. It was pleasant countryside with signs of spring, and I began to sense that the land was falling away, gently running downhill towards the Yellow River. I was thrilled to reach a stone-lined irrigation channel churning with clear, ice-cold water. After washing my head, I rinsed my socks and underpants, and then paddled my tired and swollen feet in the channel to cool off, recalling the times I had done the same in Scottish lochs and Welsh streams. Only one more thing could make this a perfect day, and that was being certain that I'd already crossed the provincial boundary. But there was nobody around to ask. Then I thought, 'Why not have a quick bath?' I quickly stripped off and took the plunge, lying on my back, going with the flow, arms outstretched with each hand holding onto the concrete sides, the water deep enough and the flow strong enough to feel as if I were in a Jacuzzi.

As I climbed out to wind-dry my body I laughed at my long dark 'gloves' and 'stockings' of deeply-tanned limbs that contrasted with my white torso and feet. After air-drying for a couple of minutes, I set off with a spring in my step, rejuvenated after my spa stop. Soon I came to a surfaced road, the first I'd seen since Wuwei. Eager for an excuse to rest again, I sat down, hoping to flag down a vehicle and ask the driver where I was.

A vehicle approached, labouring along, laden with rocks. There was no need to flag it down; it ground to halt right beside me, so close that I could feel the heat from the engine boiling beneath a great bulbous bonnet. The driver leapt down and was so mesmerised by my appearance that he didn't even seem to hear my question, repeated "Gansu? ... Ningxia?" Then, after coming to his senses he said : *"bu shi, bu shi "* (it isn't, it isn't). Surely he was misunderstanding something, or was he geographically illiterate? Then he dusted off his front number plate and said *"neimeng"* (Inner Mongolia) while pointing to a Chinese character thereon.

How had I veered so far off course? I had left the Wall in search of breakfast, then taken a rough line-of-sight short-cut back to the Wall only to be distracted by the tempting irrigation channel.

Years later, as I've recalled my 1987 journey, many people have asked "Were you ever lost?" The question has made me realise that, back then, it was quite the norm to be 'lost' for most of the time, if one defines 'lost' as not knowing exactly where I was. This attitude, feeling comfortable about being lost, was essential in the era before GPS when all there was to go by were poor maps and vague directions from locals. Of course, that's a frightening situation for most people to accept today with high-tech navigation aids at everyones' fingertips. For me, as long as I was beside the Wall, following its main course, heading east, towards the sea, I was content.

Inner Mongolia, one of China's thirty-four provincial-level administrative regions, is the long, wide, curving strip of territory that forms more than half the border between China and Mongolia. The area of the region is twice the size of France. But there was little danger of me going any further astray: desert dominated the north, while to the south the land sloped gently towards Ningxia and the Yellow River Basin, a land of fish and rice that presented a distant dark horizon of green fields to guide me in the right direction.

12

BLISTERS & PLAGUE

BEFORE LONG, I had made it back to the railway line, with its groups of maintenance workers who functioned as my lifeline in a harsh landscape. Despite the guidance provided by this permanent-way and the assistance provided by the workers, the days were long, hot and draining. Several days of high mileage, hot weather and no water for washing my feet or socks caused pairs of nascent blisters, on the balls of my feet and on each instep.

That night, lodging with quarrymen, I managed to get some pain relief by raising my feet a metre above my heart by propping them up against a wall. This stopped the blisters throbbing, but I recoiled at the realisation that I was still several tens of kilometres away from Zhongwei, my next 'open town' target, and a safe haven for an extended rest.

I swallowed a double dose of my very limited supply of Nurofen tablets after a quarryman's breakfast of steamed bread and millet porridge. By my departure time, I felt absolutely no pain in my feet, not even the slightest sting. I estimated that I'd get a maximum of five hours of pain relief. Within the hour, I was jogging quite comfortably on a footpath smoothed out by the regular passage of pedestrians beside the line.

It turned out to be a long drag into Zhongwei, passing through suburbs and local stations for more than an hour, over track intersections and across points. When it became too difficult, slow and dangerous to continue along the rails, I followed the road. Up until this stage, all the towns en route had presented a fairly standard layout, with a bell-tower or drum tower at the centre. Nearby were the main post office, government buildings and the best guesthouse that the town could offer, usually the sole option for me as a foreigner.

With the painkillers beginning to wear off, the last few kilometres into town were more agonising than those I had experienced at the end of any race. In a marathon, the crowds are there to cheer you on, but entering this town, people stopped, stood, stared, turned around, and got off their bikes. Finally, the Zhongwei Binguan, the town's guesthouse, my finishing line, came into sight. I staggered into the lobby, registered, limped to my room, swallowed two more Nurofen tablets, and fell asleep for hours. Then intense stinging woke me up.

The pain throbbed to the beat of my heart, with sharp and gouging jabs on the inside of my heels and the balls of each foot. It was clear to me that I should visit a hospital urgently, to have the blisters lanced to avoid what might be a journey-ending infection. But I was unable to even stand up.

I picked up the bedside telephone and spoke, in the best way that I was able, to the reception staff. Within minutes there was knocking at the door and I called "*qing jin!*" — please enter! The staff saw the sad state of my feet and my grimaces, which needed no explanation. Assisted by the hotel manager and a security guard, the staff carried me out and placed me in tricycle trailer, using my bed quilt as cushioning.

Thankfully, the hospital was close, and as a foreigner I was ushered to the front of the queue. A nurse lanced the blisters and cleaned them with iodine. Then I was given several folded-newspaper 'cones' filled with tablets and sealed with twists, plus

WILD WALL–THE FOUNDATION YEARS

a bundle of bandages.

I expected to be incapacitated for at least a week. I spent most of the time with my feet up in the hot, dry air and this dried the blister wounds so that they healed within three days. I hobbled gingerly to the main post office, bought postcards and postage stamps and wrote to my family. I'd covered every centimetre of the route from Jiayuguan, and had followed more than two hundred kilometres of rammed-earth Great Wall on the way. I'd overcome a multitude of challenges, one after another — self-doubt, desert survival, route finding, and dodging the Gansu police to reach the safety of Ningxia.

After Gansu's Hexi Corridor, the Yellow River valley in Ningxia was the second geographically-distinct region on my route, an area characterised by green fields irrigated by the waters of this major river. Sooner than expected, I reached 'the River' near Lingwu, and, despite the bridge being guarded, no one opposed my crossing. I was now inside the River's 'big bend', and entering the Ordos Desert, the third geographical region on my route. The Wall encountered the River in two places, and the next one, to the east, was my end-of-spring target.

Finding what remained of the Wall here, coupled with other considerations such as the southward advance of the desert, would be, I expected, very difficult indeed. However, my map clearly showed long sections of the Wall in the vicinity of three towns. These towns each had the same second character *'bian'* in their names: Anbian, Dingbian, and Jingbian. *Bian* here meant 'border', which combined with *qiang* was the primary name of the Wall, *bianqiang* — 'border defence' — used during the Ming Dynasty.

Occasionally, passing vehicles stopped, with both drivers and passengers offering me water or fruit. However, on one occasion there was an even bigger surprise: a foreigner in a car.

Steve Wetstein, from the United States, was working in the oilfield industry. His company was contracted to a Chinese client prospecting for oil and gas in northern Shaanxi. This was his day off and he'd been driven to the nearest big city, Yinchuan, the regional capital of Ningxia, and he was now on his way back to camp. He was as surprised and excited to see me as I was to see him! He was the first foreigner I'd seen since leaving Beijing five weeks before.

Steve was with a driver and interpreter, Charlie Wang. I discretely told Steve what I was doing and he became even more excited, telling me that fragments of the Wall ran right beside his survey camp. "You must call, you'll pass right by us a few miles east of Anbian and I promise you some home-treats — cold beer, bread, cookies — from our supplies sent from the US!"

I shook hands heartily with Steve and I watched his car drive off. I wondered whether I should take up his offer of hospitality — and luxuries — if I could possibly find his camp, or just stay clear away. I was concerned that the area, being closed, could be a problem: someone in the camp might report my arrival to the local police. Anyway, I decided the issue premature, as the chances of finding the camp would be slim, simply because according to my map the Wall in the region was not just one line, but two, with the remains existing in parallel.

Disconcertingly, I was a little off-colour that evening, feeling sickly, weak and nauseous. I lodged with some workers, although I had little idea what they were doing. That evening, out of the blue, a car arrived bearing an official of some kind. He explained he was representing the Yanchi County Government and I was 'welcome'. "Come with me in the car to Yanchi," he said. I resisted, repeatedly telling him that I'd reach the town tomorrow, on foot. To my great surprise he relented, assuring me I'd be given a welcome as soon as I arrived.

In the morning, I felt much better and set off. I wondered if I was heading into a trap and facing the now-expected 'U-turn treatment' of being cautioned and told to head back to the nearest open town. However, I reasoned that even if I did try to circumvent the entire town of Yanchi, my 'disappearing trick' would only add to the drama, and perhaps result in a man-hunt.

By the time I reached Yanchi it was almost lunchtime. A dark gateway piercing the town's overgrown and crumbling wall up ahead appeared jammed with people. At first I thought it was a market, with traders and shoppers milling around the opening, until a large group of students came forward from the throng towards me. I was the market attraction. "We are students of Yanchi Middle School" one of them announced loudly and nervously. Clad in 'track suits', it seemed that the best English-speaking students had been sent out on a meet and greet assignment to take me to their school. I walked and talked with them as other townsfolk excitedly joined the procession, making me feel like a pied piper.

"Are you tired?" asked one, to which I replied "No."

"Do you like Chinese food?" asked another.

"Yes."

"Are you lonely?"

"No!" I quipped. "Look around, I have hundreds of friends!"

At the school gates, a young suited man appeared and said "Hello English friend, I am Li Dong, the English teacher at Yanchi Middle School ... the county government has asked me to look after you."

Li spoke excellent English and he had a relaxed and friendly manner. "You must be tired, let's go to my home and you can take a rest there."

He led me to a low-rise apartment block beside the school and into his apartment, where I met his wife. In a room crammed with piles of books and newspapers I began to feel very happy in his foreigner-friendly home. This was the first urban home that I had ever entered in China. "Have a read of *China Daily*, they're rather old, but good for practicing," Li Dong said. Weight wise, I could not afford the luxury of a short wave radio and hadn't seen a newspaper for the best part of six weeks. I had no idea what had been going on in the wider world, so old news was better than no news.

As I thumbed through the papers Li opened a glass cabinet to get a large red box that contained, of all things, a jar of Nescafé instant coffee, creamer and two cups! "This is a wedding gift we haven't tried yet — let's have coffee!" he said. I explained how to make it, much to the interest of the couple.

Li Dong told me about his home, school, town and county, and how much the local government welcomed me and wanted to help me reach Shanhaiguan. I deemed it wise to capitalise on the welcome by showing my 'official typed letter' that had been kindly prepared at Han Suyin's suggestion.

I took up the offer of a shower and then we walked to the government-run hotel to check in and have a banquet. Several suited men and women attended, reiterating the official Yanchi welcome, whereupon I dared to present my diary. As well as containing my own notes, I'd also collected a number of written entries from farmer hosts and franks from post offices, soon to be enhanced by a prize new entry: my first official government chop (rubber stamp), a large, red, circular one, with a red star at its centre. I had to pinch myself to believe the day was going so very well, with recovery from nausea, a mass welcome and an official government welcoming banquet, sealed with a chop. And so far, no demand for an alien's travel permit nor any questioning about being in a closed area.

During the afternoon, I rested in the Li's apartment, enjoying more of his coffee and newspapers, before preparing for an evening banquet, which was equally sociable. We returned to the Li's around 8.30 p.m. with just enough time for a bedtime coffee. Then Li Dong said, "Mr. William, I'm afraid there's some bad news to tell you, I'm very worried about your safety on the road ahead."

I felt gutted at the prospect of being told that I would not be allowed to set off further into the closed area. All had seemingly gone so well, and if I was right, the government officials had left their dirty work for Mr. Li to do, and until this late in the day!

"What 'safety problem'?" I asked Li suspiciously.

"Well, I don't know how to say this in English," he said hesitantly. "It's a disease, a disease that's now in this county. It's very dangerous. I'll look for the word in my dictionary." He pulled a thick tome from his bookcase, and sat beside me, as he flicked through it, homing in on the word.

"Yes, yes, here is … it's this …."

He held his finger under the translation. When it came into focus, a shiver went down my spine. It read 'bubonic plague'.

Immediately I thought of a dead dog I'd seen the day before, or was it two days before? And my recent bout of nausea.

"The mayor told me we will soon be closing the county's border …."

This wasn't ideal bedtime news. I spent the whole night thinking about the need for another escape, not from the police, but from the plague. I decided to head off at the crack of dawn and follow the desert road to fast exit Yanchi County and Ningxia as soon as possible.

Next morning, Li Dong and his wife bade me farewell, and off I marched, out of the school compound, through a gate in the old wall on the opposite side of town, heading east.

I'd been told the day before that Yanchi meant 'Salt Lake',

and the salt industry was a pillar of the county's economy. Now I could see it. All around and above, desert and sky, was blinding white. The sun beat down mercilessly, reflecting the glare of the white salt panned plains under the brim of my cap. I trudged on, squinting, vigilantly. I thought how sore eyes, strained by the brightness, peeled to spot any checkpoints ahead, were actually more painful than heavily fatigued legs. According to my map the Wall should have paralleled the road, but I convinced myself that I would not be missing anything. I seriously doubted whether a low mound of rammed earth had any chance of survival on a landscape so decimated by the salt industry.

A moderately paced five hours of footslogging brought me to a rusted gantry which marked the Ningxia-Shaanxi border. There was no checkpoint. This was cause for celebration. Counting my short stray into Inner Mongolia, I was entering my fourth provincial region. Provincially speaking I was halfway along the Wall.

13

SWIRLING ROBES & BLINDING SAND

SUGAR KICKS FROM spearing fruit in jars were all well and good, but I was always on the lookout for real food. Anbian, meaning 'Safe Border' was the next town and I promised myself a quick stop at a restaurant. I imagined going into a kitchen and pointing to what I wanted to eat: eight eggs and five tomatoes, a handful of pork and a couple of peppers and a chunk of bean curd with four bowls of rice.

On the edge of Anbian people began to follow me, then more and many more joined. With such a throng in my wake, it would be foolhardy to risk stopping and suffer being watched while eating. This seething mass of noisy followers was certain to attract the attention of the local police. The townsfolk of Anbian obviously had not seen many, if any, foreigners before. I could only hope that they would tire of following me, then I could stop on the far side of town. I spotted another large crowd up ahead, formed for something that sounded genuinely interesting: some kind of stage performance with unbelievable musical 'sound effects'.

A travelling theatre was in town, and a play was clearly about to begin. The audience was still gathering, and behind the stage, under a draped canvas sheet, actors and actresses were dressing up and putting on make-up. Open trunks had colourful robes spilling out. Small tables were piled with coloured pastes, wigs hung on the sides of table mirrors. Strange woodwind and percussion sounds filled the air—issuing from musical instruments unknown to me. While the crowd was buzzing outside, I was capturing scenes of the prelude, using my camera to turn solo actors into duos by photographing them reflected in their dressing mirrors. A fountain of colour, a cacophony of sounds was about to explode in this tiny town on the southern edge of the Ordos Desert. For fully half an hour I was awestruck. I had left the Wall, forgotten the chase, left my worries of plague and the police behind, to be held enraptured by preparations. Then common sense prevailed. I realised that I'd delayed too long. For my own safety, and to pre-empt the local police from becoming aware of my presence, I needed to leave town as quickly as possible.

What I had witnessed was a travelling opera troupe preparing to perform a local version of Peking opera. Many regions of China have their own operatic styles, and this was almost certainly the Shaanxi provincial variety (*qin chang*).

Once out of Anbian, I was soon back in dry but pleasant countryside with patches of farmland. Ahead in the far distance, like a mirage, galvanised steel shacks glimmered in the weak afternoon sunlight. Standing beside a great structure from the past, a line of crumbling dry mud Wall swamped by sand and sagebrush, these shacks really did look like they were from another place and time. It was the seismic prospecting camp that Steve Wetstein had mentioned the week before.

That evening, I contined to escape from the constant pressure of the journey. Comfort foods, iced drinks and easy conversation was a perfect catch up after weeks of being pretty much deaf and dumb to most of what was said to me. But the relief only lasted a couple of hours. I knew it. It was bound to happen. I should have carried on past the camp and stayed with farmers.

WILD WALL – THE FOUNDATION YEARS

The police arrived to spoil the party, having likely been tipped off by Charlie Wang, the driver-interpreter turned informer. My questioning would take place early next morning in Dingbian.

I tossed and turned all night wondering how, if at all, I might wriggle out of this predicament and make a dash to reach Fugu at the Yellow River crossing. At least I had time to hide my diary and films. I loaded a new film to sacrifice, if need be, as an exposed one.

After the now-standard preliminaries of questioning I was told to write a 'self criticism', to explain and admit my mistake of entering an area closed to foreigners. I was fined 100 yuan for 'trespassing'. As I expected, I was to be sent to the nearest open town: Yinchuan, the capital of Ningxia. That meant going backwards. They would escort me to the bus station themselves, buy the ticket for me, put me on the bus, see it depart — and tell the driver not to allow me to alight until Yinchuan.

I was gutted.

"I'm so sorry it's ended like this," said Steve as we shook hands. I was too, to say the least, but I managed the stiff upper lip.

Strange, I thought, how my great, passionate and harmless dream was nearing its end in such a nondescript place. On this third attempt, my efforts since leaving Jiayuguan were rewarded by passing the 1,000 km mark, but now they were going to send me a long way back, at least 200 km, leaving the line of the Wall, driven out of the province.

I sat alone in the police car while Charlie Wang and the police officer went to buy a bus ticket for me. Hearing that a foreigner was inside, and about to kicked out of Dingbian, a crowd gathered around the car. Charlie Wang returned and we parted a way through the crowd towards a mini-bus parked out on the street. He gave me my ticket and I climbed aboard, the first passenger on the empty bus.

The driver stood outside, and shared cigarettes with Wang and the officer. They chatted happily, which I resented vehemently. I wondered what I would do, back in Britain, as a failed adventurer, defeated not by terrain and distance, but the politics of place.

Darkening my depression was the grim weather. From the ground up to the sky was brown and dusty, and a chill breeze swirled. It was another windy day in Dingbian, with less to see. Locals seemed well-prepared for it. Men wore big dark sunglasses and face-masks, and the women, like all those throughout the northwest, wrapped their heads in long cotton scarves, similar to burkhas, that only exposed their eyes.

I heard a clattering sound, as if something nearby had been blown over. People started hurrying, to get out of the wind. Sagebrush rolled across the road and a dust-devil swept past, making its way down the street. A vendor, whose wares were laid out on a cloth just outside my bus window, hurriedly gathered up each corner and with one heave moved her shop. A sandstorm was coming in, no less.

People shouted and ran. Visibility had now closed in to less than one hundred metres. Gusts of wind brought a hoarding down, crashing to the ground. Sand grains hissed against the panels of the bus, airborne vegetation and garbage hit it, things rattled. There was repetitive knocking. It was the policeman, now standing alone. He gestured something, then vanished into the sandstorm.

I'd speculated that I might encounter sandstorms, so I was carrying some large goggles, just in case. Now was the time to use them. In my imagination I said to the young policeman, "If you're going to run to save yourself, I'll do the same, to save my journey …." This sandstorm was a godsend, a veil behind which

I could make my escape.

   I rummaged in my bag and pulled out my goggles along with a T-shirt to cover my nose and mouth, then prised the door open and stepped out into the wild vortex. I don't remember making any decisions about which way to go, simply because it was impossible to see. Like a blind man, I had nothing to forewarn me of what I might hit.

14

FUGITIVE & CAPTIVE

IT WAS PECULIARLY awesome and awful. My spirit was uplifted, my mind focussed, eyes irritated and breathing suffocated. At any moment I was half expecting to be hit, be dumbstruck, maybe struck dead, by something falling or flying. I saw nothing, had nothing to focus on, and then would gain just a momentary glimpse, a view of maybe five or ten metres revealing the facade of a building, a melange of bikes crashed like dominos, a wheelbarrow, garbage bins.

I kept telling myself to keep going, because every step was taking me away. Then, very briefly, I was rewarded with my best long-distance view yet, at least 30 or 40 metres. Nobody was around. Everyone else had retreated indoors.

This slow, but ultimately effective, means of escape continued for several hours. It dragged on and on. I had no idea where I was, but kept to the road, guided by feeling the smooth tarmac underfoot. I took out my compass and was relieved to see that I was actually heading eastwards. Occasionally I saw the faint outline of a person, but for the time being, I remained anonymous. I decided that once I began to see people, and they could see me, I'd get off this main road, keep it in view if possible, and use it as my eastward guide towards Jingbian, the third in the series of three 'border' towns, and beyond there, Yulin.

Once the wind subsided and the dust settled, my adrenaline

stabilised and my euphoria passed. Then the stark reality of my actions began to sink in. I'd escaped from right under the nose of the police, under the veil of a sandstorm. Once they realised that, surely they'd start to search for me. And if they found me, I'd be in even bigger trouble. But at least it felt good to go down fighting.

As for the remainder of that day, that critical day of May 14th 1987, it's just a blur now. In all my years at the Wall or living in Beijing, a city notorious for its dust-laden spring winds, I have not seen such a major sandstorm since. What happened in Dingbian was nothing short of a miracle.

My map cutout showed how close I was to Fugu, the Great Wall's second encounter with the Yellow River—just 300 km away. If I could get there without detection, I'd be exactly on target, be able to call it a season as planned, then travel back to Beijing, set up camp at the Longtan for the summer and prepare for the autumn leg of the journey.

That evening I enjoyed just what I needed, a memorable stay, with a group of workers and their families engaged in growing saplings for the Green Great Wall afforestation project. One of the men, Feng Jinhai, was keen on calligraphy, and in his office he took two pieces of ordinary writing paper, picked up his brush, dipped it in ink and wrote 'British friend travelling the Great Wall'. Feng and his wife for some reason only had eggs to eat. So, I ate eggs. According to my diary, I ate nineteen of them.

As I made my way along tree-lined dirt roads near Jingbian, I looked around to see a motor bike. I was being followed. I continued for a while, then heard the motorbike coming up close behind me. I turned around and the two officers dismounted, spoke sternly to me and pointed to the Public Security Bureau (PSB) badges on their sleeves, which ironically featured images of the Great Wall. They wanted me to ride pillion on their motorcycle, but I refused. So, we all walked. We walked a long way, and feeling unfriendly,

I began to walk faster and faster, until eventually they had to ride their motorbike slowly behind me. As we neared the town we drew the attention of the locals, with questions and replies being shouted. Before we reached the police station news of the arrival of a foreigner must have spread widely.

I was treated well and given hot tea to drink, but I was not questioned. They locked the door of the office, leaving me alone inside to contemplate my situation and consider my next move, if I had one. I didn't.

After an hour or so the PSB officers returned and drove me away in a grey Soviet-style car with privacy provided by curtained windows. I assumed that they were taking me to Yulin, the largest city in northern Shaanxi, and that was confirmed by roadsigns on which I recognised the *lin* character of Yulin, which looks like two trees and means 'woods'. When we drove into the dusty, dull, depressing city I realised immediately that it was a misrepresentation of the modern reality.

I was taken to the Yulin Public Security Bureau headquarters, and escorted upstairs and along corridors to a large meeting room. Inside, it wasn't exactly a rally, but a gathering of about fifteen, mostly uniformed, police officers and a few plain clothes personnel. Two of these proved to be key characters in my future. One was an older man, the police chief, and one was the youngest in the room, an interpreter from the department's 'foreign affairs office'. He spoke first.

"Do you recognise that man, that policeman?" he asked, gesturing across the room.

Immediately my heart sank when I recognised him as an officer I'd seen a few days before in Dingbian.

"Mmm, no, I can't recognise him. Have we met before?"

"Hah, you should know him! He arrested you in Dingbian County."

I was asked to place all the contents of my rucksack on a large table. I emptied it out, road dust and all. When I saw all my possessions laid out there, I was amazed and proud that I'd managed on so little, and so well, over the last 1,300 kilometres.

A few officers gathered around, asking the interpreter questions as they started to fiddle with my stuff. They moved my camera, films — exposed and unexposed — and notebook to another table.

"Now, take off your shoes and empty the pockets of your shorts."

As they checked my shoes, removing the insoles, I thought how awful — and comical — it would be if they confiscated them. I had nothing to lose now, apart from those shoes, but how could I possibly escape without them? I'd trained hard for years, but was a softie when it came to going barefoot. I would not get far shod in flimsy-plastic shower slippers, the sort provided as one size fits all (about a size 8) standards for guest use in every hotel room. I took size 14s. The largest footwear I'd seen in markets looked to be no more than size 9s or 10s at best.

Thankfully, they returned my shoes forthwith. But then I remembered that they already had my passport. Like the best pickings still on the table, it was to remain in their hands, as did my fate. So there was no way — for the time being at least — that I could get out of this mess. 'How long's this going to take to sort out, and what's going to happen next?' I wondered.

"Our leader says this is a serious matter. You have flaunted the laws for aliens in China and your case will be investigated thoroughly. We will continue tomorrow, and tonight you will live in the Yulin Binguan."

I was driven in a green jeep a short distance to the guesthouse, and taken to a room on the top floor. But this was to be no conventional hotel stay.

"You'll stay locked in this room, and don't try to climb out to escape. This is the seventh floor. A waitress will bring your meals and hot water."

They left, and the manager locked the door. I sat on the bed looking down at my dusty, hairy, blackened knees and legs.

"It's over," I said.

I lay flat on my back, staring up at a grey, flaking ceiling, listening to the sounds from the street, then fell soundly asleep.

I awoke to the sound of the door being unlocked. In came a tall waitress carrying a tray of food, accompanied by the hotel manager. He said *"chifan, chifan,"* meaning "eat, eat," and then they left and locked the door.

I thought of it as a kind of last supper, imagining that the next day would probably see me being deported, at the very least. The story of John Burns, a *New York Times* journalist who'd made a motorbike trip in Northern Shaanxi—this very area—the previous year had been widely reported, and was well known among foreigners in Beijing. He had been detained for a couple of weeks and then, following diplomatic intervention, he was deported. I could only hope to make the Yulin police understand that my sole purpose for visiting here was simple—to see the Great Wall from end to end.

Dinner was most enjoyable, and I was particularly satisfied by some steamed bread that contained red dates, apparently a famous native product of Shaanxi. I often craved sweetness, silence and solitude, and for once I had them all, although not under circumstances that I would have wished for. When the waitress returned for the tray, I even managed to smile at her and say *"xiexie".*

Next morning, the young interpreter arrived to take me to the police headquarters, and so began the first of several long interrogation sessions that would be strung out over the following week.

Their study of my diary revealed that I'd travelled on foot

WILD WALL–THE FOUNDATION YEARS

from Jiayuguan to Dingbian, over a period of six weeks. I was told that all of my route, apart from the cities of Jiuquan, Zhangye, Wuwei and Zhongwei was closed to foreigners.

My diary entries were an honest record about where I'd been, what my purpose was, and how I wanted to continue to Shanhaiguan. Now they wanted me to write a statement saying that I had not studied the laws on the entry and exit of aliens in China, that I had purposely trespassed in closed areas, and that I had ignored admonishments by the police in Dingbian, escaped, and continued to trespass.

"Your case is a serious matter and is being referred to the Shaanxi Province Public Security Bureau in Xi'an and the Northwest Military Region headquarters in Lanzhou," said the interpreter. "Now we will send you back to the hotel where you can work on your self-criticism."

Back at the hotel I realised, more than ever, how much I wanted to conclude my journey in its proper place, at Old Dragon's Head, not here at the midway point. The reality was that I'd come to China too early. I'd done my best, and my luck had run out. I would have to accept whatever they decided.

Meanwhile, I had to endure the frustration of confinement, waiting for the next meal, or the next visit to the police station. I dozed on the bed. I strolled around the room.

At dinner time the waitress arrived on time, but with another girl of about twenty. She spoke broken English and was clearly quite thrilled to meet me, although I was definitely not in the mood for providing English tuition. She told me that she was a student at Yulin Teacher-Training College. After hearing the usual preliminaries of "What's your name?" and "Where are you from?" I couldn't bear to face another Chinese inquisition so told her to go, lest the police should come and find that she had been talking to a wicked foreigner.

15

Lovestruck & Deported

ON THE THIRD DAY of my detention my fate was decided. The overriding outcome was the Northwest Military Region's order that I must be stopped. The Shaanxi Province Public Security Bureau ordered that my current visa be cancelled, that I be given three days to exit China, and that I be prohibited from returning. Additional, more minor, details included paying a fairly hefty fine and footing the hotel bill for the displeasure of being locked up.

I expected deportation at the very least, but it was only when the interpreter explained the decisions to me in English did the reality hit me. My Great Wall adventure days were literally numbered.

"How can I possibly exit China, starting from here in Yulin, within three days?" I asked. By my own reckoning, it would take three days alone to reach Beijing, and from there I would need to buy a ticket to leave China.

A discussion ensued with the interpreter summarising that "comrades will discuss the practicalities of your deportation and inform you later."

Once again I was driven back to the hotel, to be locked up. For the first time since meeting, the interpreter introduced himself, as Zhou Jibin, and chatted a little, telling me that he loved the English language and how he had been taught by foreigners

WILD WALL–THE FOUNDATION YEARS

during his time at the Xi'an Foreign Languages Institute. He then surprised me by saying that he and his comrades admired my determination and respected my 'great spirit'.

The concluding scene of the Yulin incident saw me being granted a more lenient deportation margin, of seven days to leave China. Zhou Jibin would escort me from Yulin to Yan'an, by bus. I tried one last request, asking whether it would be possible to make a short visit to Zhenbeitai, a fortified platform just outside Yulin, said to be a unique structure on the entire length of the Ming Wall. "No," was the answer, "All of Yulin is closed to foreigners."

Zhou and another officer met me at 5.30 a.m. the next day and we were driven to the bus station. This was my first long-distance bus journey. It was cramped, bumpy, dusty, smoky, slimy underfoot, and took most of the day for the bus to reach Yan'an, winding along a road that picked its way across the deeply gullied landscape of the Huangtu Gaoyuan, or 'Yellow Earth Plateau'.

Zhou told me that Yan'an was the town chosen by Chairman Mao as the capital of the Communist's new base area that was established in Northern Shaanxi in 1935 at the end of a 6,000 km 'Long March'. The men stayed in the town with me overnight, because Yan'an was also closed to foreigners. Next morning they put me on the bus to Xi'an and finally returned my passport. I opened it to see the changes. I no longer had a visa allowing me to stay in China until such a date. That was obliterated with what I'm sure was a 'void' chop. I had a new chop with six day's validity, my deadline to get out of the country.

Another long and cramped bus ride, lasting until about 4 p.m. took me to a terminal bus station in the suburbs of Xi'an. Despite the heat and humidity I decided to continue my deportation journey by walking, not knowing or caring where I was heading.

I needed to use my legs and return to that familiar, therapeutic motion that my body was so accustomed to, but recently denied. This was my second visit to the ancient capital and, as in the previous year, large-leafed French plane trees stood like giant parasols shading the roads. Realising I was in limbo, I flagged down a taxi and repeated *"huochezhan"* (train station) to get on with the necessary, leaving China for good.

Outside the station, a young man who spoke passable English pushed and shoved his way through an unruly queue to get me a last-minute ticket on the next train to Beijing. It would be an eighteen-hour-long overnight journey, with no sleeper berth, but at least a reserved seat. After six weeks of being a roving British ambassador, staying and eating with farmers and seeing the country's open-door policy truly in action, my feelings for China had changed in the short space of a week from enthusiasm to despondency. As China turned against me, I'd turned against China. But this stranger's help with the complicated ticket-buying process was yet another example of the genuine friendship shown by ordinary people who upheld the country's true heart and soul. It was a timely reminder that I should not bear grudges.

With three hours to kill before departure, I decided to seek out a deserved treat. I remembered the impressive facade of the People's Hotel, so jogged down Liberation Road determined to have a beer or two before the long train ordeal. The cool, marble-floored lobby bar provided a pleasant refuge after two days of being cramped on buses, and my seven days of solitary confinement before that. A gorgeous waitress, who smelled as good as she looked, poured me an ice-cold Tsingtao beer and said, "Enjoy please. Happy hour." It was indeed, for I hadn't seen such refined beauty for a long time. I downed beer after beer, each pouring accompanied by another bonus glimpse of the long

WILD WALL-THE FOUNDATION YEARS

narrow side-split of her *qipao* (cheongsam) that extended several inches above her knee. An hour later it was back to hell, on the train without a sleeper berth. The heat, the stench of sweaty and smokey travellers and the mess all around made me realise that footslogging my way along the Wall was much better.

I arrived in Beijing the next day feeling like death warmed up. I walked from the station to Chongwenmen, where the CITS office was located, where I asked as usual to be accommodated at my Beijing basecamp — the Longtan Hotel.

Having been deprived of sleep, I collapsed onto my bed and slept most of the afternoon. I woke up with a thick head, feeling drained, angry and culture-shocked at being back in the Beijing metropolis after seven weeks in the relatively empty west. Bodily I felt wretched, ragged, and filthy. I decided to go out for a jog, then come back to take a cold shower, before having dinner and a Beijing Beer in the hotel's acceptable restaurant, choosing a few of my favourite dishes.

I made my way down to the lobby and did a little stretching there in the comfort of the air-conditioning, before stepping out into the heat. I pushed the door open and was ready to break into a jog when I saw a gorgeous girl of about twenty years old standing on the steps beside me. As an excuse to linger, I crouched down to fumble with my shoelaces to get a secret look, at her legs, her knee-length white dress with a green and black design, her black hair falling straight down her back. I stood up as she turned around, as we looked directly into each other's eyes.

"Hello! What do you do China?" she said, smiling warmly.

I was lost for words. "Hello! I'm, er, I'm writing a book ...." I said.

"A book? What's the name of your book?" she asked.

I didn't have a name for it, because to be honest I wouldn't be writing a book any more, not about half a journey. So I quickly made up a title, there and then.

"Maybe 'From the Desert to the Sea'," I replied.

"My name Wu Qi," she said, pouting her lips to emphasise the tones, and offering me her hand.

I took it, noticing her slender arms, wristwatch and particularly the absence of rings.

"Hello, I'm William," I said.

"Welcome to China!" she beamed.

A taxi pulled up in front of us. "I go out now for dinner," she said, "bye-bye." And off she went, skipping down the steps and into the car.

There comes a day for each of us when nothing will ever be the same again. Today was that day for me. It would either be heaven with her or a life of regret without her. It was love at first sight. I started my run in a trance. I didn't notice the heat, or the need to keep in the shade, or to dodge people. I just thought of Wu Qi, her name and her looks. I lingered in thoughts of her radiance, her mesmerising beauty, elegant posture, vivacious eyes, explosive smile and shy giggle. Although we only touched hands, and tantalised for less than a minute, it was a special, never-to-be-forgotten moment, one to be treasured forever.

As I returned to the hotel I felt a sense of panic, that I should do something, at least wait for her to return, or live with disappointment for the rest of my life. Then reality over-rode my passions. We were simply ships in the night. Two strangers meeting briefly in front of an hotel, soon separated, me scheduled to depart, never to return to Beijing, never to see one another again. It was a beautiful encounter and my only consolation was that I had looked deeply into her eyes and seen a loveliness that I'd never forget. In my eyes, Wu Qi would always be 'Miss China'.

WILD WALL–THE FOUNDATION YEARS

On Monday morning I was at the Midland Bank office at nine o'clock sharp, waiting for opening time. Lance Browne was away on a business trip, so Jennifer and Stephanie helped me pack all my things together and make some telephone calls. The good news was that all three cloth bundles containing exposed films had arrived by China Post, from Jiayuguan, Wuwei and Zhongwei. The bad news was there were only two British Airways flights each week to London, on Sundays and Thursdays. I needed to be out of China by midnight on Wednesday. My only option was to head for Hong Kong, so I decided to travel by train, first from Beijing to Guangzhou, then across the border at Lo Wu into Hong Kong, which at that time was still a British colony.

As I left the Midland office Stephanie asked, "Will, when will you come back?"

I had to admit that I would probably never be back.

Outside Beijing Railway Station, I stood on the crowded plaza looking up at the clocks on the towers as they struck nine and played the tune 'The East is Red'. Two months earlier, I'd been in the same place, about to head out west to Jiayuguan. Now I was about to head south, to see a different face of the country.

As I watched China pass by the carriage window, crossing first the Yellow River, then the Yangtze River, I had many flashbacks recalling different aspects of my journey. I'd seen hundreds of kilometres of rammed earth Great Wall in Gansu, Ningxia and Shaanxi. I had seen Great Wall *life*, by staying with farmers living right beside it. I had reached Dingbian, a mere 250 km or so short of my end-of-spring season target, Fugu, on the Yellow River. I hadn't missed a centimetre of the 1,300 km between Jiayuguan and Jingbian. Every day had featured a battle for the mind or body. I'd overcome innumerable uncertainties, managed with pitifully inadequate maps and basic language skills, survived vicious dogs, avoided bubonic plague, overcome infected blisters and multiple attempts by the police to stop me. I'd dealt with loneliness and fear, had become accepting of being lost, and used the police as my foil. This success was too much to abandon under any circumstances. I could hardly say that luck was against me, either. My escape, under the veil of the sandstorm was a morale-booster, even though it only prolonged my journey for a week. I had turned a defeat into a victory. The Great Wall, the people of the Great Wall, my destiny were beckoning me back. But how could I possibly return?

16

DECEPTION & BRAVERY

AS MY TRAIN approached Guangzhou my mind was made up. I would go to the passport office in Hong Kong and apply for a replacement travel document, claiming loss of my current passport. That would allow me to return to China to spend the summer as originally planned in Beijing 'beside' the Great Wall, improving my language skills. I wanted to avoid going back to Britain at all costs, for fear of getting cold feet and losing my nerve.

Although both sides of the border were inherently Chinese, the Mainland Chinese side and the British-ruled Hong Kong side were very different. Despite the black marks in my passport, my exit from the People's Republic via the busy Lo Wu crossing was surprisingly smooth. Shortly after my arrival, I was walking up Nathan Road in Kowloon, looking for accommodation. I had read a great deal, both good and bad, about a tower block called Chungking Mansions that provided cheap accommodation in a very expensive city. Deciding to check it out, I penetrated its labyrinthine floors and corridors, an experience not unlike entering a honeycomb. Access was via a ground floor mall full of shops selling the cheapest goods and eateries specialising in all kinds of Asian, Middle Eastern and even African fare. I stopped by at the Bombay Mess for a late breakfast.

Guesthouses on the upper floors were only accessible by a couple of elevators, for which one had to queue. The walls beside the elevator doors were covered with metal plaques of grandly and auspiciously named lodgings, surrounded by more recently added flyers and name-cards touting all manner of business services. These included 30-minute name card design and printing, round the clock takeaway meals, call girls as diverse as the cuisine, two-hour laundry services, two-month shipping schedules, miraculous cures for assorted ailments, and 'overnight unsolvable visa solutions' — something I might be interested in.

Eventually I found lodgings at the Peninsula. Not the famous heritage hotel on Kowloon's waterfront that looks across Victoria Harbour to the island and its 'Central' skyscrapers of the main business district, but the guesthouse in Chungking Mansions of the same name run by Mr. & Mrs. Wong. The Shanghai couple had fled from their home city decades ago and had never returned. They thought me both brave and mad for simply travelling in China, without me even telling them how unconventional my travels actually were.

Accommodation at the Peninsula was a compact experience. My room was the size of my single bed, plus an additional 'frame' of space measuring about one foot. A television was attached to the wall and the shower, outside, was communal, about the size of a telephone box. Air conditioners whined constantly, set on 18°C but pumping out more like 28°C, although the mere sound felt in some ways coldly convincing. I showered, shaved and changed, then made my way as swiftly as possible out of the building, proudly smelling of soap and shampoo rather than the essence of Chungking Mansions — spicy food, stale sweat on T-shirts and damp plaster. I headed across the road to my lodging's 'sister' property, thinking myself deserving of a silver-service afternoon tea of smoked-trout finger sandwiches, scones with butter, cream and jam, cake from the trolley and a pot of refreshing Broken Orange Pekoe. The calm environment

WILD WALL-THE FOUNDATION YEARS

in the elegant lobby helped me to clarify my thoughts. It was straightforward. Without further ado, first thing next day, I'd go to the passport office to check on the requirements for obtaining my new alphanumerical identity.

When I got there, I found crowds of people outside. They weren't queueing up, they were picketing. The passport office staff were on strike. As for how long the industrial action would continue for, nobody knew, but the workers didn't seem very happy. Me neither. Plan A was scuppered.

Despite the perceived pitfalls, I now had to consider the dreaded Plan B, of returning to Britain, applying for a new passport there, then getting a China visa before returning to Beijing. Yes, I would feel an initial thrill of getting back, being on 'home leave', but then I'd be faced with the challenge of returning to battle. The very thought of being seen as a serial trespasser in China did nothing for my confidence. I had to avoid any such coming-to-my-senses at all costs. I had to somehow stay detached from reality, in my bubble, focussed on my dream, come hell or high water.

The British Embassy in Beijing was an outside chance. Plan C would not only provide a fairly swift solution and involve a shorter travel distance but importantly ensure me staying where I needed to be. But to get there, I would need to obtain a China visa here in Hong Kong, and in a passport that already had 'black marks' in it. Then, if I surmounted that hurdle, I'd need more luck on my side at the border. How could the immigration officer possibly miss the 'black marks'? Even though my chances of pulling off the two, getting a China visa and gaining re-entry were incredibly slim, I thought it worthwhile to try.

There was no shortage of choice when it came to visa services in Hong Kong's narrow Kowloon streets. From the name, the 'Happy China Visa Service' on Peking Road seemed a good omen. As I took the narrow staircase up to the second floor, I wondered how I might deal with that standard, but now most pertinent, question on all visa forms—'Have you ever been deported for any reason whatsoever from any country?'

A fat man sat behind the reception desk playing some kind of game on a calculator-looking device.

"I want a China visa, but I've got a" I began, before he cut me short without even looking up.

"Do you want Ord-in-ary, Es-press or Su-pa Es-press Service?" he asked in a classic Hong Kong English metronomic tone.

I chose Super Express, to minimise the pain of waiting. There was no form to fill out, which came as a big relief, no photograph needed, no signature required, just HK$800 to pay.

"No visa, you still pay the money, okay?" he said looking me straight in the eye for the first time. "Tomorrow 10 a.m."

I just hoped that the office issuing the visa was too busy to bother looking through my passport. But I was not optimistic.

Next morning, just before 10 a.m., I returned nervously to the office. My heart was racing. I handed my receipt to the same fat man, still playing his game. He rummaged inside a holdall that appeared to contain scores, if not hundreds of passports. There were a few anxious moments of nerve-racking silence.

"A British, right?" he asked.

I very much expected him to look up and say something like 'sorry no vi sa'. But he tossed a British passport down on the desk.

"Check right, okay?"

Low and behold, inside my passport was a new visa, valid for three months! I felt overjoyed, in a state of semi-disbelief, as I examined this priceless addition over and over again.

In ecstatic spirits, I took the Star Ferry across Victoria Harbour, heading for the Thomas Cook office. It wasn't going to be the sad farewell that I'd prepared for, but a joyous return. I thought it both politic and polite to do some PR, for both them and me. Thomas Cook agreed and arranged interviews with reporters from the *South China Morning Post* and the *Hong Kong Standard*. I effused about the Great Wall landscapes that I had traversed, how I'd been adopted by dozens of farming families and work gangs who had supported me with friendship, food, water and shelter. However, I kept completely silent about the numerous hassles with the police in closed areas, and of course the dramas of my detention and final deportation.

The resulting newspaper coverage that appeared over the next few days was perfect publicity for me and TCTC. This time, I was featured on the front pages for the right reasons, announcing my achievements rather than my aspirations. To my delight, I was accorded additional space for photographs on the inside pages. 'Lindesay is back,' was the main message. There was little but a passing reference to David Griffiths' plans of the previous year.

I bought a rail ticket from Guangzhou to Beijing, and prepared to take a local train to the HK-PRC border at Lo Wu, and attempt entry there. The night before, I had spent some time opening and closing my stiff-boarded passport (the old dark blue pre-EU design) until it opened naturally at the page bearing the new China visa. My hope then was that the border officials would be sufficiently busy that they would limit their scrutinising to simply checking for a valid visa and matching the person before them with the identity page. If there was an entry problem, I would, as calmly as possible, step back into Hong Kong.

I thought that I had a perhaps 50-50 chance of getting through without incident. I was exceptionally nervous. I could feel my heart pounding super fast, as if I was running up a mountain. I felt drops of sweat form and fall from my armpits. A perfunctory flicking of pages, a glance up, and … an entry chop. It was all over, done in an instant. I was back in China!

Ten days after taking the train south from Beijing to Guangzhou in a mood of despair, I was heading back north on the same tracks in a state of elation.

Ahead of me lay a long, hot summer in Beijing. As usual, I headed for my familiar basecamp, the Longtan. It was mid-June and a highly eventful, but physically inactive, three weeks or more had passed since I'd been picked-up by the police in Shaanxi. I had at least ten weeks ahead of me in Beijing and looked forward to early-bird training in the cool of dawn.

Longtan Park opened its gates shortly after sunrise, at 5 a.m. which allowed me time for a good run along its cool, shaded paths, beside the lake and through rockeries, before heading back to the hotel for a long cold shower. By then, I was more than ready for breakfast. I always looked forward to the Longtan's comforting Western breakfast, but this morning was a new beginning, in more ways than training.

I entered the empty dining hall and saw just one person having her breakfast: it was 'Miss China'!

"Hello! D'you remember me? We met about two weeks ago. I'm back from Hong Kong now. I'm William."

"Yes!' she said, "and my name ...."

"Wu Qi!" we said together, laughing.

"So, you remember me?" she tantalised.

"Yes ... of course!"

"*Shi ma?*" (really?) she sang in Mandarin.

Wu Qi was wearing the same white, black and green dress and looked even more attractive with her just-got-out-of-bed appearance. She looked dressed to go to an office.

"Are you going to work?" I asked.

"Yes, I am secretary."

"Where do you work?"

"I work *Guoji Dasha* in Jianguomen Street. Do you know it?"

Guoji Dasha, meaning 'The International Building,' was the Chinese name of the CITIC Building where the Midland Bank rep office was located.

"Yes, I know it, my friend's company, his bank, it's in that building, on the 11th floor," I said.

"I work Daiwa Securities, on Floor 27."

"Maybe I'll call to see you one day ... if I'm nearby."

"Maybe it's okay. Oh, dear me, the time flies, I must go my office now, I ride my bicycle," she said.

We shook hands, and said *'zai jian'*, the Chinese 'bye-bye', which actually means 'see you again'.

And I couldn't wait to see her again! I kept seeing her refreshing smile and expressive eyes, and hearing her lovely English. I already wanted more than casual, although enticing, exchanges with her, I wanted to get to know this cheerful girl. I'd have to be brave and bold. I'd have to go to her office, knock on the door, and invite her out, perhaps to dinner. Was that acceptable in China? I had no idea! Would it be a clear signal that I fancied her? Was it taboo? I had to be brave, and just do it, or regret it.

Next day, after splashing out on a 10 yuan FEC haircut and wet shave in the plush barber salon in the Beijing Hotel, I walked as calmly as I could along Chang'an Avenue to the CITIC Building. Entering the elevator, I pressed 27, not 11. I felt a nervous excitement, knowing how important this was. My heart was thumping in my chest and I coughed to make sure that my throat was clear. In front of me was the door of Daiwa Securities, firmly closed. This, I thought, is going to be the ultimate test of China's open door policy! A foreigner knocking at the door of a prestigious office in the capital to ask a gorgeous Chinese girl out for a dinner date!

I took a deep breath and knocked firmly on the door. A

moment later it opened, and a small Japanese man stood there, and bowed.

"Hello, I'm sorry to disturb you," I said, "I'm here to see Miss Wu Qi." He bowed and grunted, turned away and in the background of the open-plan office I could see Wu Qi spring up from her desk and walk towards the door. She looked very surprised, happy and nervous as she stepped outside and pulled the door to, blushing. I took a deep breath.

"I was just in my sponsor's office and thought I'd call and wondered if would like to come out to dinner?"

"Dinner, ummm, very sorry I'm a bit busy."

"Well, maybe in a few days?"

"What day?"

"How about Thursday, that's tomorrow."

'No, busy, busy all week ...."

"How about next week then? Monday?"

"Yes, Monday, we'll have a dinner then, you mean?"

"Yes. Let's meet here, this building, at the main door."

"My work finish at six o'clock. I meet you at the west door."

"Great! See you on Monday then, at the door, west door, at six!"

I was so relieved at the good news, and she looked pleased too. And ravishing! But I had to endure four burning days and nights waiting for our date. To divert my attention, I set about contacting foreign correspondents with the aim of getting my story publicised.

I soon discovered that Beijing correspondents and reporters in Hong Kong had quite different levels of understanding of, and attitudes towards, China. Hong Kong reporters were pretty much China-ignorant, because they were based in a Westernised financial hub on the edge of the vast country. A China visit was about the last thing their editors and readers were interested in. In contrast, correspondents in the Chinese capital were fully engrossed in the country's politics, economy, culture and society. Most of them spoke Mandarin and some were literate, to a degree. Many had studied in Beijing on student exchange programmes.

As soon as I produced my map and showed the journalists the territory that I'd crossed on foot — Jiayuguan to Dingbian — they were amazed. Knowing the ground, their first question was, "How did you possibly do that through closed areas?"

In confidence, I divulged my full story, and explained my philosophy of trespass. Fully appreciating the great political sensitivities involved, they agreed to report what I had achieved and be vague about exactly how I'd done it. They were fully aware of the 'ground rules': a list of just 325 open places. They knew that China's door wasn't wide-open by any means, it was opening slowly, and from their first days here they had been restricted from going here, there and almost everywhere. Some had purposely strayed off course without asking for permission, and recounted experiences that paralleled my own — of fines and detentions, confiscation of films, and tedious self-criticisms.

But while we shared common ground and had received similar admonishments, mine had been far more numerous. They advised me to proceed with caution, warning me of the possibly serious implications of repeated trespassing. Although I seemed to have, so far, got away with my escapades relatively unscathed, the correspondents were of a consensus that somebody, somewhere in the capital's sphere of foreign affairs management (*waishi*) would be collating a dossier on me. They strongly advised me not to push my luck any further and risk aggravating, and thus humiliating, the authorities any more.

The big four British 'quality' daily newspapers — *The Times, The Daily Telegraph, The Independent* and *The Guardian* — all printed photo-stories, while Reuters News Agency filed a story worldwide. Reports made much mention of British eccentricity, of dysentery and stress fractures, of blisters and bubonic plague, sandstorms and inquisitive peasants, and made only scant mention of Chinese officialdom. Headings included *'Telepathy keeps Wall runner in touch'* (Robert Cottrell, *The Independent*); *'The Great Haul of China'* (Michael Duffy, *Manchester Evening News*) and *'The loneliness of the long distance runner'* (Tim Luard, *The Daily Telegraph*). But the headline that best summed up my journey was *'Putting Pub Promise into Practice: A journey across China tests nerve – and feet – of Briton'* (Robert Grieves, *The Times*).

A quite different test of nerve now confronted me, that of getting to my date with Wu Qi on time. It was a five-kilometre bicycle ride from the Longtan Hotel to the CITIC Building. I left with two hours to spare, allowing time for common cycling problems such as a puncture or my chain coming off.

First dates are exciting enough in themselves, but this first date with a woman beyond my dreams was something else. Apart from her irresistible beauty and natural charm, she was foreign, exotic and mysterious. And she spoke English!

The big moment approached, six o'clock at the west door. A few office workers began to emerge from the elevator and leave the building. They were not ordinary Chinese office workers. This was the only international office building in the whole of Beijing at the time—it was itself the CBD—and the women working here were all classy. They wore the best clothes, they had the shiniest hair, they were fragrant, they could walk. And I mean 'walk'.

I paced back and forth nervously, towards the elevator, then back towards the door, seeing who was coming, seeing who was going. Then I turned and Wu Qi stood right there.

"Hello Mr. William! I carry my dictionary to help me speak

the right words!" she giggled nervously.

For a brief moment we looked deeply into each other's eyes and I felt a jolt of excitement. We then began to walk eastwards along the main avenue to the Jianguo Hotel. As we strolled, our conversation flowed easily and humorously and I felt more than on top of the world, more like the focus of it. People normally stared at me anyway, but walking along with a beautiful girl, the attention was far more obvious.

"People think I am your interpreter," said Wu Qi, giggling.

We initially sat in the hotel lobby. The Jianguo Hotel was Beijing's first Sino-foreign 'joint-venture' hotel, modern and low-rise, a five-star oasis of luxury, air-conditioning and tranquility. The lobby had a shaded glass sunroof, letting in natural light, and a long reception desk, behind which stretched a scroll painting of the Yangtze River. A female pianist played a medley of romantic classics. It was the perfect ambience. I ordered two ice-cold Tsingtao beers.

We talked about names. I explained that William was my given name and Lindesay was my family name, and how many there were in my family.

She explained that Chinese peoples' names were the other way round. "So, Wu is my family name, and Qi is my second name ... it means a kind of beautiful jade."

I was stunned, entranced by the meaning of her lovely, perfect name. To me, jade personified beauty and was a quitessential Chinese treasure.

"Can you write some Chinese?" she asked.

"I'm better at speaking than writing," I said.

"Show me! Speak Chinese to me!" insisted Wu Qi.

I unleased a rapid-fire selection of my stock phrases, statements and questions on her. *"Wo zou wanli changcheng lu cong Jiayuguan dao Shanhaiguan ... wo hai meiyou jiehunle ... wo e-le, kele, leile ... changcheng zainar? Duoshao gongli?... dongnan xibei ... tingbudong!*" which roughly translate as 'I'm following the Wall from Jiayuguan to Shanhaiguan, I'm not yet married, I'm hungry, thirsty and tired. Where's the Wall? ... how many kilometres? North, south, east, west ... I don't understand!'.

"Yes! Speaking very good!" she said, clapping her hands together. "Now I want show you how to write my name."

On the back of a drinks coaster she began to write, while counting numbers. "The teacher tells the students that Chinese characters must be written correctly and beautifully." She picked up her dictionary saying "I need to look the words ...." After a few moments, the lesson recommenced with her talking about 'the strokes' and 'the stroke order' of characters.

"There it is ... my name ... Wu Qi," she said, handing me the coaster.

"Thank you! I'll keep it and learn it. So can I call you Qi then?"

"Qi? Oh no! Chinese people only call people with their second name if they have some kind of special relations between them," she explained.

Wu Qi told me she had studied history at Northwest University in Xi'an, her hometown, which explained why her employer, Daiwa, paid her an accommodation allowance to stay at the Longtan. I knew that talk of family was important in China, and had brought my family photograph with me to show her. Our dinner date of two hours together ended suddenly just as I was thinking about ordering something sweet. She looked at her wristwatch and said "It's eight o'clock, I should go home to my hotel. Thank you, nice to meet you Mr. William."

"How about we cycle back together?" I asked.

She wore a hesitant expression. "Maybe not. You know, staff at hotel will gossip ...."

17

LOVERS IN A FORBIDDEN CITY

WITHOUT ANY MEANS of instant communication back in those days, the only way for me to contact Wu Qi was by meeting her face to face. It was hard to resist looking for her at breakfast right the next morning, but I decided to give her the chance to take stock of what was a very adventurous date for both of us.

I managed to hold off for just another day before bumping into her again at breakfast. I didn't want to wait days for another dinner, so I tried for a lunch date. She accepted! For the rest of her working week, we met once a day, and on the Friday I asked about her weekends.

"I sleep in lazy!" she said, "I get up at two o'clock."

We laughed.

Early on Saturday morning, we met at the gates of Longtan Park, and cycled to Tian'anmen Square, to the Houhai lakes area north of the Forbidden City, and then to a popular tourist attraction, the former residence of Soong Chingling, the wife of the leader of China's 1911 revolution, Sun Yatsen. The bike parking lot was so large that owners were given small numbered bamboo wedges as receipts and a guideline to relocating their bikes amongst the hundreds of others. Wu Qi stood directly in front of me, close up, and pressed her wedge onto my cheek, then laughed madly.

"You are sweating!" she flirted.

She looked so playful and happy that I thought momentarily of snatching a kiss, but I dared not. I didn't want to scare her away. More subtle gestures might be the best way of telling her that I had fallen in love with her. On the way back to the Longtan, we called in at the Beijing Hotel on the pretence that I wanted a drink in the lobby café, but I went there to buy her a silk dress. She accepted, and turned into a beautiful jade covered in orchids.

After our first weekend date together, I dedicated the coming week to acquiring a new passport. My first port of call for advice was at the British Embassy Visa Section. I began to tell my story but the Vice Consul raised her hands to her ears, shook her head, signalling me to stop.

"We can only issue a new passport to replace a lost or stolen passport—but before losing it, you should photocopy the ID page and your China visa and entry chop. Only then can we issue you a new document. In an emergency we can do this within 48 hours."

I did exactly as instructed and received my new passport within the week! Now I had one more hurdle to face. I needed to take the empty passport to the police department that dealt with foreigners' visa problems, a courtyard on Nanchizi Street to the east of the Forbidden City. Thankfully, they accepted my application and photocopies. The long drawn-out process of acquiring a new passport with a valid visa was finally completed, and my original plan of summering in Beijing was ensured. And, in the process, I'd met the girl of my dreams, and made up my mind about her. Just a summer with Wu Qi would never be enough. She was the only one for me, for the rest of my life.

Early one evening, I was at the Longtan, idly staring out of my window on the 7th floor. People were emerging from their afternoon of refuge from the heat and employees were returning to their homes. To my great joy, down among the masses, I spotted Wu Qi, walking back towards the hotel. Although we had just had lunch together, I just couldn't wait until the next day to see more of her.

After dinner, I went out to buy two cans of Coca Cola and made my way to find her room, on a floor exclusively for Chinese hotel residents. Each floor was watched and serviced by a *fuwuyuan*, a security-cum-housekeeping employee, usually a woman, who typically sat imperiously behind a desk beside the entrance to the elevator. Her job was to keep a record of the name, number and gender of guests visiting each room, as well as to open doors and provide boiled water for tea.

I asked for Wu Qi's room and the woman, more friendly than fierce, led me there, shouting "*Wu Qi! ... nide waiguo pengyou laile!*" (your foreign friend is here) from the hallway.

Wu Qi opened her door, looking happy, although more than a little embarrassed, to see me.

"It's okay to sit in my room ... as long as we keep the door open," she said blushing, "because you know, in China a lot of people watch, and gossip, get jealous, and spy, and might say or do bad things against you."

For those same reasons, when cycling back to the Longtan, we always separated at the end of the road, first stopping to say '*zai jian*', and pre-set the where and when of our next rendezvous. One evening, I lifted her hand off her handlebar and, staring into her eyes, caressed it, saying, "Wu Qi, I really like you, like you a lot ...." She looked surprised, smiled and then cycled off.

Perhaps she responded to my gesture later, in a more tantalising way. The next day, as we walked from the CITIC Building to the Jianguo Hotel for lunch, she shyly asked me the meaning of a rather sensual word. I tried to explain as we walked, and our mutual laughter seemed to show that we were both hiding and signalling a secret love for each other.

That evening, without 'booking', I visited her again in her room, abiding by the door-ajar etiquette. We sat opposite each other on the twin beds, with our legs crossed, our feet just inches apart, separate but close, facing each other, talking with our eyes and body language. I could barely keep my eyes off her long, pale legs. Wu Qi flicked off one of her sandals, and eased mine off, and we touched, playing footsie for a few moments. Then we couldn't hold back the pent-up inhibitions that we'd felt from the moment we first met. We tiptoed to the door, locked it quietly and began our first night of forbidden love together.

As we met every lunchtime and evening, Qi told me that we should stay secret lovers. "If people think I am your interpreter, then that's good, that's safe," she explained. When she reminded me of all this one evening, I suddenly said "I don't want you to be my 'interpreter', I want you to be my wife!"

Qi was taken quite aback. "But ... you're a foreigner!" she said. "I'm not sure if Chinese and foreigners are even allowed to get married."

It was a shocking thought. But yes, this was the People's Republic of China, with its Forbidden City, its forbidden Great Wall, and now, forbidden love with a Chinese woman.

We walked around Ritan Park, behind the CITIC Building, watching other courting couples. Parks are traditional places for couples to date and stroll and talk about marriage. But our stroll ended pessimistically with Qi saying that no matter how much we loved each other, love between Chinese and foreigners was unacceptable in China.

A few days later, in the same park, I asked Qi again. "I'll do anything to be married to you, even if I have to smuggle you out of China," I vowed, reminding her how I'd persisted in making my way along the Great Wall. But Qi looked dejected.

"Even if we could get married my mother would surely

WILD WALL–THE FOUNDATION YEARS

disagree—she thinks foreigners are spies."

Just as all this uncertainty clouded our future together, significant changes were imminent. Qi's half-year secondment to Daiwa was about to expire, along with her housing allowance. She planned to leave the Longtan to lodge with a girlfriend elsewhere in the city before returning to her permanent job in Zhengzhou, Henan Province. At the same time, I would be leaving the Longtan too, not to recommence my journey—for it was still only late July—but to travel to a few locations along the Wall with a British cameraman to film library stock footage for Thomas Cook PR purposes.

Once I left Beijing for Jiayuguan, and the day Qi moved out to her friend's flat, we would be completely out of contact. All I had to find her with in this country of 1.25 billion people were ten Chinese characters—an address somewhere in Beijing's Dongcheng District.

Two weeks later I arrived back at a different Longtan, one without Qi. I decided that first thing next morning, I'd start to search for her by taking a taxi to the address on the paper, but that evening my plan changed. The *fuwuyuan* on my floor, who knew me quite well by now, came running down the corridor, calling my name. "*Nide pengyou lai dianhua!*" she said, (there's a friend on the phone for you).

I hurried along the corridor to the *fuwuyuan's* desk and picked up the receiver.

"Hello … William? … this is Qi," she said.

I was ecstatic just to hear her voice! "Yes Qi, I'm back, I can't wait to see you …."

"I want to tell you something," she said. "I want to see you, as soon as possible. I miss you very much."

We agreed to meet at 9 a.m., in front of a huge billboard expounding the unity of the 56 Chinese nationalities, close to Beijing Concert Hall on Chang'an Avenue. We'd met there previously, before a concert, and it was a fail-safe location.

I arrived early, but Qi got there before me. She was standing beside her bicycle, wearing the white, green and black dress she wore when we first met, knowing it was my favourite.

"Hello William!" she beamed. "I want to marry you! We can try!"

We were euphoric! We rode our bicycles eastwards, along Chang'an Avenue, across Tian'anmen Square, to the coffee bar in the Beijing Hotel, where we could at least sit close together, secretly holding hands under the table. At the jade counter of the hotel, I bought Qi an engagement ring, a single jade stone set in gold. It was August 14th, our *dinghun* or 'booking marriage day'.

We were not sure when we could get married, where we might get married, or even if we could get married. We didn't know where we would live if and when we were married, or what we would do to make a living. We just agreed to do it, come what may, because we loved each other, and because we believed that our love would indeed conquer all.

18

BACK TO THE WALL

THE LUNAR CALENDAR has guided farming life in China for millennia. Of the twenty-four solar terms that it reveals, it was *chu shu* or 'limit of heat', which falls in the third week of August, that I was anxiously awaiting. By the end of the month the humidity fell, temperatures eased to fairly comfortable levels and the nights became noticeably fresher. It was time for both Qi and I to get going, though neither of us, strictly speaking, would be going back to what, or where, we'd left.

Qi abandoned her plan of returning to the work she'd been assigned in Zhengzhou after graduation. Her life would soon be heading in a new direction with me, to Britain, and to prepare for it, she signed up for a semester-length English-language training course at a school in the city's university district.

I had also abandoned any thought of returning to where I'd been forced off track and out of China. To go back to Yulin, or anywhere in Shaanxi, would be foolishly provocative. Strategically, I now had to re-examine my map to find a detour route: there was now no possibility that my unbroken route, a solid line of travel that I'd covered on foot all the way from Jiayuguan and Jingbian could be maintained. The least disruptive option would be to re-commence my journey in the area to the immediate north of Yulin, in the Inner Mongolia Autonomous Region. Using a ruler, I drew a straight, longitudinal line, northwards from Jingbian, and saw that it passed through Dongsheng (since renamed as Ordos), about 160 km away. That translated as 'East Victory', surely a good omen. It was also legally accessible, open to foreigners, as was Baotou, a large industrial city to its north that was on a direct train line from Beijing.

For the first time on my journey I was footslogging: not scenic footslogging across a glorious landscape nor beside the imposing Great Wall, but just churning out kilometre after kilometre, alone, along a hot and stoney desert road that headed eastwards from Dongsheng to Jungar Qi. My head was down, watching my own footsteps. But I was good at dealing with repetition and monotony. Amidst this vast nothingness I knew full well that the thousands of kilometres that I'd run in training during my 'before China' years, five thousand plus in both 1984 and 1985, were paying such great dividends. Those years of hard training I had endured, without making any excuses, day after day, whether dog-tired or just exhausted, whatever the weather, had built a rock-hard strength of mind within me that allowed me to do anything I wanted. I knew I could trust my self-discipline to get me there, anywhere, hopefully to Shanhaiguan!

Of all China's Great Wall provinces and regions, Inner Mongolia claims a greater remaining length of Great Walls than any other, but day after day I saw nothing to arouse my slightest interest, save an occasional stump of a watchtower. Eventually, I reached my relocated second encounter with the Yellow River at Lamawan, and then headed northwards towards Horinger, finally sighting from afar that unmistakeable line that represents the essence of the Ming Great Wall in North China.

"There it is!" I called out.

It was still a rammed-earth Wall in these parts, curving way across rolling hills. But unlike the bare desert surroundings of the Wall in Gansu, Ningxia and Shaanxi, here it was encroached

WILD WALL–THE FOUNDATION YEARS

upon by cultivated fields. Some were being harvested as I passed by, while some were already gathered-in and ploughed, right up to the Wall's edge. Making my way over dried clods of earth was hard-going underfoot, and coming on top of my recent high daily mileage hurrying across Inner Mongolia, I began to feel a tenderness on my shin bones, an early warning of shin-splints to come.

On the other side of this Wall, the inside, lay the fifth province of my journey, Shanxi. It had an ever-so-slightly different spelling in *pinyin* (as a way to indicate a different tone on the first syllable) to its western neighbour, Shaanxi, the province that I dared not re-enter. The Wall itself marked the boundary between Shanxi and Inner Mongolia. I followed its snaking way southwards, aching as I went, heading down to a village in a wide valley.

A memorable photographic moment presented itself. A tiny woman, at least in her seventies, lugged a large bundle of cornstalks on her back. From behind, she appeared like a corn stack on legs, and I felt rather than photographing her back-breaking labour I should really have helped her, despite my own pains. She told me the village below was Shahukou. Later I'd learn that it had a slightly different former name, and the old and new preserved and concealed a war of words. In Ming times, the original three characters of *sha hu kou* translated as 'Killing Barbarians Pass'. But in the succeeding Qing (1644-1911) times, the Manchus, originating from the 'barbarian' side of the Wall themselves, made a political correction, changing the original *hu* character which meant 'barbarian' to a different *hu* that meant 'tiger'.

I stopped at a tiny roadside eatery, intending to fill up with a bowl of noodles before continuing. But I was so troubled by the aching of my tender shins that I just couldn't get myself going again. I rested there for the afternoon and, even worse, decided to stay the night. Then, to my dismay, the police arrived.

Surprisingly, I'd trekked about 400 km since leaving Dongsheng, virtually untroubled, and here the police reappeared to question me, then left. Beset by the threat of them returning in their familiar way, I set off that evening and walked through the night. By the next morning I had obviously not got away far enough. I was apprehended beside a road near Youyu, questioned, warned, and put on a bus heading to Datong. The cat and mouse game had begun again.

At the very beginning of my journey, I'd often said that I had no loves or loans to hold me back. During the spring, stage of my journey, stoppages by the police, though annoying, proved to have quite the opposite effect. By trying to block me the police themselves became the metaphorical Wall, the real barrier to be overcome, in one way or another. Instead of a breaking force they became my driving force. Back then, I had absolutely nothing to lose.

But this autumn, during part two of my challenge, things were different: I now had a love. Also, the foreign correspondents in Beijing had warned me to proceed with great caution, given that I had by this stage accumulated a notable police record. If I ignored future orders to move on from a closed to an open area, I'd be risking another deportation, even causing a diplomatic incident and perhaps reaching a point of literally 'no return' to China. If I couldn't return to China, I couldn't marry Qi, and our future together would be severely jeopardised. The stakes were much higher now that I did have a love to lose. Returning to the Wall for my autumn stage I really did have my back to the wall. I didn't have any margin for further errors.

Datong was the place where I realised that I needed to adopt a new survival strategy. From now on, I wouldn't be backtracking to fill any gaps in my route. I had to accept that my broken line would become a dashed line. A victory without some losses

WILD WALL–THE FOUNDATION YEARS

wasn't possible. I convinced myself to forget about one defeat, the loss of a single battle, but instead focus on the overall outcome of the protracted campaign, which was to reach Shanhaiguan with as many on-the-Wall or beside-the-Wall kilometres as possible.

The cat and mouse game continued as I tried to advance from Datong towards Beijing. Datong lies in the middle of a large enclosing loop along the line of the Ming Great Wall. This provided a double-layer of defences to the west of Beijing, the dynastic capital for most of the Ming period. I initially chose to follow the northern, Outer Wall, towards Zhangjiakou only to be arrested in Fengzhen. A few days later, having been forced to return to Datong, I made my way out towards Lingqiu, heading for the southern line, or Inner Wall, only to be stopped and questioned yet again. But my interceptor was indecisive. I fled once more, fugitive that I was, and endured two freezing nights literally on the run. I spent the first night in a dug-out cave and the second under a 'bash', a makeshift shelter of cornstalks before being arrested again and taken to Xuanhua.

It was in the mountains to the northwest of the capital, in Yanqing District, that I first met the classic Dragon Great Wall built of brick and stone, dotted with watchtowers along its length. I had not previously seen such a magnificent Great Wall landscape as the one which confronted me here! Thinking about the illustrated cover of the book — that I'd now definitely decided to write — I set about the task of producing the perfect cover photograph.

I didn't have a tripod, so I made a platform upon which to place my camera by stacking loose bricks lying in disarray on the Wall's pavement. Using the camera's self-timer mechanism, I had ten seconds to rush into position having once framed my shot and then tripped the shutter into action. This second part was far trickier: a quick dash back of fifteen metres, a rapid

U-turn, and then a 'natural' running action towards the camera. My aim was to be photographed looking neither straight down nor directly up at the camera, but to capture a posture with my gaze fixed naturally ahead, just far enough to where I might safely plant my feet (which was also essential to avoid a twisted ankle). Time and time again I tried, at times thinking that I'd run too far back, or too close to the camera. I was also conscious that even if my position was good, my legs and arms might look awkward or 'unorthodox', or I might have blinked. In the end I used up an entire roll of thirty-six exposures. I unloaded the film, hid it deep within my bag, safely stored inside my tiny first-aid kit, then crossed my fingers and hoped for the best.

A few kilometres east of my 'hoped-for' cover shot location, I confronted a broken-down fence erected straight across the Wall's pavement, from outside battlement to inside parapet. This structure marked the beginning of the rebuilt section of the Great Wall at Badaling, the location featured in a 1972 photograph of President Nixon, one of the first photographs of the Great Wall I ever saw, and the place where I made my first miserable visit to the Wall some eighteen months earlier. I had passed by much Wall since that day! I was now a discerning Wall devotee. Crossing this fence wasn't just another two metres forward, it was a leap from the past to the loss of originality, from the original ruins to a rebuilt structure. Behind me, stretched the decayed Great Wall, strewn with broken masonry, overgrown with grass, shrubs, stunted trees, but proud like a war veteran, at peace with its aged and bloody past. Ahead snaked a new subspecies, one that had only evolved since the 1950s, cleared and cleaned, solid and safe, not a place where you could imagine seeing the ghosts of ancient guards, but a contemporary structure festooned with 20th Century guardrails. Ravages of time—cracks, collapses and cave-ins—had been filled-in or patched-up. In my eyes the change was a contradiction, but, I conceded, it was acceptable as a one-off project, a necessary sacrifice to allow for the secure strolling of timid tourists and fragile heads of state. Sometimes one has to be cruel to be kind, and make a decision, despite the associated dilemmas. To be cruel to the past or kind to tourists? To be cruel to tourists, or be kind to the Wall?

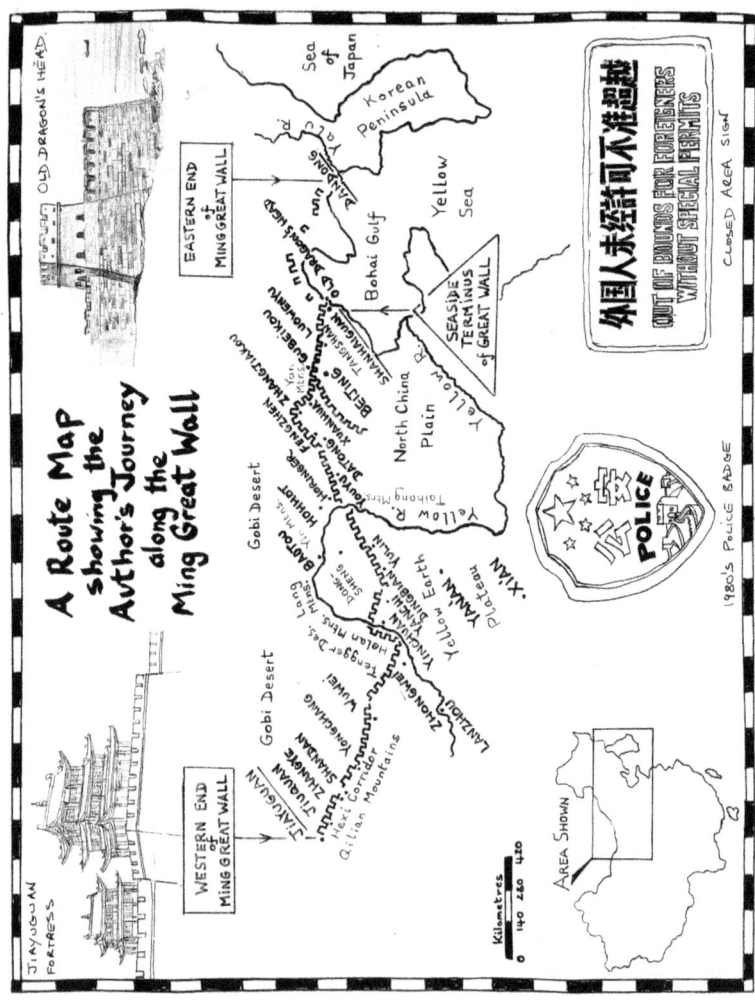

19

Vertical, Wonderful, Monstrous & Forbidden

From the high points at Badaling, with good eyesight and in clear conditions, it is easy to see the strategic importance of this the Juyong Pass. Geographically, it was imperative that Ming emperors should place their most secure defences in this pass, to erect the strongest, highest barricades to exclude their northern enemies. The Wall here seals the entrance to a valley that runs southeast-wards through the Yanshan, or 'Swallow Mountains' to the North China Plain. From ancient times, nomadic peoples from the north had sought to enter China via this inviting route, exploiting a natural weakness through the range of precipitous granite mountains. If forced to avoid the fortified pass and cross such brutal high terrain on its flanks, even the most-determined warriors mounted on Mongolian horses, the strongest in the equine world on rough ground, might take days to advance a few kilometres. In practice, many horses would be injured while men would run out of food, water and determination well before reaching their objective.

I found the course of the Wall to be disorienting and confusing at Badaling. From some vantage points it seemed to be surrounding me; at times I began to question whether it was singular or plural, thinking that perhaps there might be multiple lines, or enclosing loops. However, as I progressed it proved to be singular and twisting, and in three places at least, to be discontinuous. The gaps between the sections were, I surmised, entirely by design, apparently concessions to terrain so precipitous that no man-made additions were considered necessary. The steep cliffs, deep chasms and jagged rock faces were perilous barriers in themselves.

As I untangled the convoluted route of the Wall, another great engineering marvel revealed itself as a fairly old resident of the valley. From 1909, travellers have been taking trains from old Peking's Qianmen Railway Station to alight for Badaling at the Chinglungchiao, or 'Clear Dragon Bridge' station. It lies nestled within a V-shaped canyon — surely one of the world's best-hidden railway stations — unique in its setting, where ancient and modern Chinese wonders of stone and steel cross paths. The newer railway line takes the low, flat route, the older stone Wall being forced by considerations of war onto a high and precipitous route. From the crossing, the great hulk of the Wall climbed up at an angle of at least 45 degrees on both sides, and then away in a manner that I had not seen elsewhere. Here, and throughout the valley, I caught glimpses of a Wall that no longer seemed to slither across the terrain with ease. Rather, it was forced to make sudden, sharp and steep ascents and descents, showing its climbs, falls and turns in the shape of huge lopsided letters, deformed Vs, Ws and Ms, that I imagined had been scrawled by a giant hand. I found myself trying to read this landscape message. I realised that the letters corresponded to adjectives that perfectly described the outstanding characteristics of the Wall: Vertical, Wonderful and Monstrous.

The Beijing-Zhangjiakou railway line — known as the Peking-Kalgan line to foreigners in the early 20th Century — was China's first home-engineered and constructed permanent way, designed by Zhan Tianyou (1860-1919), whose statue stands at Chinglungchiao station. The line was built to facilitate the transportation of coal and timber to Beijing at a time when 10,000 camels a day were said to ply the route. An unanticipated benefit of the new railway was that it could transport tourist passengers to the Wall, reducing the round trip time from four full days along dusty and rocky roads, to nine hours by the smoother railway. Badaling, or 'Nankow Pass' as it was known then, became a convenient and spectacular day trip from the capital, and soon established itself as the site where increasing numbers of tourists from around the world would obtain their first glimpse of the Great Wall.

A few kilometres further south the Wall came to an abrupt mid-slope halt. Ahead, and roughly corresponding to a map of the Beijing Municipality that I had acquired over the summer, there appeared to be a long gap without Wall for close on 20 kilometres. At the time I could neither understand nor explain the reason for such gaps. Unlike out West, where the Wall was originally built of rammed-earth and had likely been eroded without trace from the landscape in many places, the edificial Wall of stone and brick of the East could never succumb to such a fate. Rather, there had never been any Wall built here, because the mountain was a defence in itself and had been strategically 'borrowed' to save manpower, materials and money.

I headed to the main valley floor and walked south along the narrow road. The sun dipped out of sight early, behind the high western mountains, and the temperature fell sharply. After several kilometres, when I thought all the Wall of the valley was behind me, I spotted more long fragments of it coming down from both sides, all of it though well-camouflaged amidst bushes in autumn leaf and in a sorry state of dereliction. The road passed right through the centre of this strange cluster of ruins, and where it first met them, I saw what was, and remains to this date as I write 35 years later, one of the steepest sections of the Wall that I had seen, or would ever see. I estimated that it was

WILD WALL–THE FOUNDATION YEARS

constructed at an angle of 70 degrees from the horizontal.

It transpired that I was passing through the badly-damaged remains of the Juyong Fortress, located within a six-km-long loop of isolated Great Wall, ellipsoidal in shape, that stretched across the valley floor and up onto the adjacent mountainsides. This was the military headquarters that administered the army garrisoned throughout the Juyong Pass. It once featured offices, barracks, stables, an arsenal, temples and a school.

Only parts of the base of the Wall could be seen, here and there on the surrounding valley sides: the upper walls, the brick battlements, and the watchtowers (as well as the remains of the ancillary buildings mentioned above) were apparently destroyed during the Sino-Japanese War. Subsequently, much of the loose Wall material that had been lying around as rubble was removed by locals to build their own houses and sheds.

A little further on the road curved around a large, and clearly ancient, stone-built edifice that was penetrated by an arched north-south tunnel, hexagonal in shape. Magnificent bas-reliefs of Buddhist deities are carved on its facades and ceiling, and deeply etched inscriptions of mainly unfathomable texts adorn the walls of the tunnel. The original rock-slab road that led through its centre was deeply gouged by the passage of countless nail-studded cartwheels. This was the Yuntai, 'Cloud Platform', a type of structure known as a 'crossing street tower'. Built in the Yuan Dynasty (1279-1368), when the Mongols ruled China, it was originally the base for for a pagoda. The tunnel bears six different kinds of writing — Chinese, Tibetan, Sanskrit, Tangut (of the Western Xia), Uyghur and Phags-pa. They are, with one exception, the scripts of five peoples subjugated by Mongol armies, whose conquests added up territorially to become the Empire of the Great Khan that extended across China and around it during the late 13th to the mid-14th Century. The exceptional script is Phags-pa. This was created as a new, unifying script at the command of Kublai Khan, who aimed to replace the many scripts of his empire with one. It became extinct as soon as the Mongols were ousted from China. This tunnel of history thankfully remains. It was dubbed the 'language archway' by foreign tourists in Peking in the late 19th Century. The texts within are principally Buddhist sutras and incantations which are, surprisingly, juxtaposed beside more worldly records-of-merit, about the building of the pagoda. More interestingly in my mind, and absent from these records — because the structure, being built circa 1340s, pre-dates the Ming — is any record of the pagoda overseeing the Wall which surrounds it being constructed. It was an event however that was seen by the stones. It must have been quite a sight.

A kind family in the village on the southern edge of the derelict Juyong Fortress took me in, and I clearly remember enjoying the pickings of their apple harvest on that chilly evening in late October. As usual the yard was full of people, but the neighbours had another reason for flocking here with their small stools. My hosts owned a television and had a working electricity supply, so in the evenings their home became the village cinema. I remembered Qi telling me about how Chinese families, and especially a newly-wed couple in the 1980s, wanted to display their success and level of achievement by acquiring 'four big belongings': a bicycle, a wristwatch, a television and a fridge. Of these four, this family on the edge of Beijing had made the best buy, a television, which had apparently replaced the sewing machine as one of the most wanted. More amazing was the fact that there was someone on the television speaking English. My ears pricked up and I moved closer to watch.

Now the tables were turned. The farmers were greatly amused that they were unable to understand the dialogue, but I was. It was a once-every-five years Chinese Communist Party

WILD WALL-THE FOUNDATION YEARS

Congress, the 13th in the Party's history since its founding in 1921. And surely it was the first congress at which a General Secretary of the Communist Party spoke in passable English at a press briefing for foreign journalists. What a remarkable sign of the times, of changing China!

The newly-appointed General Secretary was Zhao Ziyang, chosen by Deng Xiaoping. The 13th Party Congress would be hailed as a landmark meeting of the reform era, which began with the milestone Third Plenum of the 11th Congress at which Deng had taken over the reins of power. Many of the elders opposed to acceleration of reforms were being forced to retire, thus beginning the transformation of the Communist Party from that of the Long March and ageing revolutionary veterans to a Party led by younger and better-educated technocrats.

Next morning, I completed my traverse of the Juyong valley, emerging onto the edge of the vast plain that stretched south towards Beijing. Hugging the break of slope at the foot of the mountains, I walked eastwards looking for the next inroad to the mountain range to rejoin the Wall.

It was initially a long, uninteresting march, but a great historical treat lay ahead. That afternoon I arrived at a large memorial archway standing amidst pear and chestnut orchards, a *pailou*. Usually made of wood and featuring intricate joinery, the typical *pailou* is a brightly-painted masterpiece of Chinese architecture. However, this one, being in such an important place, was replicated in solid marble. This imposing structure marks the edge of the imperial mausoleum of the Ming emperors, a valley that would become known as Shisanling, or 'Thirteen Tombs' — because thirteen of the fifteen Ming emperors were entombed here.

Over the years people have repeatedly asked me: "What's the best thing about living in China?" One of my answers is "Finding amazing things, historical and traditional, just around the corner, unexpectedly."

The marble *pailou* was just the beginning. All fatigue vanished as I encountered more monumental antiquities lining the road ahead. Huge inscribed tablets on the edge of the precinct had centuries ago told approaching processions to dismount (*xiama*). Ahead, a marble guard of honour stood in attendance along an avenue called the Sacred Way. Pairs of identical statues, a little larger than life-sized, faced one another across the road, a narrow tarmac strip. Apparently, the first group of carvings, depicting various native animals, were chosen to show the vastness of the Ming Empire. There are camels from the desert in the west, horses of the steppe to the north, and elephants from the jungle in the south. Was there also a concern for early animal rights, I wondered, because there were four examples of each, one pair standing, 'on duty', one pair sitting, 'resting'. Meaningful iconography continued all the way along the avenue. Mythical unicorns (*qilin*), symbols of good government, stood ahead of Confucian scholars with their tablets in hand ready to take note of imperial orders, and then generals with their hands-on-hilts, ready to draw their swords in defence of emperor and empire.

During the period of its use, from 1424 until the fall of the Ming in 1644, the valley was guarded, a no-go area for all but the royal family and their entourage attending the occasional funeral ceremonies and participating in annual ancestor-worshipping rites. During the Qing Dynasty that followed, the Manchus observed the Han Chinese tradition of honouring the imperial lineage, and the valley, like the palace in Beijing, remained forbidden. Now, peasants live in villages dotted across this 'tombscape', a word that occurred to me there and then, for it aptly describes an extraordinary view: burial mounds, stele towers and worshipping halls whose summits and roofs project above the orchards of this once funereal, but now rural, landscape.

WILD WALL-THE FOUNDATION YEARS

Trucks and bikes trundle down the road between the statues. Even the name of the Yongle's Emperor's tomb, Changling, had been adopted by the nearest village. Now, nothing is forbidden. Well, so I thought.

Little more than fifteen kilometres away over the hills ahead stood another section of the Wall. Revived by my historical diversions I decided make a determined effort to get back to the Wall by nightfall, in the vicinity of a dot on the map called Huanghuacheng.

As I was leaving the village of Changling, I saw a cast-concrete roadside plinth that read 'Access Forbidden to Foreigners Without Alien's Travel Permits', in English, Chinese and Russian. Oddly, this was the very first such warning sign I'd seen so far, having already trespassed for approximately 2,400 kilometres through closed China. I then realised, with both shame and pride, that I'd been apprehended by the police eight times, far more times than seeing any 'no go' signs. Then it dawned upon me why I hadn't seen any signs—if they were placed everywhere they were required, then literally tens of thousands of signs would be needed, because 99% of the country was closed. So, why then, I wondered—I worried—had they taken the trouble to erect a sign beside the road in Changling? My conclusion was to ward-off any wandering foreign tourists on the Great Wall-Ming Tombs combination tour.

Within the hour, I began to doubt my simple explanation of the sign's placement. Before it was too late to avoid I walked straight past an imposing gate guarded by soldiers. Minutes later, further down the road, a uniformed officer got off his bike and started ranting at me. I was obviously an unwelcome visitor, but I just carried on walking, until he backed off and rode away. It was wishful thinking the encounter was over. Shortly afterwards, he returned with a superior officer riding in the sidecar of a motorbike. I was forced aboard and that afternoon transferred in a rickety Beijing Jeep to the police station in the county town of Huairou. Phone calls were made to Beijing by the only police officer I met in 1987 who spoke English. He told me what I knew already, but with a new addition. I had ignored warning signs and proceeded into a *forbidden* area (which was a more serious mistake than trespassing in a closed area). If I was to make the same error again, I would be deported.

Another unforgettable day concluded. It was my ninth altercation with the police. Next time perhaps, I risked being out for the count.

I was put on an evening bus to Beijing and over the next few days pondered and discussed my precarious situation. The remaining route of the Wall from Huairou to Shanhaiguan passed through more of the Beijing Municipality and then re-entered Hebei Province. I had already established recent police records in both regions. The 'nine lives' saying hung ominously in my mind. It seemed highly likely that if I dared to try again and was caught I would be deported. I could not afford to be caught trespassing in closed areas again.

Back in Beijing, I walked with Qi and talked over my dilemma. We managed to go on one of our favourite outings: the Sunday Matinee 'coffee morning' Concert in the lobby of the Jianguo Hotel. We'd enjoyed this regular weekend retreat into the romance of European classical music and opera almost without interruption during our summer courting season. It was a favourite social gathering for expats and weary travellers alike.

A journalist I'd met months before spotted me in the audience and came over to ask about my progress along the Wall. I told him what had just happened and where. "No wonder they arrested you," he whispered. "Qincheng, the prison. It's right there. They keep Jiang Qing, 'Madame Mao' of the Gang of Four there. You had better be very careful, my friend …."

20

From The Desert To The Sea

I BRAINSTORMED, searching for a way forward. I recalled having seen a feature in the magazine *China Today* about a group of French travellers who 'hiked the Great Wall' from Beijing to Shanhaiguan with the help of a local travel agency that obtained 'special permissions'. With Stephanie's help, I managed to track the agency down and they advised me that a small support crew of driver, cook, guide and vehicle and the necessary alien's travel permit could be provided for ten days for US$5,000.

Besides the unacceptably hefty price tag, it wasn't quite the ending to the great solo effort that I'd envisaged. It was simply a safe way, an ordinary means to my end compared with the extraordinary way of getting to Old Dragon's Head that I had taken so far. I'd be traversing selected sections of the Wall en route, but missing out many more. For that reason, I procrastinated. But time was running out.

While I walked, street scenes all around signalled that winter was coming. Trees were leafless; days shorter, nights longer. It had been a city of individual Beijingers a month or so ago, but now they'd transformed their outward appearances, returning to thickly padded coats against the cold and wearing masks as protection against the coal dust, becoming faceless Beijing again. A kind of hibernation was at hand. For the first time, I saw people forming orderly queues beside trucks piled high with hundreds of large cabbages. They patiently waited in turn to buy a score or more cabbages — the main winter vegetable — to get them through the cold months ahead when no other greens would come into the city. *Li dong*, meaning 'the start of winter,' was now, said Qi, and tradition reminded everyone to eat *jiaozi*, dumplings most commonly made from ground pork and some of their cabbage supply, or risk having their ears freeze and drop-off.

I couldn't deny the undesirable outcome of another trespass: deportation. Then I'd face 'double hopelessness': be a non-finisher of my Great Wall journey, and be a non-starter in my planned marriage to Qi. I wanted double happiness: to conclude my Great Wall journey and to continue my life's journey with Qi. I had to lower my expectations. It was better to have a dashed line of a route than dashed hopes. I decided to take the US$5,000 option.

Qi took me to a 'free market' strung along an alleyway between Jianguomenwai Avenue and Guanghua Street. There, a few dozen entrepreneurs had set up market stalls to sell unusual or fashionable items of clothing, said to be 'trade samples' of products manufactured for export in Guangdong Province's Special Economic Zones (SEZs). (Years later, the alley became Beijing's 'Silk Alley').

I bought a thick down jacket. I was now ready to go, but I had to wait. The travel agency was still in the process of applying for an alien's travel permit on my behalf. Meanwhile, the 'first light snow' (*xiao xue*) forecast by the lunar calendar had fallen and stayed, while the wheels of bureaucracy churned agonisingly slowly.

By the time I was finally able to recommence my journey, the roads leading out of the city were completely iced-over. At that point I was greatly relieved to see the driver stop and fit chains to the tyres. We headed first for Mutianyu, a newly renovated

WILD WALL—THE FOUNDATION YEARS

alternative to the most visited tourist Wall at Badaling. The latter had been repaved as early as 1957 to make the way safe for a visit by President of the Soviet Presidium, Voroshilov. Thereafter it was repaired little by little as Badaling became the place where most visiting heads of state would be taken to see the legendary edifice, up to and after my own Queen just the previous autumn. The rationale behind the refurbishment at Mutianyu was different. It came in the immediate wake of Deng Xiaoping's calligraphy in 1984 that called on patriots to 'Love China, Rebuild the Great Wall'. Originally conceived as a campaign to raise awareness among overseas Chinese about China's need for, but lack of, finances to rebuild more of the Great Wall at Badaling, the call went further and wider. The overwhelming response triggered the implementation of a number of other rebuilding projects that I was soon to witness along the course of the final leg of my journey. These were at Jinshanling, at Shanhaiguan's Jiaoshan, and at the Old Dragon's Head itself. When I reached these locations in 1987, the bricks had barely cooled, the mortar was barely dry, the gates were still to be erected, and the tourist tickets were yet to be printed. But of all the sections that I hiked along on this final stage, it was a short length of Wall in Hebei's Zunhua County that would surprisingly distinguish above all others. Luowenyu was the most significant photographic location on my journey, the most important place I walked, stopped and stood on the entire length of the Wall, for it was here that I met another William. A William from a different era. A William who also travelled along the Great Wall, eight decades before me, viewing a younger and less ravaged Great Wall.

What sprang into life came directly out of the badly-ruined Wall at Luowenyu. While my minders and driver stayed huddled in the warmth of the minivan I trod carefully through the virgin snow that blanketed the steep Wall, concentrating on staying upright, avoiding slipping and falling. After days of grey and bone-chilling cold, the sun shone brightly, barely raising the air temperature but warming my enthusiasm for recording what I saw. Yet why I decided to try and include myself in this photograph, I do not know, for that too would be profoundly significant, adding a mysterious element to the story that was destined to unfold slowly, stage by stage for years to come.

To take a photograph by self-timer was a time-consuming and labour-intensive palaver. As usual, I built a small square platform of loose bricks and placed my camera upon it. For my cover shot (or not) some weeks earlier at Badaling I'd taken a full hour to expose an entire roll of film, but here in this finger-numbing cold of around minus 15°C there would only be the time and warm blood available for a single shot, be it good or bad. Removing my gloves to focus, tilting the lens barrel to the correct angle, composing the frame, and finally tapping the delayed shutter-release were delicate procedures; my fingers soon felt to be on the verge of frostbite.

In total, I had ten seconds to get into place: not much time to accomplish so much in these demanding conditions. I gently touched the release, and hearing it whirr, started to count down. Taking great care not to slip, I shuffled away — seven, six, five, four — taking as many short steps, then I turned to face the camera, looking up, walking slowly with a swing of my arms through three and two, then at zero, the click, hoping for the best.

So much about this photograph seemed almost worthless, in one way or another, at the time. Whether a hit or a miss, the photograph would not be able to capture anything impressive, apart from the blue sky and bright snow. It was obvious that the Wall was a shadow of its former self, well past its best-before date of 1644, completely ravaged by the sweep of the following 343 years.

WILD WALL-THE FOUNDATION YEARS

But in time, a very different story would be told. It was destined to become a classic example of less turning out to be much-more—once the 'other half' was placed alongside. By itself, my photograph didn't show a great deal, and that's precisely why it would become so important. I'd see the photograph processed within a month or so, but the 'other half' wouldn't reveal itself for more than six years.

Little did I know at the time that I had crossed paths with a certain Dr. William Edgar Geil here, in that 79 years earlier, he had taken a photograph at the same spot during his own east to west journey. A very slow incubation began, and then, through an act of third-party generosity in 1991 we were to be introduced, virtually: and a eureka moment would occur in 1993. Years later in 1999, inspired by the rapid pace of time—not merely the passage of one year to the next, or even century to century, but no less than a leap from one millennium to the next—we two Williams saw an opportunity and need to collaborate, by using his old photographs and my retakes of the same locations to evidence change. I will leave the details of this developing story for a later and timely telling.

Within a week, I was nearing the sea, back to where my adventures on the Wall had begun on Jiaoshan, the mountain that rises above the coastal plain that extends down through the town of Shanhaiguan to Old Dragon's Head on the coast. That was August 1986, now it was December 1987. It was a torrid 38°C back then; now it was minus 15°. The landscape view had changed from a velvety green bathed in warm dawn sunshine, to frigid and white. I searched for the place where I'd taken an unforgettable sunrise photograph that perfectly captured the meaning of Shanhaiguan, the pass between the mountain and the sea. It was my first photograph of sunrise on the Great Wall, and one yet to be surpassed.

I found the location, more or less, and took the same view under winter conditions. Although the two photographs were taken only fifteen months apart they would, when compared, reveal changes. There had been more repairing and rebuilding of the Wall at Jiaoshan. This too was a great view! Clear skies, with the white-looking Bohai Gulf, an arm of the Yellow Sea, on the horizon. It was time to go there. I knew the way. It was cold, so I could run, every step of the way. What was exhausting back then would be easy now, heading down towards the sea. It would take me less than two hours.

I'd spent so many days alone on the Great Wall, and soon it was about to conclude. Ahead lay the seashore, the long-perceived, oft dreamt-about finishing line. That was one of the features that first attracted me to this journey — it was a route with a definite starting and finishing line. For so long, I had yearned to get to this point, to cross the line and then go back home. My intention had been to return to 'real life', planning to restart my career, perhaps in academia, to hopefully find a suitable girl and get married, then buy a sports car, a house and live happily ever after. How things had been blown so wonderfully off course!

Without any doubt, as a foreigner I'd made the longest, most-continuous and most-successful journey on foot along the main line of the Great Wall, the Ming Dynasty line of defence. This is the one marked on contemporary maps of China, extending between its two main termini of Jiayuguan in the west and its seaside terminus of Shanhaiguan in the east.

For years up to this point in my life, as I reached the end of a week, a month or a year, I'd make a note of my accumulated running mileage in a diary, meticulously recorded, neither overestimating nor underestimating the totals. I also recorded other pertinent information, rest days, if any, averages, and highlights, such as races. A few days before, I'd started to do the

WILD WALL–THE FOUNDATION YEARS

same for this Great Wall journey.

Last time I was here at the Old Dragon's Head it lay as ruined blocks on the seashore. I had called it a 'Headless Dragon'. Now, ahead of me, backlit by the setting sun, it had risen its head. Today it stood upright, rebuilt, proudly projecting seawards into the ebbing waves. I made my way towards it along the snow-covered beach, doing the final accounting.

By my reckoning, I'd trodden 2,470 km on foot over a period of 78 days between the Dragon's Tail and Head. I'd been beside or upon some 600 km of it, while the rest of the time I'd been between sections, sometimes lost, sometimes avoiding the police while searching for the next stretch. Lodging with farmers, herders and workers had been highlights for 60 evenings. The police arrested me nine times and deported me once. I used two passports, obtained three visas, and made three marriage proposals, all to Wu Qi who eventually said 'yes'.

I fully intended to tell the stories between and behind these figures in a book, and I thought I should keep my word about its title. The first time we'd met I'd told Qi that it would be called 'From the Desert to the Sea'. That was still my plan.

21

Press Blitz

I WAS UNABLE to telephone Qi. I knew her college location near Chegongzhuang, and we'd set it as our default meeting place whenever I finished. I was there next morning at 11.30 when class was over, waiting at the gate. Along cycled Qi in her wintergreen coat with matching knitted scarf and hat: the moment we were reunited goes down as one of the happiest moments of my life. I'd finished the Wall—for now—and was with Qi.

Thomas Cook and their PR agency advised that it would be better to break the news of my achievement after the Christmas and New Year holidays. This idea was no hardship for me because it meant I could enjoy another month in Beijing before returning to the UK. My brothers David, Nicholas, and his wife Elizabeth decided to fly out to Beijing for a pre-Christmas week, to join the celebration, visit the Wall, and most of all to meet their sister-in-law-to-be, Qi.

Qi's father and sister also came up to Beijing, which signalled the family's blessing to our planned marriage. Mr. Wu was a keen calligrapher and he brought along his brush, ink and paper and wrote a poignant piece of Chinese wisdom as a treasured gift, still cherished to this day: 'To see far you must climb to the top of the mountain'.

Meanwhile Stephanie, on hearing of my planned visit to Hong Kong to do some PR there, thought it a great pity that my news had no outlet in China. She contacted the domestic news department at Xinhua, the 'New China' News Agency, to see if they were interested.

Two journalists came to interview me, and I told them various stories and showed them my diaries. I'd managed to get many of my farmer hosts to write down their names, village name and comments about their lives beside the Wall. I'd also collected postmarks of places I'd passed through, although I regrettably let the practice slip during the second half, the autumn leg of the journey for fear that lingering in the centre of a large town increased the risk of being arrested for trespass. The journalists asked to borrow the diaries to show them to their editor as confirmation of my claims. A day later they returned them stating that news of my journey would be released imminently.

A few days later when Qi and I were strolling in Longtan Park, Qi bought a Chinese language newspaper to see if the story had been published yet. We were thrilled to see it there in black and white! "According to the report, William Lindesay, an Englishman, is the first foreigner to make such a long and successful journey on foot along the Great Wall," read Qi, beaming with delight. A fact that I knew only full well!

An English version of the same news story, *'Foreigner completes run along Great Wall'* released by Xinhua ran on the front page of *China Daily*, one of my regular reads whenever I could obtain a copy. I also saw a news brief therein announcing that the Tian'anmen Rostrum would be open to the public for the very first time on New Year's Day. Qi and I decided to be among the first to go there, for it seemed a memorable way to begin 1988 together.

It was a crisp, clear freezing-cold winter's day when we walked up the steps to the rostrum. Chairman Mao Zedong had ascended these same steps on October 1st, 1949 to announce the foundation of the People's Republic of China. This momentous day came after years of bitter conflict against the Chinese Nationalist government, then the invading Japanese, and finally winning the civil war. As Qi and I were among the first one hundred visitors we were given red metal badges dated 1988.1.1 as mementos.

"I collected Chairman Mao badges just like these when I was a little girl," said Qi.

We were now standing directly above Mao's portrait, with Chang'an Avenue below us, and beyond the expanse of Tian'anmen Square. I felt as if I was standing at a junction in time. Behind us, to the north, was the red-walled and golden-roofed Forbidden City, the residence of the Ming emperors who had ordered the building of the best-known Great Wall. In front of us to the south was the Square, bordered by the Great Hall of the People on the western side and the National Museum of China on the east. These imposing buildings were the new face of China, a country that was bound to be a major part of my life from now on, my future life with Qi.

Qi had found out, much to our considerable relief, that marriages between Chinese nationals and foreigners had been legalised in 1983, and that neither bride nor groom needed parental permission. Marriage planning for us in 1988 was ultra complex in procedure and minimal in spending and show, compared to the minimal procedure and maximum show-off spending of today. These days, couples usually begin by taking wedding photographs at various sites, wearing different outfits at each place, then they book as large a restaurant as can be afforded, receive envelopes of cash from attendees, and start married life in a fully furnished and self-owned apartment gifted by the parents. They will often have courted for months or even years, and investigated each other's height, education level, social background, salaries and savings to make sure that they are 'suited'.

Marriage planning for Qi was entirely different, a major component being getting together all the documents needed to satisfy China's most prolific industry, bureaucracy. Chinese red tape created innumerable and seemingly insurmountable hassles and hurdles for the populace. We simply wished to get married, which in essence involved persuading the Ministry of Civil Affairs to issue us with a marriage certificate. This was our sole aim, our only concern and our single hope: we never gave any thought to housing, income, heights or social backgrounds. We didn't dare to think what we might do, or could possibly do, if for some reason we were unable to satisfy the powers behind the bureaucratic desks.

Before our attempted marriage, I had to leave China and Qi, and return to Britain where I had to perform various obligations for my sponsors, tell my story to the media, and hopefully get a publisher interested in the book that I was now eager to write. It would be a painful three months of separation, although almost every day during the period, the postman would take a letter to, and bring a letter back, from China.

A few days before my flight back to the UK, I received the astounding news that Thomas Cook TC had arranged a press reception at the Chinese Embassy in London, an event to be hosted by the Chinese Ambassador to Britain, Ji Chaozhu. Ji had been at Premier Zhou Enlai's side as his interpreter during Nixon's China visit in 1972.

Although I was initially elated at receiving this news, I soon came down to earth when I considered the possible adverse consequences of such an event. Potential embarrassment, for both me and the Chinese Ambassador, crossed my mind as I considered the political implications if any details leaked out about how exactly I had managed to trek across 2,500 kilometres of closed China — by trespassing. After considering my possible answer to the question 'how?', I decided that it would be along the lines of 'with the warm hospitality of the people living close to the Great Wall'. I only hoped that there would not be a question like 'How did you get permission for your journey?'

Ultimately, if things did get out of hand, then my return to China in the spring might be jeopardised. If my visa application was turned down I would be unable to get married. Nonetheless, I cautiously agreed with Thomas Cook that the Chinese Embassy was an appropriate venue for the news briefing. I was, after all, wanting to tell a Great Wall friendship story, a Great Wall love story. The date was set, and impressive Embassy invitations bearing the national emblem of China were sent to the press, media, sponsors and family members. We would be gathering in Portland Place on the January 6th, 1988. Auspiciously, this was an historic anniversary in UK-China relations: on this day in 1950, Britain and the newly-founded People's Republic of China initiated diplomatic relations.

I landed in a freezing cold and wet London. The days ahead were a frenzy of jet lag, reverse culture shock and exercises in carefully choosing the right words to describe my journey to journalists. Reports about my achievement hit the top spots, featuring as the human-interest tail-enders to both BBCs national *Nine O'Clock News* and ITVs *News at Ten*. My sponsors, especially Thomas Cook, had hit the jackpot. The 'if' in my original expedition prospectus was now a thing of the past, the objective had been achieved.

Most of my family, mother and father, brothers and sister, and three of their children — nephews and nieces — came down to London for the main event. Thankfully the doors of the previously impenetrable Chinese Embassy that I'd visited earlier

WILD WALL–THE FOUNDATION YEARS

in pursuit of my first China visa were now wide open. Inside, we all assembled in front of a magnificent painting of, most appropriately, the Great Wall. The reception was given British Government approval by the attendance of Lady Chalker, MP for my hometown of Wallasey, then Minister of State for Europe. Speeches were made, cultural friendship praised, and anecdotes told, the most well-received being the tale of me 'borrowing a wife and son' to gain kudos as a married man with a family in the eyes of my Chinese farmer hosts. Photo calls followed. Me and my big, bare feet. Me bathing my sore feet in a bucket of water. Holding the Chinese flag aloft. Standing with my borrowed wife and son, sister-in-law Hilary and nephew Bob.

All had gone exceedingly well, but sadly was not set to end well. Two of the journalists sidled up beside me and asked for a 'private word'. Their tone was ominous. The embassy had prepared an interview room, so I stepped inside with the reporters, one from the *Daily Mail*, one from *The Times*. They were in joint possession of a disturbing piece of paper, a fax received from China.

"I'd like your comment on this fax from the China Sports Services Company in Beijing," said one of the men.

I hadn't heard anything about the company since my days in Hong Kong, although of course I remembered that they had been contracted by David Griffiths to provide logistical support for his planned Great Wall expedition, complete with 'official permissions'.

The reporter proceeded to read the fax. "Recent reports in the Chinese media claiming that William Lindesay has completed a 2,470 km journey on foot along the Great Wall are a complete fabrication. According to public security organs in Yulin, Shaanxi Province, Lindesay was deported from China in May 1987, and could not have returned to continue his journey."

"What do you have to say, Mr. Lindesay?" asked the other reporter.

"Part of the fax is true," I said. " I was deported from Yulin in Shaanxi in late May, but I re-entered China and continued my journey in the autumn, and I did cover 2,470 km along the route of the Great Wall between Jiayuguan and Shanhaiguan."

"Can you prove it, Mr. Lindesay?" was the follow up.

"Yes of course … my complete story will be in my book, coming out next year."

"Why next year, Mr. Lindesay?"

"Well, the Great Wall's long, isn't it? And my story of finding it, and following it, and fighting my way along it, is a very long story as well."

"You fought? You fought who? The authorities?"

"Ahaha, no. Metaphorically speaking, I had to fight all kinds of things — fears imaginary and real, like vicious dogs, through sandstorms, avoiding bubonic plague, dealing with fatigue and blisters, dysentery and stress fractures, all kinds of things…."

"Thanks for your time, Mr. Lindesay. Just a couple of last questions. What's the title of your book, and who's publishing it?"

Xinhua reporters had asked me the same question in Beijing. When I'd replied "The Great Wall: From the Desert to the Sea" they suggested a slight edit.

"My book's going to be titled *Alone on the Great Wall: From the Desert to the Sea*, and it looks as if my publisher will be Hodder & Stoughton."

22

BEAUTIFUL JADE

ONCE THE MEDIA frenzy had subsided I set about obtaining all the necessary papers that I required as a foreigner to marry a Chinese citizen in China. One was a personal statement, translated and notarised by a bilingual solicitor in Manchester's Chinatown, declaring that I was single, had never married previously, and intended to marry Wu Qi and support her. Another was my birth certificate. The most problematical requirement was the 'proof of gainful occupation', because I didn't have one. I couldn't just describe myself as 'Adventurer, no salary as such, but enormously popular, writing a book, potential bestseller'. A family friend, Peter Hill kindly helped by giving me a job, on paper at least, as a spectacle-frame salesman! I would arrange the final document on arrival in Beijing, a 'Certificate of No Legal Impediment to Marriage', which had to be posted on a notice board in the British Embassy for three weeks and receive no public objections.

I arrived back in Beijing as the first signs of spring were beginning to show: the magnolias on Chang'an Avenue and in the parks were just coming into bloom, and Qi looked fabulous. We did two of our favourite things in Beijing, before heading to Qi's hometown of Xi'an. First, we went to a Sunday coffee-morning concert at the Jianguo Hotel, and second, we went for a walk at Xiangshan, or Fragrant Hills, on the western edge of the city.

Chinese law required that a marriage—in legal terms the issuing of a marriage certificate—should take place in either the bride's or the bridegroom's hometown. 'Hometown' is defined as the location of one's *hukou*, the place where the person is registered – all Chinese people have to have a *hukou*. For Qi and the rest of her Wu family their *hukou* was Xi'an. As a foreigner, I was unable to stay as a guest in her family's apartment on their university campus, so I lodged in a nearby 'hospitality house' (*zhaodaisuo*) for 10 yuan ($1.25) per day.

While Qi did the final rounds to collate the required papers on her side—educational records from middle school to university and character references from employers—I began to write my book, and I really did 'write' it, with pen and paper. Hodder & Stoughton, a very reputable London publisher with an impressive exploration and adventure catalogue, had expressed interest in my story after seeing my journey reported on the BBC's national news. Before any deal could be signed, however, I had to submit three sample chapters. If they liked my writing, an advance of £5,000 was suggested. The prospect of half of that windfall—a wedding gift—on arrival in Britain with my new wife was a great motivation to a near-penniless adventurer.

I started to write. The waste paper basket filled-up. I cleared my head with frequent cups of Nescafé and long runs. Qi brought me a takeout breakfast from her home every morning, and cooked dinner in my room on a simple electric cooker. The menu was always egg and tomato noodles, but it tasted great every time.

By mid-April, believing that we had collected all the documentation required by law, we prepared to go in person to the ministry building in Xi'an to begin our formal application to be married. What a lot of papers there were! We placed them on the bed in my room and they completely covered it! However, Qi told me that I had just one more thing to do before we could finally submit our application. I had to go to the hospital for a 'health check'.

"What kind of check?" I asked suspiciously.

Qi started to giggle. "Well, you know, related to marriage. A man health check, checking down there is working ...."

"Okay! okay!" I said, "whatever it takes!"

It 'took' a bit more nerve than I imagined. There wasn't one doctor, but two. And they were both women, aged about 55! Thankfully, they were just as embarrassed and as anxious to get the procedure over and done with as I was. With a quick drop of the trousers and a cursory nudge and glance the whole examination was over within a few seconds. What a relief! I was passed 'fit to marry'.

We cycled to the People's Government of Shaanxi Province building, passing the Big Wild Goose Pagoda on the way and entering the Heping (Peace) Gate in the city wall. But on arrival at the government building, we were met by a closed gate: foreigners were not allowed to enter! Negotiations on the internal phone ensued, and the problem was soon resolved when the marriage affairs counsellor came down from her office to meet us and personally escort us inside. She didn't look too pleased about the situation. As we walked through the labyrinthine building, I thought it quite possible that she might be spiteful and find fault with our application.

We entered her office and handed over our precious brown envelope full of papers. A large golden 'double happiness' character on a red background hung on the wall behind her. Qi and I sat silently, nervously, watching her scrutinise our documents one by one.

"Mr. William, Miss Wu, thank you for waiting," she said

calmly. "I have now checked your documents and they are all in order and so I can accept your application to marry."

We were immensely relieved! This seemed to be a good start.

"I have taken notice of your background histories. I think Miss Wu and Mr. William are very well suited to marry," she said, "I see that you are similar ages, you both have university degrees, you come from good families, and I can see you love each other very much."

Qi and I beamed at each other with delight. The officer then handed us each a printed sheet.

"Please study our country's policy of family planning and support the Party and Government in its work. If you agree, you may return here tomorrow for issuance of your marriage certificates."

"Tomorrow?!" we said, looking at each other impatiently. "Yes! ... No, wait, maybe not," I said to Qi. "Tomorrow is the 13th, isn't it? How about the day after tomorrow? The 14th, that's a better day."

So April 14th was set to be our wedding day.

Having seen my two brothers and sister get married in typical British style, after months of preparations, rehearsals, dress hire, car fleet hire, banquets, lewd best-man speeches and so on, I always dreaded the day if and when my turn came round. Most of all, I disliked the stiffness of it all, and felt sorry for the exhausted couple enduring such a public day, and pitied the near-bankrupted parents who had to pay the large bills. But for Qi and I, our wedding day would be quite the opposite: personal, private, relaxing and inexpensive.

Qi wore a neat navy-blue skirt and matching top that I'd bought for her from Marks & Spencer. I wore a pair of new Levi chinos, old Timberland shoes and a striped Jaeger shirt. Immediately after getting married, we planned to walk just 200

WILD WALL–THE FOUNDATION YEARS

metres to the People's Hotel to begin our life together. We left our bikes behind and took the bus into town instead, another unique aspect of our big day!

The marriage counsellor had solved the gate entry problem in advance and was ready to receive us in her office. There were just a few things left to do. Sign a form, have our fingerprints taken and pay 10 yuan each for our certificates.

Fifteen minutes later, we stood at the reception desk of the People's Hotel and asked for one room, with a double bed. "One room?" croaked the receptionist with a puzzled expression. Then she said: "Show me your marriage certificate please."

We did. Proudly.

When I tell people that I first met my mother-in-law the day after Qi and I got married, they think I'm making a typical British mother-in-law joke. But it's true. Once married, our relationship was accepted, legal and respected, and in Qi's mother's mind I was transformed from the stereotypical foreign spy of the movies to being a pampered son-in-law.

Both Qi's parents were teachers, her father a professor of microwave science, her mother a middle school mathematics teacher. I was warmly welcomed to the Wu family apartment, and was pleased to see large maps on their walls, of China and the world. They reflected not only our mutual interest in geography but the international view of the family. However, Qi explained that the primary purpose of the maps was to cover up the dirty walls and its patches of flaking paint.

Qi and her sister, Wu Xiaoping, helped her mother cook the lunch, while I taught Zuo Na, our niece, English. The lunch undergoing production line-like preparation was *jiaozi* – meat dumplings. Qi told me that they were a favourite food when the family reunited at festival times, because labour-intensive and time-consuming processes bound the family together.

Dumplings require teamwork: mixing, kneading and resting the dough, fine chopping of cabbage and mixing with ground pork, rolling out the pastry into a tube shape, cutting into small lumps and rolling out into circles, then filling and sealing up, boiling and eating. Only then did I realise just how honoured I was back in September 1986 when a Gansu family had fed me *jiaozi*. They were the first homemade dumplings that I'd eaten, and I hadn't eaten any like them since.

We planned to visit some big cities on our, not honeymoon but honey month. Many of the places were chosen because they had featured in our courting conversations over the months. Shanghai, with its Oriental charisma was the city where Qi and I had dreamt of spending a romantic weekend. We 'saw' the Yangtze River flowing along a scroll in the Jianguo Hotel lobby and promised ourselves that we'd take a voyage along it, in style, in a first class cabin.

We managed to get soft-sleeper berths on the Xi'an to Shanghai train, which took about twenty hours. Staying at the glitzy Jinjiang Hotel was memorable — it distinguished itself as the only Chinese hotel that did not require us to show our marriage certificate! Things weren't as straightforward down at the Yangtze River Ferry Terminal where we tried to secure a first class cabin for the entire navigable route from Shanghai to Chongqing. The vendor insisted that the ship had only second class and third class cabins, and there were no first class cabins. The term 'first class', Qi thought, was considered bourgeois, and the name prevented government officials from claiming expenses, while 'second class' presented no such problems. So we started our second class voyage aboard the 'The East is Red No.17'.

When people ask me "Have you seen much of the Yangtze River?" I jokingly reply that Qi and I honeymooned on the river, had a great time and hardly saw anything. But my answer has another meaning in that the weather along the river is notoriously misty and grey. And there were other unforeseen challenges for newlyweds, hilarious now but infuriating at the time. For one, our cabin door didn't have a lock. The conscientious crew member who's job it was to keep the cabins clean and tidy and ensure that everyone was supplied with boiling water, had no respect for the privacy of passengers and would just walk in unannounced. We obviously needed to set up an early-warning system. The furniture was screwed to the floor to prevent it moving on choppy waters, so we barricaded the doorway with luggage. Another issue was the intrusive loudspeaker system, programmed on the universal assumption that all passengers should rise and shine at the crack of dawn. Loud martial music was blasted throughout the ship. PT-type orders were shouted. 'Wake up! Open the door! Air the cabin! Brush your teeth! Drink hot water! Take a stroll on deck!' Muffling the speaker in our cabin did little to silence the strident female announcer. Eventually I resorted to using my Swiss Army knife to cut the flack.

After six days upon the river we disembarked at Chongqing, a vast urban sprawl that is so far inland it was chosen as the Chinese government's wartime capital from 1937-45. There we spent a few days enjoying the fiery food of the city before continuing our honey month through Yunnan Province to Chengdu in Sichuan. The most striking sight there for me was an enormous statue of Chairman Mao Zedong, one of only a few I'd ever seen, for most were quietly removed under cover of darkness in the late 1970's after his death. It even attracted the lenses of a group of young shutterbugs armed with Seagull brand cameras. We exchanged shots and smiles, some English and some Chinese, in front of the statue for a while, before I was distracted by the building right behind it, the Sichuan Provincial Exhibition Hall. Feigning interest in the dull manufactures on display, Qi and I made our way to the top floor. There I reached an open window to take the photograph that I wanted, showing Mao's point of view, standing high above street level, looking down on the ant-like cyclists and the wide avenue below, sweeping away into the city haze.

Our honey month finally came to an end but, as in all good marriages, the honeymoon never ends. Qi and I had two more bureaucratic hurdles to overcome on our return to Xi'an: firstly, to get Qi a passport, and secondly to obtain a spouse's visa for the UK. Both tasks were considered fairly difficult at the time. Few Chinese citizens applied for personal passports. Most Chinese who travelled overseas in the 1980s did so either on public business or for international study.

While we waited for her passport application to be approved, I returned to book writing. Qi began the unenviable task of sorting out her belongings. This comprised dividing her possessions into four categories: those to take to the UK, things to be left behind in China, things that were no longer of any use so were to be thrown out, or possessions that couldn't be thrown out so were simply left in the clutter corner.

One group of objects in the questionable category was a box of 'Mao badges'. Qi had first mentioned these to me on New Year's Day when we visited the Tian'anmen Rostrum. Issued on high days and revolutionarily significant days, these red and gold badges were worn religiously during the Cultural Revolution. "They're useless now, nobody would think of wearing them," said Qi, "But very few would think of throwing them away. We couldn't even throw a newspaper away during those years because every page had something about Chairman Mao on it."

I found the badges fascinating. Kitschy and gaudy, they were standard in most ways yet different in minor details. Mao's head was almost always in gold, set against a red background. One reason for their production, superficially, was to mark an event or commemorate an anniversary, and so they were surprisingly informative. Another reason was adulation, a campaign primarily organised by Mao's heir-apparent, Lin Biao. A popular design commemorated the establishment of the Chinese Communist Party in 1921. Another showed the town of Yan'an in northern Shaanxi, with its landmark tower that I'd seen myself when the police escorted me there during my deportation. Another showed the 'Bethlehem' of the Mao cult, his birthplace, the family home in Shaoshan, Hunan Province. There were scores of different ones. Some badges displayed numbers, dates: one was marked '1893.12.26'.

I asked Qi about its significance. "All Chinese know that date. That's when Chairman Mao was born," she said.

My great grandfather, Johannes Crescentius dos Remédios (1846-1913), born in Macau, China. He lived the four quarters of his life on four continents.

My grandfather, John Middleton Lindesay (1879-1955), born in Christchurch, New Zealand. He captained eleven ships during his naval career.

The SS Falkland, my grandfather's first ship as a cadet in 1895.

My grandmother, Etheldreda Lindesay with sons John Hamilton (my father, standing) and brother Fred; New York, c. 1924.

My family; from left to right, David, Nicholas, me and Dorothy-Jane with our mother and father; Wallasey, c. 1960.

In my first tent; Wallasey, 1963.

With Mum at Chester Zoo, 1965.

My St. Aidan's class, tower-roof of Liverpool's Anglican Cathedral, 1967. Headmaster 'Maccie' is on the left. Young William is beside Mrs. Collinson, at far right.

Receiving the Victor Ludorum *from Miss Walker (St. Aidan's headmistress, left) and Mrs. Fraser; Belvedere Fields, Wallasey, 1967.*

Clean sweep at St. Aidan's Sports Day in 1967.

Moor training, heading to Peel Tower, near Ramsbottom, Lancashire, during a 35-km loop of the 'Three Towers', 1983.

Winter training; Yorkshire Dales, 1984.

Preston Half Marathon; Lancashire, 1983.

Racing (No. 272) in the 'Hyde 10K', one of six 'Tour of Tameside' races over seven days; Manchester, 1983.

Brother Nicholas and I running the 140-km Ridgeway National Trail; Wiltshire, 1985.

Running Hadrian's Wall at Cuddy's Crags, near Housesteads, Northumbria, July 1984, (Nick Lindesay photo).

Breaking news: William is going to run the Great Wall; photo in Liverpool Daily Post, *Dec. 31st, 1985*, (Bob Bird photo).

Cantonese Chinese and chopsticks lessons from Chef Luk Shan Lau; Mr. Chow's Restaurant, Liverpool's Chinatown, 1986, (Tony Kenwright photo).

First day in Peking photograph, cyclists and 'Long live Marxism, Leninism and Mao Zedong Thought!'; Chang'an Avenue, March 1986.

Billboard reading 'Support the international proletariat in the struggle against imperialist oppression and colonialism to achieve liberation and social progress!'; Chang'an Avenue, March 1986.

The Tian'anmen Gate, Peking, March 1986.

First steps on the Great Wall; Badaling, March 1986.

Old revolutionaries Marx and Engels out for China's National Day, October 1986.

Ruins of Old Dragon's Head, the 'seaside terminus' of the Ming Great Wall; August 1986. It was rebuilt in 1987.

Shanhaiguan's main gate-tower, 'The First Pass Under Heaven'; August 1986.

The Wang family; Qingshui; Gansu, September 1986.

My first 'Wallscape' photo, sunrise over the Shanhaiguan coastal plain; August 1986.

The cliff-edge western end of the Ming Great Wall; Jiayuguan, Gansu, 1986.

Leaving Jiayuguan in April 1987, taken by self-timer. (Inset), 'Area Closed to Foreigners' sign, a police museum exhibit, Beijing.

High and continuous rammed-earth Wall in the Hexi Corridor is breached by the Lanzhou-Urumqi road at Changchengkou (top inset). I lodged nearby with the Yin family (lower inset); Shandan, Gansu, April 1987.

The Wall in the Hexi Corridor blanketed by snow, April 1987.

Herders (left) and rammed-earth Wall (centre); near Xiakou, Shandan. (Right), Moslem herder; Ningxia, May 1987

Children going to school; lee of Wujiao Hills, Gansu-Ningxia border, May 1987.

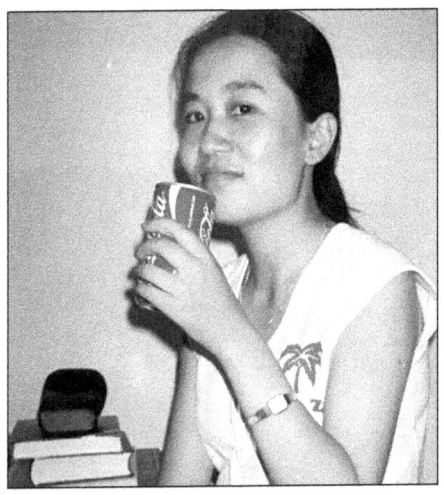

My first photograph of Wu Qi; Longtan Hotel, Beijing, June 1987.

Qi in her signature summer-of-1987 dress, Tian'anmen, August 1987.

'Stock photo' for the press, taken summer 1987, near Badaling, (Oliver Photo).

Student days; Qi studying at Xi'an's Northwest University, after the resumption of national entrance exams in 1977.

At Beijing's Western Hills, August 1987.

Sighting the Wall again; near Horinger, Inner Mongolia-Shanxi border, September 1987.

Near Shahukou, 'Kill the Barbarians' Pass; Shanxi-Inner Mongolia border, September 1987.

The *Alone on the Great Wall* book-cover photo, the best of a whole film taken using my camera's self timer mechanism; west of Badaling, October 1987.

The most important photograph of my Great Wall journey, at Luowenyu, Hebei, November 1987. Explorer William Geil had taken a photograph here in 1908, (see inset). This perchance 'meeting' eventually led us to collaborate in 'rephotographing the Wall'.

Somewhere in eastern Hebei, November 1987.

Running competition from a local; newly-rebuilt Wall, Jiaoshan, Shanhaiguan, December 1987.

Painting to mark Deng Xiaoping's 1984 directive 'Love China, Rebuild the Great Wall'.

Jiaoshan, from the Wall on the coastal plain; Shanhaiguan, December 1987.

Qi's father presented me with his gift calligraphy on our first meeting, which reads: 'To see far you need to scale high mountains'.

Qi and I with my brothers David (front, centre), Nicholas (right) and his wife Elizabeth (left); Badaling Great Wall, December 1987.

*The 'good family man' photo, with 'borrowed' sister-in-law Hilary and her son Bob; Chinese Embassy, London, January 1988, (*Mail on Sunday *photo).*

The 'amazing 'feat-feet' pose; Chinese Embassy, London, 1988.

Time to put my feet up; Chinese Embassy.

The Lindesay family with Chinese Ambassador Ji Chaozhu; Chinese Embassy, London, 1988.

With Roger Stebbing (Midland Bank), Baroness Lynda Chalker (MP, Wallasey) and Ji Chaozhu (China's Ambassador to the UK); Chinese Embassy, London, 1988.

Cycling around to gather last-minute paperwork needed for our marriage; Bell Tower, Xi'an, April 1988.

Our self-timer wedding portrait; the People's Hotel, Xi'an, April 1988.

Qi gets ready for a honeymoon dinner; Jinjiang Hotel, Shanghai, April 1988.

Portrait for 'True Love' feature in the UK magazine Bella; Seacombe waterfront, Wirral, September 1988.

Starring live on the BBC 1 primetime show Wogan; Shepherd's Bush Studios, London, August 1988. (Screenshot courtesy BBC).

Qi on the Tian'anmen Rostrum, on its first day open to the public; New Year's Day, 1988. To mark the occasion we were given badges as souvenirs.

The Wu family, with the three girls all wearing their Mao badges, (from left to right), Wu Lin, Wu Qi and Wu Xiaoping; Xi'an, 1966.

A street-side photo display on the life of Chairman Mao; Chongwenmen, Beijing, 1987.

Qi with some of her family's Mao badges; Xi'an, 1990.

A class of schoolchildren visiting Mao's family home; Shaoshan, Hunan Province, 1990.

Guide at Mao's family home in Shaoshan holds straw sandals, footwear widely used by soldiers on the Long March; Hunan, 1990.

Shaoshan Railway Station in Mao's hometown, built big for the mass influx of red guards on 'revolutionary travels'; Hunan, September 1990.

Qi and I with veterans of the Long March; Ruijin, Jiangxi, October 1990.

Xu Youwan, artilleryman on the Long March, aged 83; Ruijin, 1990.

Tiled-facade showing Mao Zedong, aged 41, at the start of the Long March; Ruijin, Jiangxi, October 1990.

23

A Great Wall Love Story

Qi's passport application went through surprisingly quicky and unquestioned. We had just one more procedure to tackle, to obtain a settlement visa for entry to the UK, and for that we travelled back to Beijing and made an appointment at the British Embassy. Her 'interview' was, and remains to this day, the smoothest, most pleasant visa application one could ever imagine. It consisted of a cordial conversation over afternoon tea with the Consul, Catherine Nettleton. This red-carpet treatment wasn't in recognition of me, a British citizen, being the first foreigner to explore the Great Wall for its full length, it was purely an indication of the small number of personal visa applications by Chinese individuals at that time.

Qi and I happened to get engaged on the 14th day of the month, chose to marry on the 14th, so unsurprisingly we chose to fly to the UK on the 14th. For Qi, it was probably the equivalent of that day back in 1986 for me when I gathered up my hopes and fears and boarded my first-ever flight to China. This was Qi's maiden flight.

It was also a landmark day for my family in Wallasey. All three of my siblings had married spouses sourced within a five-kilometre radius of the family home. While one occasionally heard of someone from the UK marrying someone 'from the continent' (meaning Europe), further international marriages were rare at the time, but here was William bringing home a wife from China, 8,000 kilometres away. Qi and I were long-range indeed, truly intercontinental!

The best description of Qi's first day in Britain is 'traditional'. It was a Sunday, so my mother, as was her custom, prepared a sumtuous roast lunch. In the afternoon, my brothers, their wives and children took Qi and I to Harrison Park where we played the quintessential British game of cricket.

Reconciling my mother and father to the reality of a Chinese daughter-in-law had been left in the capable hands of Dave, Nick and Elizabeth. However, we would eventually appreciate the wisdom behind the Chinese character for peace, which shows one woman under a roof, and not two! The family were most conscientious in helping Qi get used to Britain and our ways, or as my mother put it 'getting Westernised'. Our two cultures and countries could not be more different. Thinking back, one major reason for our happiness and the longevity of our marriage is that Qi has always embraced British ways and traditions while remaining completely Chinese. Similarly, I have willingly adapted to China and embraced its history and culture while remaining quintessentially British. We've never felt the need to push any aspect of our respective origins and backgrounds down the other's throat. The result is that we tend to share the same Western breakfast and the same Chinese dinner, but at lunchtime we go both west and east, as I make a sandwich and Qi prepares some fried rice.

Having been out of gainful employment for almost two and half years, I was penniless and thus had no option but to ask for my parents' help in accommodating us in the family home, at least for the foreseeable future. I envisaged that this situation would persist until my book was published. So, there I was, aged 31, having travelled in a huge life-changing circle from Wallasey to the Great Wall of China and back to Wallasey again, now on the threshold of an uncertain future.

I had no difficulty drumming-up renewed press interest with Qi at my side. *'From Wallasey to the Wall, winning a Chinese bride'* screamed the *Liverpool Daily Post*. My adventures were one important aspect of my achievement, but that journey coupled with an Oriental romance was just what the British press loved: a Great Wall love story. People from mainland China were virtually unknown in the West in the 1980's, so the curiosity value of Qi appearing with me on television and radio was a winner. She was everything an ambassador should be, showing Britain that China was coming back into the world, and of course always looking beautiful.

Nick called me one morning about a month after we'd arrived back and said "Will, they want you on *Wogan*!"

Wogan was a thirty-minute chat show screened on the BBC 1 television channel at peak time, 7 p.m. on Mondays and Wednesdays. Hosted by the chatty, humorous and hugely popular Terry Wogan, it consistently ranked as the most-watched TV programme in the UK. Qi had co-starred with me on local television shows in Liverpool and Manchester, but this one was in a different league in terms of national visibility! To avoid Qi getting nervous, I told her that it was just another TV appearance, but this time down in London.

But her suspicions that this was an altogether larger event were aroused as we travelled First Class on the train to London and raised further when a chauffeur-driven limousine met us on the platform at Euston Station for the transfer to the Park Lane Hilton Hotel. We only had time to shower and change, me into my best suit, Qi into her 'honey month' *qipao* (cheongsam) before being driven to the BBC Shepherd's Bush Studios. After a quick chat with Terry in the green room, we were set to go live. We

WILD WALL–THE FOUNDATION YEARS

walked out on to the stage-set amid rapturous applause from the ticketed audience, our entrance being broadcast to eight million viewers up and down the land. Qi's jade quality and charm shone throughout.

A sense of the show's enormous reach came first thing next morning as I walked with Qi towards Parliament Square. As we crossed Westminster Bridge, I told Qi of my London Marathon finishes there, and while doing so, a suited businessman doffed his hat, smiled and said "Saw you both on *Wogan* last night. Congratulations!"

24

ALONE ON THE GREAT WALL

MY CORRESPONDENCE with Hodder & Stoughton, the publishers, had been progressing well and my sample chapters were well-received by one of their top editors, Margaret Body. She invited me down to their London office for a discussion. Sensing that I was on the verge of landing their substantive offer, I borrowed the cash for a rail ticket from my brother Nick and took the first train from Liverpool, travelling by myself to save on a rail fare. As I emerged from the Tube station at Great Russell Street, adjacent to the imposing British Museum, I encountered droves of commuters rushing to their offices. It wasn't a pretty sight and it caused me to reflect on my bold decision to go against that flow, to follow my dream of the Great Wall and pursue it with dogged determination. Beside me was the world's greatest museum, and here I was, having explored the world's greatest *open-air* museum, on my way to Bedford Square to see one of London's top publishers!

Margaret Body had a tiny office literally stacked with books from floor to ceiling. The stars on her shelves were titles she'd edited since the 1960s, their spines announcing the pinnacles and places reached by a host of explorers, adventurers and inveterate travellers, whose ranks I was on the verge of joining.

Margaret talked about the kind of book Hodders wanted: about 80,000 words, with eight pages of colour photographs,

WILD WALL-THE FOUNDATION YEARS

as soon as possible, before the Great British public forgot about me and my exploits. I had about eight months to deliver a double-spaced, typed manuscript, by April 1989. Margaret then confirmed the 'business side', an advance against sales of £5,000: I tried not to gasp in excitement.

Half would be payable upfront on signing the contract with the rest to be paid on the day of publication, tentatively in autumn 1989. A few days later, I signed, purposely dating the contract 8.8.1988, an auspicious date for my hoped-for bestseller. The number eight, *ba*, is a lucky number in Chinese because it rhymes with *fa*, which means wealth, fortune or to prosper, so the more eights the better. A few weeks later, my first cheque arrived. I was now solvent and able to support my wife. My parents were pensioners, so we contributed £50 each week towards the cost of our stay.

For the first time, Qi and I started working together, remotely, on the Great Wall. My most pressing task was to submit potential photographs to Hodders for inclusion in their 1989 catalogue of new publications, and also for the design of a dust-jacket with the book scheduled to be printed in September. The whole roll of film that I'd shot for that purpose had proven to be well worth the effort: the 36 exposures included one perfect shot. I was captured in the ideal spot and at a realistically athletic moment, with my arms, legs and head all looking good and the Wall zigzagging away in the background. The picture accomplished exactly what a book cover photograph should do, to tell readers what the story inside was all about. It showed me alone on the Great Wall. All that I had to do now was to write the rest of the book.

I wrote with a ballpoint pen on A4 paper. My 'desktop' was the dining room table, my heritage was in the photographs on our piano, and my story was in my head and legs, on my maps, and in Qi's eyes. I had a handful of history books, mainly to check dates, and a basket always overflowing with screwed-up or torn-up sheets of paper. Once I'd completed a chapter, I had to rewrite it clearly and neatly for a typist who used an electronic 'word processor'. A local lady, Joy Grainge, did *Alone on the Great Wall* for me. She slashed her per-page price to ensure that she could have a hand in her first-ever book publication with, no less, the famous couple who had been on *Wogan*! But only when she returned the neat-looking typescript did I discover that, reading it typed compared to hand-scrawled, seemed to convey a completely different flow and feel to the words. And so yet another stage in the process emerged, that of written amendments and re-typing. Finally, and ahead of schedule, in February 1989 I packaged up a photocopied complete manuscript and mailed it 'Recorded Delivery' to London. I waited nervously for Margaret's reaction. She told me the race was now on to edit, page set and print over the next six months to ensure that copies would be distributed nationwide by November: the sales team predicted that it would be the perfect Christmas book, an ideal combination of adventure and romance.

In the meantime I got down to a few of the most pleasurable jobs left to do for the book, drawing maps, choosing photographs, writing captions and thinking who might write a foreword. I chose Han Suyin, who graciously agreed and penned this:

> '*Three years ago, fortuitously, William Lindsay and I were together in Manchester – or was it Birmingham? – waiting to appear on a television programme. As usual we, the consenting sheep, huddled in rubbery armchairs, waiting while the media lords were preparing to praise or maul us. William and I talked. I found him a man of disarming simplicity. He wanted to run the Great Wall of China.*
>
> *"How are you going to explain to the people you meet in*

WILD WALL-THE FOUNDATION YEARS

China what you are doing?"

He showed me a little pocket book on which he had scribbled, in his not too legible writing, that he was William Lindesay, and running the Great Wall.

"This will never do," I told him, full of my knowledge of how the simplest things can become awkward when meeting with unbudging officials. "No one reads English very much in China's hinterland ... you should have a letter, in English and in Chinese, stating that you are running the Great Wall for fun and for friendship. You will meet bureaucrats, they are there to obstruct, deny, suspect, retard, interrogate, never to encourage something they cannot understand. You need a nice letter for bureaucrats."

"Who is going to do that?" asked William, a bit puzzled.

"Me. I know how to deal with them. I'll write a nice letter, and I have a friend who will do it on his computer typewriter, so that it is easy to read, and looks more important. In both English and Chinese."

So it was done. My friend produced a perfect letter, suave, bland, speckled with appropriate clichés. Off went William Lindesay, and ran the Great Wall.

But it was not the letter, it was William's wonderful candour, that purity of mind and aim, which brought him success. He met affectionate care all the way, and this book is not only his own odyssey but the great story of the people of the Wall. A bright child of the cosmos, William ran for all of us who in our hearts dream that each day of our lives might be a step of love'.

Dr Han Suyin
Lausanne, 1989

For more than three years, my life had been lived at full speed, all for the Great Wall, and now I had nothing urgent to do, only to wait for the return of the edited manuscript. When it came back I saw that it was decimated. I hadn't seen such so many red-ink scrawlings and lines since my worst school-exam days. It was a blood bath! Margaret said it was far too long, and had to be culled. I fought tooth and nail for retaining details, but she insisted they should be saved for my memoir in 30 years' time. I was forced to concede. And so you have them here.

Qi began to join me for short runs and long walks along the Wirral coast. As we walked, we discussed our plans for our future. Should it be in Britain or in China? Should I try to return to the conventional, or continue with the unconventional? Could I manage to become conventional after being out of that loop for so long? But how could I be unconventional without another novel idea?

Meanwhile, Qi's looks and skills were in demand, beginning with a telephone call from out of the blue: a photographic agency had seen her picture in a newspaper and wanted her to be model in an advertising shot for a business centre. ICI, the big chemicals multinational was expanding its market to China and appointed Qi as a translator. But for most of her time Qi was a student again, enrolled on an English writing course at Birkenhead College. There she made friends with a Xiu-Ai, a woman from Taiwan, and Yoko, a woman from Tokyo.

Our maintenance costs, transport fares, typing and college fees had by this time almost exhausted the Hodders advance. Just in the nick of time, Midland Bank began recruiting part-time staff. Having secretarial experience and a postgraduate diploma in finance, Qi applied and was accepted for the job, working in Liverpool. However, I was reluctant to 'leave' the Wall.

The prospect of publicity around the book's publication would

WILD WALL–THE FOUNDATION YEARS

present an opportunity to capitalise on my achievement and growing fame, and also of monetising my specialist knowledge. I believed that Great Wall tourism might be our future. I designed a limited-edition tour guiding travellers along the length of the Great Wall 'from desert to sea', from Jiayuguan to Shanhaiguan, via Xi'an and Beijing and a few other open places. Bales Tours, a high-end tour operator, was my first choice of travel agent to market the tour: Anthony Bales loved the idea of Qi and I hosting it and agreed to get it up and running. We scheduled an autumn 1989 departure date, priced it at £2,375 per head, and printed an attractive brochure.

China was rarely in the UK news, and if there was a China story in the press, my brother Nick would always telephone me. But from May 1989, it became headline news. Peking University students first mourned the death of Hu Yaobang, the former General Secretary of the CCP and a committed reformer. The mood of memorial gatherings then swung from solemn to critical, and they became protests against corruption and for a more open society. Massed demonstrators gridlocked Beijing. I wasn't overly concerned: I thought that the imminent arrival of summer would make it too hot to continue the protests, the students would then go home for the vacation and the movement would fizzle out.

Meanwhile in London, the book cover design was finalised and I received a colour proof by post. It looked excellent: my name in block capitals, in blue font, 'William Lindesay' above the title in red, '*Alone on the Great Wall*'. The sky was photoshopped to blue from its original greyish-white, which the designer said was 'too cold', and I accepted the change. Keen to make progress with the publicity, I tried the cover on a book of the same size and thickness, and began to think about a set-piece photograph that would help sales, come the day. It was an easy decision as to where we should go for the photo shoot: up to Hadrian's Wall for the weekend to show Qi my big stepping stone.

Then all of a sudden, after a telephone call, 'come the day' took on multiple meanings. The situation in Beijing had exploded. Chaos erupted as the army was called in to restore order. The day after the massacre, on June 5th, Margaret Body telephoned to "discuss the rationale of not publishing anything about China this year" as she put it. The sales team strongly advised postponing publication for several months, at least six, maybe twelve—to allow time for the turmoil to subside and book buyers to forget what had happened.

"Nobody's going to be buying China books right now," Margaret professed pessimistically. "Could you possibly wait until next year for us to publish? Or are you going back to China?"

Anthony Bales was the next person to telephone, not surprisingly to cancel the Great Wall tour idea. Tourism, it seemed, would not be our immediate future.

But it was during that chaotic 1989 summer, with our backs literally to the Wall, that I began to take steps towards my next China journey.

III

Following in Footsteps
1990-1991

25

My 'Appointment' With The Long March

ONE LATE SUMMER afternoon in Beijing in 1987 while I was waiting for Qi to join me after work in our usual meeting place, the Jianguo Hotel lobby bar, I began chatting with a British businessman at an adjacent table. A few cold beers on his expense account lubricated our conversation, which progressed from small talk to why we were in far-off China. After telling him the gist of my Great Wall story he said something like, "Next you should look at today's China, and study Mao Zedong. He's the man who really made modern China."

But why Mao now for me, and how?

I remembered that one of Qi's many 'Mao badges' was stamped with the Chairman's date of birth, in December 1893. That meant the centenary of his birth would be 1993, just over four years away. Seeing the other badges in the box and discovering the revolutionary events they glorified was an accessible way of framing the story of modern China for me. I knew that if I was ever going to 'study' Mao it couldn't be from a purely political standpoint. I do not like politics, nor do I enjoy standing still. I would have to study Mao in my own way, in a way that he'd not been studied before, by following him, retracing his footsteps, going the way that I preferred, under my own steam. That's why I began to think about retracing the Long March, on foot. How else could one understand such a feat of endurance? And

WILD WALL–THE FOUNDATION YEARS

as for what the Long March led to, the foundation of the People's Republic of China, episodes in that phase of the story could be personalised by my researching and retelling of Qi's own family's stories from the Mao era. The components of a new journey were coming together. It promised not only to satisfy my ambition, but to fulfil my duty, to know the story of my wife's own country, of the China made by Mao.

I'd known of 'the Long March' for many years, but was unaware exactly what it was, or how significant it was in the story of 'New China'. The legendary military pursuit by the Nationalist government forces of the outlawed Communist guerrillas was played out across 6,000 km of rugged terrain, from southeast to northwest. The Long March involved 80,000 starters and only 4,000 finishers, although it was far more complicated than that simple summary. Among the finishers was Mao, the founder of the People's Republic, and Deng, who was destined to revive the the country decades later. The March lasted one calendar year from 1934 to 1935, and it began on October 16th—my birthday. I became proudly aware of this nugget of information as a boy through my desire to learn what other great events had occurred 'on this day in history'. That was years ago, in the mid 1960s. But yet another sign had emerged recently. The March concluded in northern Shaanxi, at a small town called Wuqi, and that sounded like Qi's full name, although the written characters are different.

What better sequel to my Great Wall journey than another Chinese historical epic: the Long March? Another challenging journey, but through different regions of China. Another historical traverse, but through different times. A very good reason for Qi and I to return to China.

My response to Margaret Body's question about our availability in 1990 was definite: "We won't be in the UK next year, we'll be back in China, unable to do any book publicity."

The ultimatum worked. Hodders agreed to adhere to the original launch date for *Alone*.

As publication day neared, Qi and I went down to Hodders in London to collect the books hot off the press, the day advance copies arrived by courier from the factory. More good news awaited us: the publicity department had decided to invest in a UK promotional tour. This was a fantastic opportunity for Qi to see Britain from south to north in a way that we were unable to afford ourselves.

Outside the office, sitting on a park bench in Bedford Square, we pored over the book in the winter sunlight. Another surprise, printed inside, lay in store for Qi. I handed a copy to her, open at the dedication page: 'To Wu Qi'. The book I'd mentioned to her when I first saw her, my love at first sight, was there in our hands!

We were launched into the publicity tour in November, in London, getting off to a brilliant start with a lunchtime interview by the charming and witty *Daily Mail* columnist Lynda Lee Potter. She exceeded her usual word count with an article (including great pictures) splashed across two pages, titled '*The Long, Long Run of Love: The Couple whose Destiny was Sealed by the Great Wall of China*' (*The Mail on Saturday*, December 2nd 1989). BBC Radio 2 prime-time shows followed, with pithy chats to top presenters Derek Jameson and Gloria Hunniford — and perfect musical accompaniment with Phil Bailey's *Walking on the Chinese Wall* and, it seems hard to believe, 'T'pau' with their No. 1 hit from just weeks before, *China in your Hand*. A home city interview in Liverpool with Harold Brough yielded my favourite headline by its reference to the Chinese police, who wore green uniforms in the 1980s: '*Running Away from the Little Green Men*' (*The Daily Post*, November 15th 1989).

Our tour continued across the Pennines in Newcastle where

WILD WALL–THE FOUNDATION YEARS

David Whetstone reported my *'Taste for Wall to Wall Adventure'* (*The Newcastle Journal*) and featured my photograph of Qi reading 'the book' at Hadrian's Wall. North of the border in Glasgow at Café Gondolfi we had a memorable and hilarious interview with Alisdair Marshall who produced his *'Wonder of the Wall'* (*Glasgow Evening Times*, November 25th 1989) piece divulging a fundamental secret of my success: 'having more training mileage in my legs than the average ten-year-old car'. Our roadshow was truly snowballing now, and we capped off the tour just before Christmas in festive style back in Wallasey. After a morning run with my brothers to buy multiple copies of *The Times* we returned home to quaff champagne before a smoked salmon and scrambled eggs breakfast with the whole family while reading a full-page of extracts headed *'Sports Book of the Week: Alone on the Great Wall'* (December 23rd 1989). Finally, I took Qi to Eire (illegally, as she didn't have time to apply for the visa that was required at that time) to bring our whirlwind round of publicity tours, as well as the 1980s, to a close with a fun appearance on RTE's *Kenny Live* show in Dublin.

It was an enormously successful and fantastically enjoyable book tour. For the record, Hodder's PR department collected all the newspaper clippings, cassettes of TV appearances and radio shows, ranking them according to readerships, audiences and viewership reached. By an entirely different means of measurement, however, it was the interview I gave at BBC Radio Oxford on the morning of November 15th 1989 that would prove to be the most significant of them all. It reached one person in particular who decided that she should introduce me to someone similar.

An elderly local lady had heard me speaking, would buy my book in 1990, read it in 1991 and then write to me, c/o Hodder & Stoughton. What she wrote, and her subsequent generosity in sending me another book, an old book about the Great Wall, written by 'the other William' (whom I mentioned earlier) would eventually inspire me to make another journey that was to play a major role in exposing just how much of the Wall was destroyed during the 20th Century, and elevating its conservation towards the top of China's cultural relics protection agenda. But it would almost another four years before the book was in my hands.

As the new decade approached, it was a change in my course of history that began to occupy more and more of my thoughts. Reporters were asking me "What are you doing next?" Early in the new year, on the strength of good sales figures, I mentioned my new book idea to Margaret at Hodders. This was not only a simple matter of courtesy, but also a condition of my contract with Hodders to give them 'first refusal on any subsequent work'. Margaret liked the idea of *Marching with Mao*, but said she would prefer to wait to see if we managed to land any international editions of *Alone*.

26

Living Between Journeys

BETWEEN THE TWO New Years of 1990, Western and Chinese, I tried to make a living by giving illustrated talks and selling books at each venue. Preparing the slide show was a lengthy and extremely fiddly chore, one that I dreaded for days in advance, rather like the approach of a dental appointment. Being a newcomer to the public speaking circuit, I foolishly used my original transparencies. The rigmarole of placing the best selection in the carousel of the slide-projector, and hoping that it rotated and changed the slide when a button was pressed, became a nerve-wracking experience. These devices were very susceptible to jamming. Both slide mounts and the slides themselves were easily damaged during attempts to extricate them from the clutches of the hot mechanism! However, while these machines had their infuriating moments, troublesome audience members could be far worse!

After the equipment was all set-up, I would sit behind a table that was piled with neatly-arranged copies of *Alone on the Great Wall*, purchased at an author's discount of 50% of the retail price, i.e. £7.50. As most talks didn't offer a speaker's fee I depended on a small percentage of the audience buying books to cover my costs and make a profit. One thing remains in my memory about these talks. There would always be someone, of the self-centred persuasion, who wished to hog my attention to the exclusion of all others. They mindlessly monopolised the book-table conversation. They would ask question after question while flicking cursorily through my book and making ignorant, irrelevant or foolish remarks. Examples include inanities such as 'Well of course it didn't stop Genghis Khan' or 'It didn't work' and 'Actually it was built to keep the Chinese in', or the most irritating, 'A friend of mine's been to China and he's also walked the Wall'. This kind of person never once bought a book and would typically, after about ten minutes or so of time-wasting, conclude by saying something like, "Very nice book, I'll definitely order it from my local library!"

The word 'library' spoken in this context made me wince. My concealed thoughts (that I can finally get off my chest!) would be along the lines of: "Well, this book took almost a year to write, it records a journey that itself took two years, and you are about to see a one-hour performance from the heart free of charge, so can you imagine how delighted I am to learn that you intend to borrow this book from the library?"

I suppose such a rant, private as it was, reflected a mounting frustration: the reality of earning a living from being an explorer-author was difficult, unsustainable. Sometimes I sold ten books, and once I sold only two. Fortunately, Qi kept our ship afloat with her bank job in Liverpool. After months of doing paperwork in the back office, she was moved to the front counter as a clerk. It proved to be a 'promotion' that brought her more tears than it was worth. Her problem with the general public was different to mine.

"I just can't understand what half the customers are talking about," Qi wept.

I didn't want Qi to get upset over her inability to understand Scouse, so she resigned to enjoy a few months at home. To make ends meet, I began looking for any kind of job, and was

WILD WALL–THE FOUNDATION YEARS

invited to interview for a temporary post with Wirral Borough Council based at Wallasey's impressive town hall, just beside the Seacombe 'Ferry cross the Mersey' over to Liverpool. Although strictly overqualified with a bachelor of science degree, I lacked two 'basic' new skills—I couldn't type, nor could I use a word processor; files, file names, saving to memory and 'floppies' (short for floppy disk) were all alien to me, and I frankly admitted it. But I was still offered the job! Later, my boss Paul told me that he selected me for my honesty! It would be my last experience of working in Britain. I spent an enjoyable five months there as an office employee, and most of all was able to commute by running ten milers, along the prom all the way from Wallasey to Seacombe via New Brighton, savouring the sea breezes.

By early summer, Qi and I had worked out our Long March strategy. We were ready to formally pitch the new book idea, giving Hodders first refusal. I'd used office lunch hours to type my proposal. In it, I explained that I intended to explore the Long March from the unique perspective of the route itself, placing it in the context of what events had led to the Long March—civil wars—and what the Long March had led to—the foundation of the People's Republic of China. Our timing proved to be impeccable. *Alone* had sold almost all 3,000 copies printed, and a US publisher was said to be interested in a paperback edition. Margaret Body confirmed the Long March deal, offering me another £5,000 advance, as before in two stages.

With money due to be deposited in the bank, we began to plan in concrete terms, looking at the logistics of how I'd be able to stay long term in China. We would need a place to live, and I would always require a visa, perhaps every few months. At that time, the authorities did not give any visa privileges whatsoever to spouses of Chinese nationals resident in China. Compounding this headache was the news that, on our leaving China two years before, Qi's mother had assumed that we would settle in Britain, so she had cancelled Qi's *hukou* in Xi'an. This meant that while she remained a Chinese national she was no longer registered as a resident with a *hukou*. To solve my problem, Qi suggested that I look for a job as an English language teacher at a university in Xi'an, where we could rely on family help. This would give me an official status as a 'foreign expert' with a work visa and residence permit, a place to live, long vacations at Chinese New Year and in the summer, and a not-too-burdensome twelve hours of classes per week.

I agreed that this was a practical solution to our dilemma. Thus, we decided that I would begin retracing the Long March on arrival in Beijing in the autumn, then start work at university after the Chinese New Year winter vacation in February, returning to the Long March in the summer vacation. Any spare time in between would be used to research and write the book. Family connections (*guanxi*) cranked into gear and Qi's sister, Xiaoping, soon found me a job at the Shaanxi Institute of Mechanical Engineering in Xi'an.

Our days in Britain were now counting down. Apart from the book tour, Qi and I hadn't had a vacation since arriving two years earlier, so decided that it was time we did. We chose to walk one of Britain's long-distance trails, the West Highland Way in Scotland. Walking and running in the Great British outdoors had transformed Qi into a lover of the wilds and nature. Our summer trek through the Highlands, covering the 154 km route from the northern edge of Glasgow to Fort William in five days and camping all the way, was definitely a most-cherished time in Britain—and doubtless the countless midges that joined us felt the same.

More good news came from Hodders: the US edition was confirmed with Fulcrum Publishers in Colorado, and that meant another moderate payment, and a boost to morale. I had long romanced about an overland trip to China, and especially travelling on the Trans-Mongolian railway from Moscow to Beijing. For most of my life thus far, so much of that quadrant of the world map was overlooked; because all that lay beyond the Iron Curtain was impossible for Westerners to reach. In 1989, that began to change: in the second half of the year, the rise of a trade union in Poland, the fall of a wall in Germany, and the execution of a dictator in Romania, all set in motion the beginning of the end in the Cold War. An historic chance was now within our reach.

Rail tickets were twice the price of flying, and trains took ten times longer at the quickest. We'd need fifteen days or so for the journey, making it a whistle-stop rather than a non-stop tour. We would only have time and money for a quick look at three major cities en route, national capitals that were in a state of flux. On and off trains, just the two of us, would be a hassle, but would be easy compared to a future travelling with children. The Trans-Mongolian wasn't just a way of getting there, it was more about the act of being on the way there. All in all, it was not only a momentous time in history to travel overland, but the perfect time for us.

27

THE BERLIN WALL

I'D WATCHED the widely reported fall of the Berlin Wall live on television, in November 1989, and the topic had naturally cropped-up in interviews during the promotional tour for my book. I'd also watched the Tian'anmen protests live on television. The Square, part of our courting ground, had become a battle ground. Thankfully we weren't there, and that conveniently allowed me to state in advance to interviewers that I was not qualified to discuss an event that I didn't witness. "It's an irrelevant question," I said, "I'm here to talk about the Great Wall, not Tian'anmen Square." I wasn't going to jeopardise my personal plans by airing my views on such a politically sensitive question. In private circles, in the pub, things were different. I told friends that Communist Party leaders had been humiliated. A bite back was inevitable. A scapegoat was necessary. And what if the movement had overthrown the Party and state? How could those students possibly govern a country of 1.25 billion? Civil and ethnic wars would have erupted.

Now, here I was, in Berlin standing in front of their Wall — and behind it, for both ways were now possible — curious to see what was left of it.

Although superficially scarred, most of it was still standing. Official demolition had only just started, and it would take almost 18 months to remove the long-despised 155 km barrier, a

WILD WALL–THE FOUNDATION YEARS

painful memory and monstrous eyesore for Berliners.

My immediate impression was that one couldn't compare it to the Great Wall, in any respect: its length, height, material, method of construction, and purpose differed markedly. It looked more like a flimsy concrete screen, and it was much lower and thinner than I'd expected. It was, after all, merely a divider to deter individual escapees and defectors, not a defensive wall put up to stop whole armies. And most importantly it was devoid of the fundamental requisites upon which the aura of the Great Wall is grounded: antiquity and the mystery of exactly how it was built. In Berlin we know exactly how, because it was as recently as 1961, and the West filmed the process. It was assembled using pre-cast concrete blocks that were lifted into position by cranes with the individual sections cemented together. And of course, the major operational difference between the Berlin Wall and the Great Wall was its primary purpose, that of keeping people in, rather than keeping them out. Only a fool ever asked, "How many West Germans tried to escape to the East, over the Wall?" while many a fool has ventured to suggest that one purpose of the Great Wall was to keep the Chinese population in. My response to that tired joke has been to ask: "How many Chinese fled north, across the Great Wall to enjoy a harsh life of herding on the steppe?"

But moving up close and pondering, there were some interesting features that would eventually provoke more profound thoughts. The Berlin Wall's original smooth surface was already heavily defaced. The West-facing side had been daubed with graffiti ranging from moving creations to worthless sprayings, the former by avant-garde artists, the latter by vandals and drunkards. Time changes everything, though. After the fall, *any* painted part still in situ was at a premium, a collector's item, a piece of Cold War history, there for the taking simply by renting a hammer and chisel (including 'free' goggles), a sledgehammer, even a stepladder, from one of an enterprising number of East Berliners who, early on, had seen the potential of setting up a 'CIY' (chip-it-yourself) service. And if the battered and scoured complexion of the Wall in front of us was any indication, they must have been doing very good business. The Berlin Wall was the only solid drape along the entire Iron Curtain, while the rest of the ideological East-West divide, along the 9,000 km front from the Barents Sea in the north to the Adriatic Sea in the south was defended by soldiers, watchtowers, barbed wire and mines. The drape was now in tatters, pock-marked as if afflicted by a disfiguring disease, holed as if moth-eaten. Gaps had appeared where sledgehammers had broken through at the weak points, the cemented joints. Here the Wall was literally fraying from within, its contorted rebars exposed like ribs of a skeleton.

As I recount this experience, thirty years after the fall and coinciding with it being in the news again in 2020, I am wiser, having gleaned greater knowledge during my own 'career' progression from a Great Wall explorer to a Great Wall scholar and conservationist. In hindsight, I'm shocked by the short-sightedness that led to the immediate destruction of the Berlin Wall. Only a few short sections and ancillary components, totalling less than one percent of the original barrier, now remain. The longest is a 1.3 km 'gallery' that mainly features worthless spray-can art, the likes of which you can see in every city around the world. Wasn't it rash of the German government, of Berliners, of local entrepreneurs, and of avaricious tourists, to unite and destroy it? Now that so little is left, time once more changes everything, as it always will. Berliners of the future will surely lament the destruction of this historical Wall by their fathers and grandfathers, just as the Chinese now despair at the loss of large parts of their Great Wall by their forbears during a period of revolutionary rage, when they were sucked into the

WILD WALL–THE FOUNDATION YEARS

maelstrom of ideological madness prevalent at the time.

To celebrate the redundancy of the Berlin Wall, which not only divided a city but also a nation and its people, was right. To rejoice in the abandonment of its checkpoints and the demobilisation of its jack-booted guards, that was a victory. To be blinded by the destructive fervour of the moment and to not have the foresight to preserve the structure as a monument for future generations, to celebrate reunification, to remember the re-creation of one Germany, was a major mistake.

It could have stood today as a most fitting memorial to a tale of two cities. Thankfully, stories of bravery of those who escaped, and of those who failed and died will endure, in books, films and museums.

Looking back, I too lacked foresight! When I visited in 1990, I should have run the whole 155 km length of the Berlin Wall, when it was still there, when my legs could have carried me along it, at a steady 6 km per hour, in around 25 hours or so. Now it's gone, marked only by a line on the ground, a tourist trail, not the Berlin Wall.

I did at least have the good sense to buy an historic postcard that shows the demolition of the Wall with an inset of a newspaper cutting with the headline '*Honecker: Mauer bleibt noch 100 Jahre*' – 'The Wall will last for 100 Years', a comment by GDR leader Erich Honecker. It ended up lasting only 28 years. Preserved as a monument it might have lasted one thousand years.

It is believed that Genghis Khan once said 'a wall is only as good as the men who guard it'. In Berlin, the Wall's men were already demobbed, and unashamedly, for they had no say in the division, they were eager to get rid of their workwear and equipment, touted from plastic bags, or neatly arranged in open car boots. Their ugly and clunky items of war and repression had their unique selling points, presently as objects of ridicule. What big hats they had all worn! How heroic they must have been, with so many medals! How brave to keep the people safe with their truncheons, bayonets and jack boots. Now, anyone with a few tens of dollars to spend could join their ghostly ranks and be sure of a prize at a fancy dress party.

28

SLOW TRAINS TO CHINA

BACK ON A TRAIN, our next stop was Warsaw in Poland. Poles still adored the British at the time, and had done so ever since we'd given Hitler an ultimatum in September 1939: get out of Poland or be at war with Great Britain. The Poles have never forgotten this, as one kind man was about to show us. A fellow passenger out of Berlin, he insisted that we stay at his son's empty apartment in Warsaw. From there, he went out shopping for us, buying bread, eggs, cheese, tomatoes and beer. What more could one ask for? Next day he guided us around Warsaw. "You must go to the top of our Palace of Culture and Science," he said. "From up there, 200 metres high, you get the best view of the city. Because it's the only place in Warsaw from where you can't see the Palace of Culture." The monstrosity was a 'gift' from their Soviet oppressors, who controlled Poland at the time. The building is wholly despised, both for what it represents and for its ugly Stalinist architecture.

It was time to move on and catch what train we could to Moscow. However, although we had a open ticket, we did not have a berth. No problem. Our friend insisted that the ticket vendor should find us sleeper berths to Moscow. He shouted at her. He told all the other travellers in the ticket hall what was going on. And he translated his rants into English for our benefit.

"I'm telling her, that you are our British friends, our best friends, and we should not forget who our best friends are, and what they did for us!"

We shared a sleeper cabin on the train with two pretty Russian girls in their twenties, obviously privileged, for they told us they had been on a shopping trip to Berlin. Like our Polish saviour, they too spoke excellent English, and like him, as is common while travelling, they showed their hospitality by insisting that we must visit them while in Moscow.

"Yes, yes, of course!" we said. Of course, neither them nor us really meant it.

Nearing Moscow, I pondered Russia's and China's political parallels across the 20th Century. China took an early lead by deposing its last emperor, in 1911, while the Russian Tsar Nicholas and the rest of the Romanov family were shot and bayoneted in 1918. The Soviet Union was a decade ahead of China with its revolution, led by Lenin, in 1917, compared with that by the Chinese Communists in 1927, led by Mao from 1935. But in the recognition of the need for reforms, to change or perish, China was ahead of Russia. Deng Xiaoping initiated *gaige kaifang* from 1978, while Mikhail Gorbachev only launched *glasnost* & *perestroika* (openness & restructuring) in 1986. Had China's head-start made a noticeable difference? Did the Chinese people's discontent of 1989 warn of what might face Russia? We were about to find out in Moscow.

Many people regard travel by train as boring, but not me! A bizarre incident was about to happen, which in retrospect seems to have been an ominous prediction about the future unity of the Soviet Union itself. The very last carriage of our train became uncoupled as we were speeding along to Moscow. This dangerous incident was brought to the attention of the driver and chief conductor by some occupants of the detached carriage. They had moved forward along the train to take lunch in the dining car, only to find that their carriage had disappeared by the time they tried to return to it. They were confronted by the sight of a door that opened directly onto the track that was speeding past beneath!

The dissolution of the Soviet Union occurred in December 1991, a year or so after this train-splitting event. But we saw much else in Moscow that predicted the coming collapse. On the city's Arbat Prospekt, dissident artists ridiculed Lenin and Stalin who were widely despised for their purges and gulags. Portraits showed them with devils' horns, covered in medals and with knobbly knees, and there were other not so amusing signs of impending change.

I have always been sceptical of statistics. Forget about economic charts and percentage growth figures, it's what's in stock on the shelves that really counts, and whether people are having to queue or not. These are the common-man's and common-sense economic indicators.

In 1980s China, queues were ubiquitous and they had 'Chinese characteristics'. Pushers and shovers were numerous, tolerated and rarely harangued. In Moscow people needed to queue because of shortages, and they did queue. They queued everywhere, for everything, in a most-orderly fashion. They even joked about it. "What's 200 metres long and eats cabbage? The answer: "A meat queue in the Soviet Union."

Long queues were also the norm outside Moscow's restaurants. But as foreigners, we were lucky. As soon as the *maître de* spotted us, she beckoned us forward, and ushered us in, providing the special English menu. Although this was several times more expensive than the local version, it was cheap in sterling terms against the near-worthless Rouble. The longest queue of all was at the newly-opened McDonalds.

All this queue-jumping was innately embarrassing for me,

a true democratic Brit, so for a change we decided to enjoy room service, 'self' style, back in the austere Hotel Cosmos. We'd brought a bag of foodstuffs from the UK and were about to begin our evening meal when a knock on the door brought an unexpected change of plan. There stood Ludmilla, one of the girls from the train!

"I've come to take you to my home to dinner," she said. "The driver is waiting below."

It was difficult to make any excuse, so off we went, to the distant suburbs of Moscow in a large black limousine. I'd read that it was Europe's largest city, now I believed it. Polite small talk kept us going, until we arrived there, somewhere, but we'll never know exactly where. The interior of the apartment was a palace compared to the austere exterior of the housing block. Inside, waiting for us, were Ludmilla's sister and mother.

A magnificent spread was laid out on the table to greet us. We drank Russian champagne, enjoyed smoked sturgeon canapés and moved on to borsht, fried pork fillet, mashed potatoes and beef stroganoff. A Brit, a Chinese and some Russians speaking English, perfect English, merrymaking in Moscow of all places! And the mother spoke most-perfect English. What a glamorous woman she was too: tall, strong and slim with meticulously groomed hair and draping jewellery. I complemented her.

"You don't speak *ordinary* English, you speak Queen's English."

"I have to," she said with a twinkle in her eye, "I'm an interpreter for KGB."

A dry Russian joke perhaps? We all laughed, but I'm sure she was not joking. After all, did the ordinary Muscovite have a chauffeur-driven limousine and access to such scarce foods? Still, this gathering, it turned out, had only one motive behind it: friendship. The way this family had opened up their home was a

WILD WALL–THE FOUNDATION YEARS

real *glasnost* experience for us, international relations at their best that we'd never forget. An hour so later, we were dropped back down to earth in the Cosmos.

Next day, our obligatory Intourist guide took us to Yaroslavsky Railway Station, gave us our tickets ten minutes before departure, walked us to our carriage, and waved us off. The big train ride to Beijing, five and a half days of window traveling, a must for railway buffs, was about to begin.

Every part of the famous line had a geopolitical motive. Following the opening of the east coast port of Vladivostok in 1860, the Trans-Siberian railway line, the longest in the world at 9,289 km, was built between 1891 and 1901 to connect Moscow to the Sea of Japan, and hence the Pacific Ocean. Pertinent to us, a branch line southwards to Ulaanbaatar, following the former Tea Route, was subsequently built between 1940 and 1949. The connection to Beijing was completed between 1953 and 1956 when Sino-Soviet relations were good and Moscow was sending train-loads of engineers and industrial equipment to China.

Qi and I shared a compartment with a young Englishman, Peter, about our age—in his early thirties—and Lothar von Faulkenhosen (how could one ever forget such a distinguished name?), a German archaeology professor at UCLA, and an accomplished polyglot. Lothar spoke English like a BBC newsreader, Mandarin like a CCTV newsreader, and Russian, which by our ears at least, sounded impressively colloquial.

The train day established a distinct pattern: we chatted, read, brewed tea and coffee and shared treats of each other's stash of goodies, dozed, looked out of the windows and walked along to the restaurant car when called.

Our first meal, some borscht, dark bread and butter as a starter, followed by a main course of potatoes, cabbage and a sausage-like object, was quite tasty, washed down with good strong black coffee. However, dinner was more or less the same, with a different-shaped sausage. So was the next day, and the next!

Every so often the train stopped, we alighted, walked briskly, flung our limbs around, and looked for local morsels to purchase while taking care not to stray too far, for fear of the train departing without us. Back in the carriage we exhumed stop-relevant snippets from our guidebooks. 'We're across the Urals now, into Asia'. 'Yekaterinburg ... the Romanovs were murdered here', ... 'Siberia ... Stalin's gulag country' and 'Lake Baikal, twenty percent of the world's freshwater supply'.

After following the Baikal lakeshore for about 170 km, the railway line turns south-eastwards to Ulan Ude, from where the line divides. The Trans-Siberian proper continues eastwards towards the terminus at Vladivostok on the Pacific coast, and the Trans-Mongolian line turns southwards towards Beijing .

Soon we crossed the Russia-Mongolia border, leaving a land of big-hatted border officials for another whose officials wore even bigger hats. Within half a day, we emerged from Siberian forests of white birch onto the rolling green steppeland of Mongolia. At last I could get a glimpse of this important region, the vast expanses outside, to the north of the Great Wall, the other side of the story.

From here on southwards we followed a route traversed throughout antiquity by nomadic warriors on horseback. The earliest journeys, made as far back as 2,500 years ago, were disorganised bids to survive, made by those who had lost their livestock on which they depended entirely, taken by drought, disease or extreme winter freezes. In the 13th Century, this same journey was made by a large and highly-organised cavalry army united by Genghis Khan's (1162-1227) manifesto. He raised their expectations above grudges of the past and overrode their

WILD WALL—THE FOUNDATION YEARS

religious prejudices and dogmas. He convinced them to ride beside him to attack, besiege, conquer, and occupy towns and cities, and to harness the labour, resources and products of the Chinese Empire and control its trading routes. He promised his followers commensurate material reward for their fighting, belief and trust. Some eight hundred kilometres north of the Great Wall I was, I believe, at the far edge of the Great Wall theatre of war, at the root cause of the Great Wall story—crossing a landscape that could be lived on, but not lived well on for long, before catastrophe struck.

For a geographer like me, a student of the Great Wall story, this was a riveting journey. I could not leave my window seat. I felt it was essential to keep watching, to note the changes. Heading south the land became drier, the grassland of the steppe thinned, white clusters of *ger* camps became fewer. Then came the notorious Gobi, a 1,600 kilometre wedge of largely stoney desert that straggles most of the Mongolia-China border, and a major element in the Great Wall story. Once nomadic people became capable and confident in crossing this natural barrier, Great Walls were needed as artificial barriers to stop them.

We reached our second border, Mongolia-China, at Erenhot. Here, there was a transport glitch, by design, incorporated by engineers to delay any modern invasion. The gauge (distance between tracks) of the railway line changed from the 1,520 mm Russian gauge to the 1,435 mm 'standard', which meant that the train could not proceed southwards until the bogies (wheel sets) were changed. This process took place in sheds, the carriages being lifted high in the air on hydraulic jacks. The heavy work was done by an efficient workforce of Chinese railway workers, men and women, who I regarded as old friends of mine.

A few hours further south the Gobi's harshness eased, for ahead was another transition zone, the northern limit of cultivation in today's China. Passengers on the train started to buzz with excitement. We'd been aboard for almost five days, eating bread, potatoes, sausages and cabbage. Everyone was about ready for some treats of Beijing Duck and Peking Beer.

At Zhangjiakou, we had an appetiser for China's long-missed vast and varied larder. Vendors waited on the platform to welcome us, neatly spaced along it, standing beside their trolleys. Each was overloaded with produce from the land of plenty: melons, tomatoes, cucumbers, roast chickens, eggs cooked in tea, beer, congee and instant noodles.

Like me, born in Wallasey, Qi too had the Wall in her DNA right from her early days. She was born in this old frontier town of Zhangjiakou just a few hundred metres from the ruins of the Outer Line of the Ming Great Wall, and I took a special picture of her standing in front of a cast-concrete station plaque displaying its name.

From here, while continuing to retrace the ancient invasion route leading from the Mongolian steppes to the northern plain of China, we also joined another important route, one that hails from a much more recent era: the first railway that was designed, built and financed by China. This was the Peking-to-Kalgan line constructed to replace the convoys of camels that carried coal and wood to the capital. Soon we'd be riding that section of the line in the lee of the Great Wall that I'd seen three autumns ago.

Bright sunny conditions prevailed: Beijing's golden-autumn weather was on seasonal schedule. A screen of rugged mountains now came into clear view ahead, making the way south seem well-nigh impossible. If it looked like a challenge for a train in 1990, then surely it was more so for a cavalry army in centuries past. But there always had been a way to pass through these mountains, a way that had evolved aeons before, slowly, carved by forces of erosion exploiting weaknesses in nature's armour:

WILD WALL-THE FOUNDATION YEARS

The Juyong Pass. For us by train, there was a newer way through, underneath, made by tunnelling in 1909. Emerging from these tunnels into the bright light, my eyes took some seconds to adjust. Then, to my great delight, I saw the Wall right outside my window as we crept through it and stopped at Qinglongqiao Station.

The Wall here, was, I knew very well from 1987, the first layer of a series of related and staggered fortifications that one encounters from north to south along the length of the Juyong Pass. By merely approaching this defile, nomadic horsemen had already endured a death-defying journey that included a crossing of the Gobi Desert, a battle against nature's hardships. As they neared the pass, they would set eyes on the uncompromising alliance between man and nature: the Great Wall. The Ming chose this location as the place to stand their ground, for just beyond the pass, a short ride across the plain, was Beijing, their capital.

Cities on the site of Beijing, albeit with different names, had functioned as capitals for a total of about 800 years, and all of them were exceptional in one way or another. If we look at the core of dynastic Chinese history, between the Qin (with its terracotta warriors as a bookmark) in 221 BC and the Qing (with the Last Emperor's forced abdication as the bookmark of 1911) for 800 of this 2,200 year-long timespan, either the northern part of China or all of China was conquered and ruled by a succession of nomadic groups from the north. First came the Xianbei in the 6th Century AD, then the Qidans in the 10th century, the Jurchens in their immediate wake, then the Mongols in the 13th Century and finally the Manchus in the 17th Century. Coming from the far north, they felt comfortable having a capital in the north of the land they conquered. Whatever they called it, Yanjing, Zhongdu or Khanbalik, it was close to their ancestral homeland. The first and only ethnic Han imperial dynasty to select the site of Beijing as its capital was the Ming, because its third emperor, Yongle (r. 1402-1423), hatched a radical plan to wipe out the Mongols (who had once ruled China) by attack, rather than contain them by fixed defence. As soon as Yongle seized the throne from his nephew, he relocated the capital from Nanjing to Beijing. Becoming known as the 'Emperor on Horseback' (*mabei huangdi*), he led his armies from the front, launching northern military expeditions from his newly-built capital city, determined to destroy his people's old enemy. He eventually failed in 1423, losing most of his army to starvation through overstretched supply lines, and his own life. He left his successors with a major dilemma—a grand capital replete with the Imperial Palace (now known as the Forbidden City), and temples behind a magnificent city wall (tragically demolished in the late 1960s), but all of it too close for comfort to the volatile frontier region. Hence the need for the greatest sections of Wall in these mountains to the capital's immediate north, to ensure no breakthroughs.

29

MY ROUTE OF BADGES

ENTERING THE JUYONG Pass and heading down towards Beijing is a memorable final furlong for everyone on the 7,826 km-long Trans-Mongolian railway journey. For Qi and I it brought double-happiness, a joyous return to *mama zhongguo* as we'd begun calling the motherland, and a very special and personal welcome back from our matchmaker, the Great Wall, the like of which we could only enjoy by travelling overland. In retrospect, this spectacular way back to China would be remembered as much more: a life milestone. I was not only changing my course of history from the ancient to the modern. We were also moving house, home, jobs and countries. From now on, China would be my adopted country, home for the rest of my life, and the Great Wall, despite the revolutionary detour that lay immediately ahead of me, was destined to be my life's work.

For the time being, though, I needed to adjust my sights. The Great Wall was now behind me, shelved, receding to the north; it was the Long March that I was now approaching, in the south. I began to compare the two. They were legendary army events, great military achievements, universal symbols of China. To me they were absolute synonyms for it, representing everything that China was, is, and will be: endurance, hard work, determination, an ability to do the impossible. For centuries, the Ming army built the Great Wall across the breadth of North China; for one year, the Red Army footslogged and fought its way from the southeast to the northwest. But in all other respects the two were vastly different.

One was tangible archaeology, the other intangible history. The Ming engineers and workers left a permanent landscape feature. Its most solid components, made of rock and brick, have survived the centuries, standing defiantly, only scathed in part. I didn't expect the Long Marchers to have left any permanent trace of their passage. The most reliable clues were temporary, ticking away by the day, the reminiscences of local septuagenarians who maybe as children stood and watched as thousands marched by, and the recollections of its veteran participants, by now octogenarians.

One was here forever, the other just for a day and gone by tomorrow. I'd followed the Great Wall because of its high visibility: marked on maps. At its best, it remained huge, continuous, dragon-like, coiling away behind and beyond for as far as my eyes could keep up, a few tens of kilometres in each direction. The Long Marchers left only their footprints, no trace. This posed a navigational challenge. As my departure day approached, I began to wonder exactly how I'd achieve the essential 'feet-on' experience in my quest to discover the spirit of the Long March. What sections would I choose? How would I find my way?

The Beijing-Xi'an train was our seventh since leaving Wallasey. Qi's family was thrilled to see her, and pleasantly surprised that we were 'back', to stay for the foreseeable future. For a Chinese to voluntarily return to the motherland in those days after spending time abroad where they could have legitimately remained, forfeiting a spouse's settlement visa and qualification for naturalisation, was a rare choice. Qi and I didn't have the time or inclination to wait around simply for her to become a

British citizen when we had far more exciting projects to pursue: to retrace the Long March and publish a book in time for the centenary of Mao Zedong's birth in December 1993.

Eager to map out my route, I asked Qi to retrieve the box of Mao badges that she'd stashed away before we left for the UK. Originally they had been produced and distributed from 1966 to 1969 to function as the popular propellent of propaganda to the masses. They were worn to show loyalty to Chairman Mao. My idea was to use these badges, focussing on their themes or the events that they commemorated, to present a way for me to proceed on a biographical journey through Mao's life and times. This journey extended from 1893 to 1976, from cradle to grave, and beyond the grave, his legacy — after-effect or aftermath — until his centenary in 1993.

"Actually," said Qi, "these badges were a very clever way of teaching people the basic facts — names, events, dates, slogans."

We began by putting some of them in their place, on my map.

"Ruijin, where the Long March began, 1934," she said. That was a town in southeast China, on the Jiangxi-Fujian provincial border, the de facto capital of the 'Soviet Republic of China' a mountain refuge of the guerrilla group named the Workers and Peasants Army that became the Red Army.

"Next is 'me' — haha — Wuqi, where the Long March ended, 1935." I knew exactly where to put that one — just below the Great Wall in Shaanxi Province. That's where the Communists established their new Soviet Republic.

"Okay, so I'll start my March from Ruijin, and end it at Wuqi," I said. Next I needed a number of dots en route, to show 'turning points', where battles were won or lost, challenges overcome.

"This one, very important, the Zunyi Conference in Guizhou Province, 1935, it's where Chairman Mao becomes the big leader of the Party and army." He held these positions for 41 more years, from 1935 until his death at the age of 83 in 1976.

We continued, searching for what I called 'dramatic badges', the places that would lead me into the March's wildest country: crossing the Yangtze River, whose upper reaches in Yunnan Province are known as the Golden Sands River, the traverse of Sichuan's Great Snowy Mountains, the highest part of the Long March, and the treacherous crossing of the marshlands bordering the Tibetan Plateau. Connecting these dots would lie at the heart of my own Long March.

Badges also gave me ideas for constructing the before-and-after. What events led to the Long March? Mao's birth in Shaoshan; the inaugural Chinese Communist Party Congress in 1921 in Shanghai and Jiaxing, and the outbreak of the Communist-Nationalist conflict, in Nanchang in 1927.

And afterwards? What did the Long March lead to? The zenith was Mao's victorious arrival in Beijing to ascend the Tian'anmen Rostrum in 1949 and proclaim the establishment of the PRC. We had a family story to personalise that event: Qi's father was a student in Peking. Several lows followed: during the Cultural Revolution he was 'sent to the cowsheds', forced to do manual work, for being an intellectual. As a teenager, Qi's sister Xiaoping was sent-down to the countryside for six years. Thankfully these were participatory experiences, not tragic ones, that I would seek to retell.

There it was, a route of badges. I'd be alone as I linked the dots, but Qi would be embarking with me, and would meet me at key locations to search for veterans to interview, to translate, and of course to relieve heartache.

30

MARCHING WITH MAO

IT WAS MY first time in south China. I had an early indication that marching with Mao here wasn't going to be easy because I couldn't understand what southerners were saying. I was led to believe that they spoke different dialects, but when I spoke to Hunanese locals in Mao's birthplace at Shaoshan, my ears heard a completely different language. It wasn't Mandarin as I knew it. Apparent that we didn't have a *lingua franca*, they often resorted to writing. The unavailability of pen and paper was no barrier. They were quite accustomed to a make-do method, a finger for a pen and a palm for a paper. In charade-style they hand wrote characters under my nose, and then looked up at me with an inquisitive expression that asked, "Now d'you know what I mean?" But as the Chinese proverb goes, they were 'playing a lute to an ox'. I knew fewer than a thousand Chinese characters. The whole performance did, however, illustrate a remarkable characteristic of the mysterious Chinese language: that the palm-writing system worked perfectly well for them. Although those living far apart in China may pronounce the same characters very differently, they at least do have the same meaning in the minds of all who read them — whatever dialect they spoke. (Nowadays, the easiest way for south and north to 'talk' is to write: text messages are okay, voice messages are a waste of time!).

To be on time for my historical appointment I busied myself

with preparations to leave the old Chinese Soviet at Ruijin in Jiangxi Province exactly fifty-six years to the day, actually night, in 1934 that the Long March began, on October 16th, my thirty-fourth birthday.

I had decided to wear and carry 'period-related' if not quite 'period style' clothing and kit, for good reason. For one hundred yuan or so I had pieced together a complete People's Liberation Army uniform, for generationally speaking the 'PLA' was the direct descendant of the Red Army. For rain I had a green cap, dubbed the 'Mao' cap by foreigners. For shine I had a straw hat, lined with plastic as farmers advocated in anticipation of heavy southern rains. My green cotton trousers were baggy enough to take knitted long johns when I reached the southwest and its colder mountain provinces. On top I wore a matching khaki shirt and drill jacket. Its buttons were of impressive-looking brass, embossed with the Chinese-style numerals *ba yi* (8.1) which commemorate August 1st as the foundation date of the People's Liberation Army, the military arm of the Communist Party, being the date of an uprising against the Nationalist Chinese government (dominated by the Nationalist Party, also known as the Kuomintang or KMT) in Nanchang.

My rucksack was also bought from an army supplies store, frameless and rubberised, and secured with old-fashioned draw-cords and buckles. Half-packed it sagged hideously in true sack style but jammed full it took on the shape of a squarish parcel that promised some buoyancy if, heaven forbid, I should fall into a river. Inside were just a few concessions to half a century's technological progress. My down sleeping bag was far more compact than the woollen blankets that Mao's orderly carried for him, but at least the duck feathers originated in China. DIY is not my forte, so to avoid doing what the Red Army did — unhinging doors to sleep on — I carried a locally-woven straw mat, a

WILD WALL–THE FOUNDATION YEARS

forerunner of the insulating ground-pads used by outdoorsmen nowadays.

How could I explain this 'Action Man' mentality? Dressing in PLA soldier-style was not re-enactment taken to fanatical extremes, nor a futile attempt to disguise myself. It was simply a ploy to minimise the uneasy fidgeting and undue fascination on the part of the people I'd meet en route. I knew just how much of a distraction it was to be an international trade show exhibit for the West's outdoor equipment manufacturers.

For safety's sake I bought a wooden walking stick. I'd use it as a pacemaker and a sergeant-major when my stride became sluggish. It could also function as a dog beater, rat basher, snake stabber. If any of these predators should overcome my stick, I didn't have much to deal with what might follow, apart from a few leftovers from our recent Scottish walk – plasters, bandages, Vaseline and the like. Qi took me to the local pharmacist's dispensary in Ruijin in search of a panacea. It was a very different experience to Boots in Glasgow. Wooden boxes and glass jars displayed a variety of floral and faunal medicinal ingredients as well as ready-made potions, pills and ointments.

"What's that? I asked. "Young male donkey urine, good for dermatitis," came the answer. "Okay, how about that one?" I pointed. "Burnt human hair paste, for boils."

I wanted something wide-spectrum to deal with a possible variety of ailments. Sitting in front of the doctor on duty seemed to be one way to start. He checked my pulse, looked at the white of my eyes, asked to see my tongue, and without hesitation scribbled a prescription. We handed it to the pharmacist behind the counter. After scrutinising it she snapped, "Can't read it." which prompted the doctor to snarl 'extract of snake bile' in reply. Hearing Qi's interpretation, I asked her to request something, well, 'vegetarian'. Without hesitation he recommended *Yunnan*

Baiyao, a secret, powdered formula concocted from the abundant flora of Yunnan Province. For internal and external use, it was good for almost anything in anybody, from period pain to sore throats, from internal haemorrhages to gunshot wounds — and animal bites. It could be taken dry, with water, with wine, or sprinkled on grazes and open wounds! I had immediate faith in this wonderful stuff to sort out all sorts: it smelt like a walk through Kew Gardens (and no wonder, many of the plants they have originated in Yunnan).

While Qi scouted Ruijin alone in search of old Long Marchers, I familiarised myself with my new old kit. The button-fly trousers were particularly fiddly: I realised that I'd have to go early to avoid a rush to open the floodgates! The main problem with the rucksack was its absence of compartments, so I used my jacket pockets instead. There was the 'way-finding' pocket containing pages from an atlas of China and an army compass. Another pocket was 'psychological'. How could the police scold me if they found a bilingual copy of 'Chairman Mao's Little Red Book' in my breast pocket? Another item in there was a snapshot to exploit the Chinese shutter-bug craze. It showed me with a group of students at an 'English Corner'. On the reverse, it was captioned in Chinese: 'We welcome Mr. William to serve in the socialist construction of our motherland by helping us gain fluency in English, the world language necessary for our country to realise the Four Modernisations' (in agriculture, industry, defence, and science & technology). Finally, I had a 'friendship pocket' containing a packet of cigarettes and a box of matches to make diplomatic breakthroughs.

Fewer than five percent of the soldiers that began the Red Army's breakout of the Nationalist encirclement in 1934 eventually reached Wuqi in Shaanxi the following October. For that reason, plus the chances of 'finishers' surviving for a further fifty-five years until 1990, I thought that there would be virtually no chance of Qi locating any living veterans. Optimistically, she cited the proverb 'withered leaves fall close to the tree', explaining that as Chinese people grow older they tend of go back to where they began: their hometowns. And she was right. She found three veterans who agreed to talk to 'her husband.' Two were 'leavers,' who set off and completed the March, and one was a 'remainer' — not a conscientious objector — but one that had to stay in the vacated Soviet along with thousands of others, the too-young, sick and too old. To ensure that at least I'd get my foot in the door before they declined to speak, Qi didn't tell any of them in advance that I was a Westerner.

While I'd be the first foreigner attempting to retrace the Long March on foot, I wasn't the first on the Long March: that was the German military advisor Otto Braun, who took the Chinese name Li De. Braun was sent to Beijing on the Trans-Siberian railway by Comintern, the international organisation that advocated world communism, and then smuggled south to the 'Soviet Republic of China' straddling the Jiangxi-Fujian border, which was encircled by Nationalist forces.

I met my first Long Marcher, Gu Yiping, in his spacious eight-roomed home on Red Capital Street, Ruijin. The home was a retirement perk for his services as a bodyguard to Zhou Enlai, always Mao's loyal right-hand man and eventual premier of China. We sat on creaking wicker chairs, beside a table of homegrown tangerines and peanuts, and beneath a large wall map of China. At the age of 78, Gu Yiping knew full well that the anniversary of the Long March departure was coming round once again and he had no trouble in recalling those autumn days a lifetime ago when it began, when he was 22 years old.

I asked him whether he, or others, knew that a march was planned. "In hindsight there were some indicators," he responded. "Peasant women were ordered to increase their output of *caoxie* (straw sandals) and to produce them to an extra thick standard."

I'd been shown examples of these sandals, still commonly worn footwear by farmers in the region, by a museum guide. Soon afterwards, I went to a market to search for a pair. I couldn't find any large enough—remember, a whopping size 14—but I did purchase, much to the amusement and astonishment of the large crowd that had gathered, the two largest pairs that the old lady had on her stall as keepsakes, items to study, admire and inspire.

Helping myself to peanuts from the table appeared to act as a prompt to Gu. "Feasting was another clue—suddenly all frugality ceased," he said. "You know there's a Chinese proverb that goes, 'only a foolish man kills an ox'—because it's more valuable as a draught animal than just for its meat. Well, for weeks our rations had included duck and pork. We were eating the producers of eggs and piglets!"

Gu Yiping played-down his surprise promotion from ordinary soldier to one of Zhou Enlai's team of orderly-bodyguards as 'one day carrying a spear, the next day a loaded pistol'. He moved around the Soviet, from one run-down farm to another, so that Zhou's whereabouts never remained fixed. It was a regular strategy, he said, as spies were active in passing information on leaders' movements to the Nationalist army who then targeted the known location with air raids. From that moment, Gu was constantly at Zhou Enlai's side, and he had only a few days' notice of the moonlit start of the March.

"In one way my job was easy, all I carried was Zhou's document case, field glasses, lamp and food-box. It was lightweight compared to the others. Just ten to twelve kilograms."

The other Long Marcher I met in Ruijin was a real heavyweight:

artilleryman Xu Youwan. He left Yudu, the second town of the Soviet, on October 19th, under a starry night sky.

"A pontoon bridge had been hastily made that evening for us to cross the river. I carried a mortar, captured from the KMT, four shells, one hundred bullets and five *jin* of rice, altogether about 80 *jin* (40 kgs). The pontoon was dismantled at dawn and the boats hidden during the day on the bushy banks."

A week of mass departures under the cover of darkness went completely undetected by the government forces. It would take the KMT three weeks to discover that the Communists had gone. Interestingly, the news was first reported to the outside world by *The New York Times*, which noted '40,000 red bandits were looting their way through Hunan'. Humiliated by the incompetence of their intelligence, the KMT moved into the Soviet to vent their anger on those who remained. A 'White Terror' was unleashed on those who'd supported and lived amongst the Reds. The 'remainer' I met, Bao Zhong fought on as a guerrilla, eventually recounting his efforts in a book *On the Banks of the Min River*. "Around 6,000 communist sympathisers were executed that first winter," he told me, "no tree could be seen without a corpse hanging from its branches …."

31

To The Golden Sands River

UNTIL I REACHED Kunming, capital of Yunnan Province, my route had meandered across a wide front. This reflected the zig-zagging paths of the Red Army itself. But from now on, heading north, my targets were quite specific. Topping my list of important sites was the riverside hamlet of Jiaopingdu on the Jinsha (Golden Sands) River. This settlement is located on the old Yunnan-Sichuan muleteer's road that was used to carry opium, medicinal flora and brick-tea to northern markets, and returning south with yak hides and Tibetan medicinal fauna. It promised to be a three-way crunch point: for the Communists it was one of only a few places for them to cross the raging river; for the Nationalists it was the perfect place to stop them in their tracks and force them to backtrack. In Chiang Kai-shek's own words: "The fate of the nation depends on keeping the Reds bottled up south of the Yangtze'. For me, it was a highlight on my route. Come police or closed areas, hell or high water, I had to get there, badge or bust.

A local bus from Kunming to Luquan left me an estimated two to three days' march away through a closed county to the Jinsha River. The initial stretch was a packed mud road as far as Sayingpan, where the road ended. I asked villagers how I might continue to the river. Vague comments, but no detailed directions, came in response, such as 'straight on', 'it's five hours away' or 'you'll get there tonight'. Then a short man in a floppy straw hat stepped forward from the crowd. "I'm on my way to Jiaopingdu ...." he muttered.

What good fortune! What more could I ask for than this man who was talking of action rather than merely offering words of advice?

"How about we go there together?" I asked.

A little beyond the village we reached a col, from where a huge vista opened out, dominated by a valley so deep and steep-sided that I doubted whether any path could possibly negotiate its slopes. No wonder there was no road! Yet on the distant mountain sides, terraces stood out like a patchwork and paths fell away threadlike to hamlets perched on the steep slopes below.

Before I even knew my companion's name or could contemplate the arduous decent, he was off, leading the way, shuffling along with his short, quick steps, sliding, yet always in control. I followed in the clouds of dust that he kicked-up. Try as I might, I always lagged behind him, for I was trying to stop sliding, to stay on my feet. The reason for the pronounced patchwork appearance of cultivation became clear: some terraces were harvested, others not. To catch my breath, and to help him lose his, I offered my walking companion a cigarette.

His name was Zhang Changyuan and he was heading home to Huili, Sichuan Province, north of the river. His few possessions were bundled in a small brown bag with makeshift rope shoulder straps. He didn't carry any food, drank from springs along the way, and walked in the 'straw sandals' of the day, thin-soled black plimsolls, nicknamed 'lazy shoes'. The Red Army had always relied on the support of locals to show them the way, while spreading their manifesto: to oust landlords and distribute land among the people. Luckily for me, by going home Zhang was going my way, the shortest way, the old mule trail into Sichuan. To reach there by bus, he told me, was a long, circuitous, and expensive journey, so he preferred the three-day walk. En route I told him the purpose of my journey, and my hopes of finding one of the boatmen who ferried Red Army soldiers across the river in 1935. To my astonishment Zhang said he knew of them! "If we want to rest in Jiaopingdu tonight, then we should hurry on our way," he urged.

The patchwork wheat plots were now behind and above us. The next zone, on the moderately steep lower slopes, was occupied by orchards of apples and pears, and below those came the rice terraces where springs oozed and provided natural irrigation. It was November and the rice had been harvested, exposing bare sheets of mud being pecked-over by ducks. Crystal clear water, filtered by 1,500 metres of rock, flowed down to join the main torrent below, grey waters that had flowed here from Qinghai and Sichuan. The Jinsha River had scoured a deep V-shaped valley with fearful force, its roaring sound amplified by the steep slopes.

We arrived at Jiaopingdu just in time, it seemed. I predicted that it might undergo a name amendment to reflect the change that was in the offing. The third character, *du*, means ferry, but before us loomed a building site. A bridge, *qiao*, was under construction and its workforce of two hundred had provided the biggest influx of strangers since 1935. The foreman kindly invited us to share their accommodations, but, appreciating the security mania surrounding key construction projects, I politely refused. I reminded Zhang that it was the *du* rather than the *qiao* that I'd come here for.

We headed off downstream on a narrow path just ten metres or so above the river. Its turbulence chilled us with a following wind. A log riding along on the waves ploughed past us at great speed. We stopped. Zhang pointed. I imitated its passage by miming a see-saw action from fist to elbow and, if Zhang's expression was anything to go by, we were thinking the same: how a log drifting free from a sawmill might become a waterborne missile. Soon Zhang stopped, turned around, pointed and nodded. Up ahead, standing in a huddled group were farmsteads: surely Jiaopingdu?

The shortage of flat ground had necessitated crowding of the buildings, so much so that what little space remained between them produced alleyways just shoulders in width. Footsteps of strangers couldn't be heard, but loud-beaked geese cackled our arrival. Zhang pushed open a heavy wooden door and I followed him inside to see a courtyard full of perhaps ten people, bowls to mouths, their chopsticks swooping over a table full of dishes.

"I've brought a foreign friend with me," Zhang said to the silent mass that looked up, agog, yet continued chewing. Once they had swallowed, and registered Zhang's announcement, an old man, and possibly his son, rose from their stools and chorused the greeting *"xinkule, zuo, zuo, chifan, huanying nimen,"* (you're tired, sit, sit and eat, you're welcome).

"That's him, he's Zhang Chaoman," said Zhang. The old man who had been singled out beamed a warm smile and he asked one of the women to scoop some rice into my bowl. I ate ravenously and washed it down with hot tea; it turned out to be more than a banquet! I had reached not only the place, but also found the man. Zhang Chaoman was one of the renowned brothers who had operated the ferry service across the river.

Dusk was falling as we finished dinner. The women cleared the table and the men lit up, Zhang Chaoman smoking a long pipe. I asked him to step outside so I could photograph him at his doorway in what little light was left. But even our simple dialogue emphasised our communication problems. His accent was heavy and he—like most people here—appeared to have been deafened by the high-level of background noise generated by the river. It was necessary to persistently shout into one another's ears. I asked if he could write down his story, but he was illiterate. So were all the others.

"Tell Pei Yingfa to come over!" they cried, and shortly afterwards a young lad by that name arrived having received the summons. He had the best writing in the village.

"Please tell me your Long March story," I said.

Zhang spoke, Pei wrote. Qi would eventually translate.

> "The Red Army's Long March reached Jiaopingdu around the 24th to 26th April in the 24th year of Republican China (1911+24 = 1935). Twenty-four scouts came to my brother's (Zhang Chaoshou's) caravanserai in Xiaolongcun (Small Dragon Village). He was petrified, he could see they weren't traders. They told him they weren't the KMT, they were the poor-people's army-men fighting to kill the tigers (landlords. officials and tax collectors) and liberate the poor. 'Find boats for us to cross the river!' they ordered. He told them 'I don't have any boats, but my four brothers, Chaolu, Chaofu, Chaojun and Chaoman (that's me) – have boats'. But the problem was the tigers made us keep all the boats moored on the north bank! Everything that floated was there. We searched and found a damaged boat, plugged its holes with material from a merchant. It was just good enough to get us across and steal the boats in time for the Red Army's arrival! A one-eyed general (Liu Bocheng) stood on a boulder on the riverbank to direct the crossing for a whole week. We ferried thousands across each day while the hillside was covered by those waiting. Not a single man drowned during the whole operation. Once they were across, the boats were cut free so that they drifted downstream and smashed up. The KMT were prevented from crossing the river themselves and chasing the Reds on the other side ...."

That wasn't quite the end of the story. The Zhang brothers were arrested and faced execution in Luquan. But after being strung up and tortured for twelve hours they were finally spared after they claimed that the Reds had forced them at gunpoint to ferry them across.

"Instead, the KMT fined us 280 *taels* (about 11kg of silver ingots), confiscated our furniture, and forced us to serve up all the mutton and wine we owned to their top brass for the next week," said Zhang Chaoman.

I had one follow-up question to the ferryman: "Why haven't you mentioned Mao Zedong?"

Zhang explained. "We didn't know who or what communists were. We thought the one-eyed general was their army's commander. Once the Red Army crossed the river and marched off into Sichuan, we heard nothing about them, we forgot about them. Only years later in 1949 did we hear of Mao Zedong, only years after that did we hear of the 'Long March'. Just think, Chairman Mao may have been in my boat without me even knowing it!"

I was given an upstairs room. Level ground was at a premium but wood plentiful, so the Zhangs, like all families in Jiaopingdu, had a double-storey home. Outside my window I could hear the river churning loudly, and see its water gleaming in the moonlight. I lay down contentedly, in anticipation, and trepidation, of crossing the river tomorrow by boat with Zhang Chaoman.

But the night turned into a bit of a nightmare. I heard footsteps, and then saw shadows, and then realised an oil lamp was being held directly above my bed. "*Qichuang! Kuai qichuang!*" (Get up! Quickly, get up!) urged Zhang's son in a loud kind of whisper.

It took a few seconds to wake to full consciousness and begin to think what was going on. The Chinese do not make a habit of early morning calls, nor breakfast in bed, so what might be happening to warrant this ritual? Perhaps a flood warning had been issued? No, to my great surprise it was the reappearance of my old adversaries, the Public Security Bureau.

My earlier Long March encounters with them, in Hunan and Guizhou had amounted to nothing, because I had nothing to lose, for nothing was at stake. Here there was a lot to lose. I had Zhang Chaoman's precious account written on a piece of paper, and I hadn't crossed the river yet.

During my questioning by candlelight, Pei Yingfa's transcript of the ferryman's recollections was duly mentioned by my hosts, demanded by the police officer, and confiscated from me. And it went without saying that I'd be denied my eagerly awaited crossing of the Jinsha River into Sichuan. My only consolation at that moment was the photograph that I'd taken of Zhang, and the need to retain it by whatever means. And while the questioning at this ridiculous hour was unnecessary, for as usual it would be repeated at a police station, sooner or later, the performance plunged into further absurdity when the officer became preoccupied with an issue on my ethnicity.

The ethnic diversity of China's 1.25 billion population at the time was 96% Han, with the other 4% being the so-called 56 'national minorities'. Going by the number of brightly-dressed locals that I'd seen, Yunnan had more than its fair share of minorities. (Later I was told it had twenty-five of them). So, while I could appreciate that people in this part of China were ethnically conscious, I was surprised when the police officer asked me "*ni shi shenme minzu?*" (what nationality are you?). I simply reiterated "*wo shi yingguoren* …." (I'm British), which was the same answer to his earlier question of "*ni shi na guoren?*" (what country do you come from?).

We entered into a frustrating loop dialogue—"What country are you from?" "I'm British." "What's your ethnicity? "I'm British …" and so on.

WILD WALL–THE FOUNDATION YEARS

"Yes, but what ethnic group are you?", he persisted to ask.

"I've told you! We don't have them in Britain."

"But that's impossible. Everyone has an ethnic grouping."

I wondered whether this policeman's world was so small that he just couldn't comprehend that someone might not have an 'ethnicity' such as *huizu* (Moslem) or *manzu* (Manchurian) or *zangzu* (Tibetan). Or did he think that because I could speak Chinese then I was Chinese in that way, and therefore subject to Chinese ethnic categorisation? Some foreigners did joke that they are members of China's 57th minority nationality!

It was 2 a.m. and I was tired and bored with going around in circles. So I decided to turn his question around and side with him. I asked him "What's your ethnic grouping?"

"I'm a Han, of course!" he replied.

"I think I am a Han as well, the same as you."

He nodded approvingly and wrote down the answer.

There was no sensible explanation for why he accepted my ridiculous answer. The reason was that as a bureaucrat he'd been well trained in the business of collecting nonsense. He had a form to fill in. There was a space for ethnicity. It couldn't be left blank.

Thankfully my interrogation had concluded for the time being, so I could return to my bed. Next on trial was Zhang the Sichuanese, to be questioned about assisting me in entering an area closed to foreigners. Chinese people speak loudly, so it was easy to eavesdrop from upstairs. "When and where did you meet?" "What did he pay you?" "Did he give you anything?" "What questions did he ask you?" And importantly, "Did he take any photographs?" My good friend answered all the questions correctly. "Yesterday" … "Nothing" … "Nothing." … "Nothing." … "No." I rummaged for my camera, unloaded the film and hid everything photographic deep in my bag among dirty tees, socks and underwear.

Next morning, I saw everything in a different light. I'd scored an uplifting victory. By marching with Zhang I'd reached the river and heard, although not yet fully understood, Zhang the ferryman's account of his participation in a critical event that he and his brothers had made possible. What would have happened if Chiang Kai-shek had kept the Red Army south of the Jinsha River? The Long March might have taken quite a different direction, and possibly unfolded in a very different way.

The police returned in a Beijing Jeep. As I climbed into the back, Zhang the ferryman readied his boat to take Zhang the Sichuanese across the river. Within a few minutes, they'd be on the other side. In a few hours, I'd be over the mountain and far away.

In Jiaoxi I was duly met by local police chiefs and a plainclothed young man who, I suspected, was the local English teacher drafted in for interpretation duty. I was wrong.

"I'm Zhao Jinghui," he spoke confidently, "a *yi* nationality representative of the National People's Congress at Beijing's Great Hall of the People ... it's very worthwhile to study Mao Zedong by walking the Long March," he said in near-perfect English, before switching over to a local language to converse and shuffle papers with the arresting officer. I saw that my passport and Pei's written account were now in his hands.

"We have inconvenienced you. Here, let me return your belongings. Now, let's go to eat, a banquet is prepared."

Zhang's historic testimony was safely back in my hands and would be duly translated by Qi, which, for want of space, is only précised above. Out of interest, thirty years later, in 2020, as I was writing this cherished recollection, I've just done a search of the internet which, we are led to believe, records just about everything known about anything. For 'Zhang Chaoman, ferryman, Long March' the only Google link turning up in English reads 'Chaoman, Zhang, boatman' as a role in a 2007 movie called 'The Long March'.

32

LUDING BRIDGE

I ONLY STARTED to understand what Zhang the Sichuanese meant about the pros of walking directly north to Sichuan when I was forced backwards to take the long way round, by road. I'd originally factored in four days for my journey from Kunming to the Golden Sands River, and then onward to Xichang, where Qi and I planned to rendezvous before I tackled the next section of my March. Deflected off course by the police, I was now back in Kunming, while Qi was 500 km away in Xichang, waiting, wondering and no doubt worrying. There was no means available for me to get in touch with her, to explain why I was late and when I might arrive.

Li Bai (701-762 AD), arguably China's most revered poet, wrote in *The Hardship of the Road to Sichuan* that travelling into Sichuan was 'more difficult than reaching the sky'. The heart of the province occupies an extensive geological basin, and its margins are guarded by mountain ranges veined by deep gorges containing wild rivers. These were spanned by precious few bridges back in the year of the Long March. It was here, on Sichuan's mid-western edge, that the Red Army faced dual battles, against nature as well as the government forces. At the same time, Mao also aimed to orchestrate a rendezvous with another band of the Red Army on its own Long March nearby.

Just as the term 'the Great Wall' leads most people into

thinking that there is just one Great Wall, when there are in fact many (at least sixteen, built by different dynasties over a period of 2,000 years), so it is with 'The Long March'. It wasn't a single military manoeuvre by one army led by one man; it was a concurrent series of multi-pronged migratory routes followed by several Communist forces, all aiming to converge in a new Soviet base area. Mao only assumed paramount leadership of the Communist Party and its Red Army in the middle of the March, in January 1935 at Zunyi, in Guizhou, and in the field he personally commanded only the 'First Front', or Central Red Army. He hoped to meet the Fourth Front Army, commanded by Zhang Guotao, somewhere in western Sichuan, thereby benefitting from reinforcements and moving as one towards the chosen destination—if indeed there was an intended one at that point.

It took me two more days to reach Xichang by bus, driving along mountain roads that were washed away by rivers and blocked by rockfalls triggered by frequent earthquakes. It took a further couple of hours to find our 'nameless' rendezvous hotel, a venue agreed in advance to be 'the biggest hotel in Xichang where foreigners are permitted to stay'. When I finally arrived there, I asked the reception for Wu Qi's room number.

"There's no guest with that name," responded the receptionist unconvincingly.

I asked repeatedly, much to her growing annoyance, but she assured me, while cursorily shuffling through untidy papers on the desk, that there was no Wu Qi registered as a guest, not now, nor in the last few days.

Was there another hotel in town open to foreigners? Perhaps she'd gone there? My frustration at being three days late grew more intense. I sat down in disbelief in the lobby, exhausted and dejected. A new receptionist came on duty, so I tried quizzing her. "No Wu Qi in our hotel' she confirmed, pronouncing hotel as 'hottle' as if it rhymed with 'bottle'. Then to my complete surprise I heard a joyful "Hello William!" from behind. I turned around to see my gorgeous Qi skipping down the staircase into the lobby.

"How long have you been here?" I asked Qi.

"Four days," she replied.

The communication problems that delayed our reunion in 1990 — detours, washouts, rockfalls, no telephones, and being mis-informed or even misled — brought into perspective the immense difficulties that orchestrating a secret meeting of two armies in mountainous Sichuan must have posed back in 1935.

What was increasingly fascinating to me about the Long March was its haphazardness; the realisation that, at the outset, nobody knew where they were going, and even en route they didn't have much idea in advance. They were living off and fighting off their wits, not looking too far ahead, concentrating on week-by-week survival, living hand-to-mouth. But it was also clear as I progressed that as places were reached, as harsher weather was encountered, as forbidding terrain loomed, some doors closed while others remained open. I tried to place myself in Mao's shoes — or sandals — to understand his predicament, his plan of action, ahead of him in Sichuan.

There was no possibility that Mao, with his surviving followers, (perhaps just a quarter of the original 80,000 soldiers who had left Jiangxi) could risk taking the easy road, the low and level road, through the middle of the densely-populated Sichuan Basin. The heavily-armed government army were surely strong there and their trucks and large guns could move swiftly across that low and flat terrain. Mao's only option was a higher road, along the side of the basin, through the mountains that rimmed its western flank, following rivers, crossing peaks.

Here, Generalissimo Chiang was presented with another cut-throat opportunity: to force the Communists further west, onto the Daxue Shan, the Great Snowy Mountains proper, where they would be doomed to suffer exposure, altitude sickness and starvation.

To avoid death by landscape, Mao needed to place his army on the 'right' side of the Dadu River, on the basin side of it in the east, and not on the wrong, left side of the Great Snowies in the west. Thus, the Dadu River was set to be the next theatre of the conflict. One of my most memorable badges showed 'The Battle of Luding Bridge', which followed an abandoned attempt to cross the Dadu river by boat. It has become enshrined in Red Army lore as a military miracle, but is dismissed by many others as exaggerated propaganda.

My route to Luding was straightforward, following the Dadu River, which I joined at Shimian, a day's bus ride north of Xichang. I set out in pre-dawn darkness and followed it for hours, by sound, until I reached Anshunchang, the original focus of Mao's plan to cross the river. Here at sunrise, the raucous, dark waters cloaked in mist were transformed into a seductive body of glistening jade waves churning hypnotically along, crested with pearly white dragons. It was December and freezing cold. The water level was low; most moisture was ice-locked in the Great 'Snowies' to the north and west. Giants' chopsticks, tree trunks, were left high and dry on midstream shoals. The Red Army, however, reached here in May 1935, when the river was at its highest, widest and wildest.

Before I'd set off from Ruijin, army veteran Xu Youwan had told me that the Dadu River was 300 metres across, from bank to bank, making it three times the width of the Golden Sands, and with vicious whirlpools. The range of his gun was 400 metres. *Yizu* nationality sympathisers had guided the crack 'Triple

WILD WALL–THE FOUNDATION YEARS

Ones' — the First Corps of the First Regiment of the First Front Army — on mountain trails that enabled them to look down on the gun positions at the ferry point. These were manned by the troops of the warlord Liu Wenhui, who was allied to the KMT. Surprisingly quickly, the battle against the KMT allies was won. The second battle, against the river, was next.

Some 20,000 men needed to be ferried across the river here. There were only three small boats available, and the landing points on both sides were at the foot of steep and treacherous slopes that had been turned into mudslides by the heavy summer rainfall. Xu Youwan saw men slide down into the river to be swept away. They resorted to using bamboo poles to 'abseil' down, and tried making ropes by weaving local plants. Soldiers desperately attached twigs and sticks to the soles of their sandals, crampon-style, in the hope of gaining more traction. For 48 hours the ferrying continued, through the night, until rain lashed down in a deluge, terminating the operation. Only 3,000 Reds had so far been ferried. On the third day when crossings resumed, a round trip took three hours. Even at the fastest rate it would take at least two more weeks to get everyone across, time that Mao could not afford. He changed his plan. The bulk of the army on the west bank would march, as fast as possible without rest, northwards for 120 km to Luding and cross the river there — if the bridge hadn't been destroyed.

More than half a century later, the Dadu River is now paralleled by a new rocky road blasted into the mountainside on the east bank. There are also bridges every ten kilometres or so; some are of the traditional iron-chain type, others newer cable suspension bridges, but most are rickety structures of rusted metal and rotten wood. To reach the new road, I chose to cross on a concrete bridge and save my nerves for crossing 'The Fixed Bridge of Lu' named after the engineer who built it in 1701. In the cold mountain air of December with its fourteen hours of darkness per day, I opted for two days' of marching (still full-on, pre-dawn to post-dusk) compared with those spearheading the Red Army's advance of one day.

When the crack troops of the Red Army arrived at Luding, the bridge was still being used. As a guaranteed form of income — all users were tolled, all transported goods taxed — the warlord-managed bridge was too lucrative to be sabotaged. All its defenders needed to do in the event of it coming under attack, so they thought, was to remove the wooden planks, leaving only the hanging chains, making it impassable. Removing just half the planks would suffice, they thought, and that's what they did. A small guard detachment would then be enough to hold the bridge, while all other armed men could defend the town against the Red bandits progressing up the east bank (the 3,000 or so who had been ferried across).

I found the bridge still very much in use, sparingly planked and a busy two-way thoroughfare linking the town on both banks. I stood at one end for a long while, watching locals, from the age of five to eighty-five, amble nonchalantly across, unperturbed by its swinging which, I observed with trepidation, became a rocking when it happened a procession of people crossed at the same time. I had good sea legs, but my rocking bridge ones were unproven. As a boy I had suffered a recurring nightmare of crossing a swaying bridge in a storm. On my first crossing I wanted to have the bridge as much to myself as possible. It was a long wait, but Luding's morning rush-hour to school and market began to slacken.

I stepped cautiously on to the structure of thirteen huge iron chains, each of its links large enough for a clenched fist to be threaded through. I immediately felt a familiar swaying motion, reminding me of my oilfield days when our drilling rig was rocked by storms in the Norwegian North Sea. But this was different. When I glanced up, the mountains seemed to be moving. The view down was even less comforting. Through the floorboards, and through the chains on both sides the white waves of the Dadu churned below. I trod gingerly towards the centre of the bowed span, each cautious step taking me further away from the bridgehead where the giant chains were embedded. Despite being alone so far, my eighty kilogram weight and gait caused the whole structure, and I with it, to sway freely. At first it swung gently from side to side, horizontally. Then it began to sway in an up and down motion, vertically, rippling in a pulsing motion. I glanced up to see that others were now coming across the bridge. As we neared, my swaying and their rippling waves integrated, and the whole bridge jiggled and rocked. The experience was exacerbated when I met the locals head on, pushing their bicycles, carrying baskets of market goods, or pulling children, for whom the crossing was great fun, like a trip to the swings. A nauseous, yet at the same time thrilling, feeling of air- and sea-sickness ensued, for this bridge was certainly not terra firma, it was a terror-inducing path in the sky. I stopped and gripped the chest-high side chain for balance, trying not to look petrified. I looked back and tried to distract myself by imagining the legendary event of 1935.

By some miraculous means — one must envisage the most dramatic scene possible from a Jackie Chan or Spiderman movie — twenty or so Red Army soldiers had crawled along these chains minus their planks, under the cover of supporting firepower from the bridgehead behind them. It was already too late for the complacent warlord guards to strip the rest of the bridge planks away, so they attempted to set them alight, but the Red charge was unstoppable. The heroic scene has been portrayed in many a film and poster, but witnesses, including Deng Xiaoping himself, claimed the battle "was a very easy military operation against warlord troops armed only with old muskets." I chucked at the thought as I finally made it to the far side.

Once the first troops were across, they found doors in the town to re-floor the bridge. During that evening and for the next three days, thousands of Red Army soldiers crossed the repaired bridge to enter Luding, and feast on pork, chicken and rice. Now Mao could lead the Red Army north again, avoiding the highest parts of the Great Snowy Range.

Fascinated by the bridge, and in need of photographs of it in good light, I returned in the afternoon, first to a restaurant near its eastern bridgehead where I contemplated my plan of Long March action. I'd completed my first season, winter was coming, and I was expected back in Xi'an to teach after the Chinese New Year (Spring Festival) break. I ate dumplings to celebrate, and continued watch in astonishment as children perhaps as young as eight years old pranced across the bridge on their way home from school, unaccompanied. The *laoban*, the proprietor of the restaurant, told me they checked and changed any damaged wooden planks every three years, and the hand-forged iron chains every five.

After I had finished eating, the *laoban* showed me a narrow path that led down towards the waterline. From there I could look up to see the winter-blue sky through the planks and the chains of the bridge. It was a superb perspective. With a wide-angle lens I photographed the full 103-metre length of the bridge spanning the gorge. Then the thinkable happened: I saw a very large dark object fall off the bridge, hit semi-submerged rocks and then be washed away into the swirling deep. I hoped it was a basket. But why was there so much screaming? Someone had fallen off, or jumped. People on the bridge were in hysteria, looking down. Men scurried down to the waterline on the other side, looking helpless, for there was no body to be seen to rescue. Above me, I saw a woman in shock being carried—manhandled—off the bridge. The wailing, the cries and shrieks rose in a haunting pitch above the rushing of the river.

Later that same dreadful day, the 'bamboo telegraph' told me via the restaurant owner that the person who had fallen to her death was a 30-year-old woman, the daughter of the old woman who had been screaming in anguish. She had tripped, fallen over, and rolled off the bridge before her very eyes. Everyone knew the drowned woman. They said she'd used the bridge twice a day for almost all her life.

I decided not to cross the Dadu again. I turned my back on the terrible river and its bridge of death.

33

CROSSING THE HIGHEST MOUNTAIN

FROM LUDING, Mao would lead his army north, but I had to return to the present. It was December and I travelled back to Xi'an to take up my teaching position there. I am postponing my telling of those amusing classroom and campus experiences, which appear in later chapters. For story-telling momentum I am continuing with my Long March, now.

I actually returned to Sichuan the following summer, marching directly northwards with the Red Army to the 'summit' of the Long March, Jiajin Shan (Mountain), a 4,100-metre peak in the Great Snowy Mountains. My home leave break put me back in seasonal synchronisation with the Long Marchers' crossing of the mountains and grasslands, which would have been well-nigh impossible in December.

Getting near the mountain in question, for me as a foreigner, was a familiar challenge. I couldn't buy tickets on public transport to enter closed areas, so I had no other option but to walk from somewhere much further away. That approach would, however, enable me to acclimatise to the increasing altitude, which effects most people from about 2,800 metres.

I'd done a considerable amount of homework on my route. I purchased an atlas of Sichuan, studied the Central Army's route and committed it to memory. With the assistance of Teacher Qi I'd learned to read and pronounce, and as a backstop, memorized

WILD WALL–THE FOUNDATION YEARS

the characters of a string of place names on both sides of the mountain. Now it was time to put my planning to the test.

From Xi'an I travelled to Chengdu by train. Next I took a long distance bus that climbed out of the Sichuan Basin, destined for Luding in the west. Much to the astonishment of the driver and all passengers, I insisted the bus stop at a junction in the middle of nowhere, from where I would head off north towards the town of Tianquan. This is where I began my second Long March season.

My approach march to the mountain, about 90 kilometres away, was now clear and on foot, providing that I could avoid the police and find a few more key turning points. Each find boosted my confidence, the next being a turn off towards a village named Laochang. There, I needed to find what appeared on the map to be a footpath or dirt road to Lingguan. My routefinding success continued to roll. I got most reassuring directions from two old men lounging in bamboo chairs, shaded beneath a line-full of drying tobacco leaves that were all shrivelled and nicotine-coloured like their faces. Their hands held their homemade product, cigarettes rubbed and rolled in local newspaper. I questioned them about 'The Red Army's route in 1935' and to my great surprise they immediately, convincingly pointed me in a reliable direction using the turn of phrase *"tamen zou nabian,"* (they went that way). I found the brevity of their response very encouraging. Spoken Chinese, which is greatly truncated in style, makes it unclear whether an action has taken place, is taking place or will take place. Their tone made me feel that the Red Army was only 56 minutes ahead of me, not 56 years, and that indeed I was right on the their trail.

I took the muddy path, rutted by cartwheels and perforated by hoof prints, that followed a small river, which functioned as a communal bath, swimming pool and laundrette. Noodle-limbed boys, wearing nothing but sun-given brown suits of summer, were diving into the waters. Like birds of feather, women, self-sorted by age or topics of gossip, flocked together at the water's edge. The results of all their washing blossomed forth on the riverside shrubs as purple singlets, army green trousers like my own, fondant pink blouses, white bodices and bloomers, all spread out on branches to dry.

The path began to meander like the river itself, which I crossed several times at fords or on spindly 'bridges', some of them no more than horizontal wire fences floored with a few thin planks. I emerged at a small village, finding my way through only by trespassing; entering straw-strewn courtyards, chicken runs and pigsties, intruding where big noses were surely seldom, if ever, seen. Cross-field walking took me through the peasants' unharvested larder. An old man picking broad beans told me to ford the river again and climb up the valley side. Before letting me go, he stuffed a kilo or so of the pods into my rucksack, demonstrating they could be eaten raw. Once I found his path, I munched on my nutritious takeaway as I walked. I flavoured them with a few bites of garlic doggy-bagged from a bus-stop *fandian* (literally a 'rice house') – which served not only as gastronomic condiment but also as a general preventative medicine. Water, collected from the many gushing streams, into which I squeezed fresh lemon – like the garlic, a natural antiseptic – completed my lunch. I carried lemon and garlic, not for salad dressing but, to help kill any bugs in the water that in the high-altitude up ahead would boil at well below 100°C.

The valley, and the path confined within it, narrowed as I climbed upward. A cliff fell away at my side, so I walked with a considerable counteracting tilt. Other walkers on the trail tilted too, bent like hunchbacks under their heavy burdens of bamboo. Freshly cut green trunks, twice or thrice the height of their carriers, were lashed together on the backs of these short porters. Their toil must have been permanently disabling. To maintain their balance, these young men articulated themselves so that their burden neither dug in to the earth behind them nor caught on the overhanging branches above. This avoidance tactic necessitated walking whilst almost bent double, with their hands on their knees. Despite the weight of their loads—they told me that each trunk weighed about ten kg and each of them carried at least six—they didn't wear padding on their backs and were shod only in plastic sandals or paper-thin, 'lazy shoes'. But lazy these men certainly were not: they crawled along like lines of worker ants carrying twigs much larger and heavier than themselves, pouring with sweat, their trousers rolled up to reveal bulging calf muscles.

Scaffolding-quality bamboo prospered on the ground floor of this arboretum, a botanist's wonderland. The middle slopes were different, dominated by exotics that I was quite familiar with, such as rhododendrons, camellias, azaleas, and japonicas, species that had been introduced into our English gardens from this region and neighbouring Yunnan. There were also complete and beautiful strangers, rarer shrubs that I'd never seen.

These primeval forests were the aerial display grounds for flying insects of dinosaurian proportions; furry, fleshy moths, like bats with open wings, lay camouflaged and confident to be still, awaiting their nightshift routines; huge dragonflies with stained-glass window wings, showered iridescence as they flew by, their segmented tails rattling as they stalled from bush to bush; and large butterflies like the Chinese kites that they inspired, flitted from flower to flower, appearing not only to pick up nectar but also to steal a pastel shade off each bloom too, so multi-coloured were their wings.

Many streams watered this garden of paradise. I stopped to

bathe naked in one of its crystal pools. Fortunately, my ablutions were completed just in time—before some peasants ambled by, completely unaware that they'd just missed a foreigner's bath time. But the risk was certainly worth it! My ten-minute plunge left me refreshed. I marched on faster, invigorated, excited to hear the roar of the Baoxing He (River), then to see it, and then to view the town of Lingguan stretching along its eastern bank.

I darted into a small restaurant, memorable for its bamboo everything, from chairs to tables to chopsticks. I wolfed down a couple of bowls of *mapo doufu*, a classic Sichuanese dish, a personal favourite made of bean-curd and ground pork awash with a chilli and peppery sauce, eaten with bland white rice. The *laoban* was impressed by the speed of my slurping and savouring of the province's famously fiery hot dish. I asked him about the way ahead: Baoxing was twenty five km away, he said. After so many months of being cooped up on campus I felt exhilarated to be marching again. Despite my fatigue I decided to press on, do a late shift to utilise the cool evening air.

The dark green woolly mountains that channelled the Baoxing River were crested with low clouds, and it began to drizzle, the damper conditions attracting some giant mosquitos out for the twilight hour. The roar of the river seemed muffled now, subsumed by the buzzing of countless insects, the peals of thunder, and the rising and falling chorus of cicadas.

Just as it was getting dark I started to look for a possible place to rest. Farms, which I'd come to regard as humanitarian temples where I had never been refused food and lodging, were less approachable after dusk. A foreign devil dropping in out of the darkness asking for shelter was, I thought, demanding too much from good Samaritans. Fortunately, I came to a riverside building named the Malou Shan River Monitoring Station where they recorded the height of the Baoxing River. My hosts there

WILD WALL–THE FOUNDATION YEARS

hydrated me with copious mugs of jasmine tea, fed me a noodle supper and provided their table-tennis table for a bed. I set off early next morning, reaching Baoxing in time for breakfast, taking my place at a handy roadside stall serving *youtiao* (deep fried dough sticks) to the many workmen and artisans who were on their way to the local marble quarry and its surrounding workshops.

Twenty five years previously, in 1966, one quarry worker told me, they had been ordered to do marble carving for revolutionary purposes. The factory's biggest and most important commission, received from Chengdu, was for a statue of the Chairman. Quarrymen fulfilled the large order by cutting an overcoated Chairman Mao to a precise height of 12.26 metres (I knew that represented Mao's birthday on December 26th). Once transported to Chengdu it was placed on a plinth 7.1 metres in height (the Communist Party's foundation day of July 1st) and then on a flight of steps 8.1 metres in height (the PLA's foundation day of August 1st). The whole stack clearly showed that Mao was the big man chorusing both the Party and the army. "All we work on now are small Tang beauties, Buddhas, and guardian lions for doorways," the worker lamented. "But you can still see our Mao statue in Chengdu. It was too strong and large to be toppled after the Cultural Revolution, it would need a big earthquake!" I'd seen it a couple of times, as recently as a few days ago whilst passing through the city. Its sheer size demonstrated just what Mao had become—or had been made into—by the time the statue was transported and erected in 1968.

As I was recalling this story, I wondered whether Baoxing was still famous for its white marble, and what it might be making in 2021. So, I turned to Google: the quarry now produces top-quality bathroom floor tiles that are widely available through merchants selling on Alibaba. What a fascinating change in business, from the cult of Mao to down-to-earth, yet no doubt highly lucrative, luxury floor-tile production.

Some easy marching followed, along the misleadingly-named North River, which actually flowed east. It became a long uphill grind though a gorge to Minzhi, which I estimated to lie within striking distance—about a day's hiking away—of Jiajin Mountain. I began to ask locals about the conditions on the mountain. "It's difficult, there's snow," was a fairly standard answer, but so stereotyped that I took what I heard with a pinch of salt. There was one hopeful exception, an old man. He was somewhat amused by my PLA clothing, so I told him my story to explain my choice of attire.

"Look!" he snapped. "In the 24th year of the Republic the Red Army came here, and now, what is it, the 80th year, the 'Foreign Red Army' has arrived!"

The gathered audience found his creation so amusing that I decided it was too good a gem to leave behind, and so I adopted it then and there as my Chinese name. For the rest of my journey and for a few years after, I introduced myself as 'Yang Hongjun', Foreign Red Army.

To mark the naming event, I asked the old man to sign my dairy. He continued his story, saying that it was village folk here who gave the soldiers strings of chilli peppers, root ginger and garlic to make a soup to resist the cold. The soldiers stopped for a time while the locals weaved new sandals for them. Some villagers joined the Red Army and some set off to guide them over Jiajin Shan and into Xiaojin County. It was a well-trodden trail, he said. I gave the old man—Zhang Dajian my Chinese 'father'—a warm hug, much to the crowd's happiness, and set off again.

To the north of Huangdianzi, about fifteen km from the mountain, I stopped at a timber yard. I'd only been there a short while when a jeep pulled in, and out jumped three men, one in police uniform. One of those in plain clothes was the middle school English teacher, from Baoxing, requisitioned by the PSB for the interrogation. He said that rangers at the nearby giant panda reserve had alerted them about a trespassing foreigner walking through an area where my likes were an even rarer species. It took them two hours to drive me back to Baoxing: it had taken me eleven hours to cover the 65 km on foot. In the foyer of the hotel it was reiterated that I should go to Ya'an by bus next morning, and that not only was Jiajin Mountain closed to foreigners but it was 'too dangerous, even for Chinese'.

I had not underestimated the physical challenge of reaching the summit of Jiajin Shan, even in midsummer. My caution was fuelled by the depiction of the event in *The East is Red*, a revolutionary opera. Veterans I had met likened the mountain's fickle weather to a child's face—smiling and bright one minute, then throwing a tantrum and whipping up a snowstorm the next. They recounted stories of their comrades losing fingers and toes to frostbite, while others slid down icy slopes to their death.

I retreated to my room to work around a familiar problem. The only Mao badge I carried showed the Great Snowy Mountains: my Long March would be incomplete without crossing Jiajin Shan. The only questions in my mind were 'when?' and 'how?' I'd go in the middle of the night, I decided. I was on the ground floor, so could climb out of the window. Anticipating that the gate of the hotel compound would be locked after dark, and not wanting to disturb the night watchman's sleep, I made a reconnaissance of the yard and found an easy place to hop over the back wall. I set myself an early departure time of two in the morning.

All around seemed pitch dark at first, but I hoped my eyes would soon accommodate, and I dared not use my torch. Out on the road, I thought it would be safer to walk in the middle, far from the sides where I might to stumble on bicycles, boxes or baskets. For safety, I moved slowly with my arms stretched out in front, using them as feelers, expecting that I might still bump into something, and then I did. It struck my knees and legs so hard that I went head-first into a sprawl, almost smashing my teeth. I'd collided with some kind of concrete bollard in the middle of the road!

I walked at a snail's pace for a long time, licking my wounds, and when dawn began to break, I flagged down the first truck to come along. More than an hour later, we drove past the place of my arrest. I allowed a safety margin of about one kilometre before asking the driver to stop. Jumping down from the cab, I felt a huge rush of adrenalin as if I had escaped, climbed the fence and thrown off the shackles. Now it was time to run. Almost immediately, the metalled road became a rocky, rough track along the west bank of the East River, now a gushing mountain stream. Ahead stood Jiajin Shan, the peaks clearly visible! The sun shone brilliantly, igniting the dew on the pines into a blaze of fragrance.

Despite what appeared to be ideal conditions ahead, I foraged for some twigs for possible use as makeshift grippers, before passing the tree line. As I was doing this, a young man clad in a dark blue Mao suit came swiftly up from behind. He was clearly going somewhere rather than tracking me: he was laden with a sack of rice, knotted at each corner and made into a rucksack with grass-wound rope.

"Where are you going?" he asked.

"Jiajin Shan," I replied, and turning the question around asked, "And you?"

I beat him to the Golden Monkeys (cigarettes) and tossed him one. He pointed with it and said "Dawei." That was the town on the far side of Jiajin Mountain, renowned as the place where Mao's First Front had managed to link up with Zhang's Fourth Front Army.

We set off together. Ding Li chatted incessantly. He told me he'd crossed Jiajin Shan more than thirty times before, twice a year, often with his brothers and sisters of whom he had eight.

"Is there any snow?" I asked.

He chuckled, pointing skywards. "No snow, not in summer."

Ding Li led the way purposefully, hopping over puddles, across streams and patches of mud, then breaking into bouncing and rolling strides: I sensed that he was trying to race me, expecting me to lag behind at a pedestrian pace. If I hadn't known anything about the altitude, I don't think I would have particularly noticed anything. But I was somewhat breathless walking quickly uphill and trying to talk, and understand, all at the same time.

He quizzed me about Britain. What did the peasants grow? Did they own their land, have machines, televisions, telephones? Did every family have a car? Could I drive? Was there any birth control? This really strained my vocabulary but made sign language interesting. What did I like doing in my spare time? Which sports? I made the mistake of answering "marathon running", a reply that Ding Li interpreted as throwing down the gauntlet. "We'll run then, shall we?" he said, breaking into a jog that he kept going for at least one kilometre. Still together, but now gasping for breath, we stopped and called it a draw. We sat on a large boulder and praised each other's fitness, then drank from a gurgling spring and picked over a crimson carpet of wild strawberries. After the short rest we marched on in silence. For just a short while.

As a distinct mountain ridge came into view, the hills were enlivened by the baritone echoes of Ding Li bellowing *Chairman*

Mao Our Dearest One, which he continued to sing, all verses of it, until we reached the summit.

We shook hands before looking into a small shrine, a rock-built shelter that housed a wooden image of Buddha seated amid a plethora of altar offerings. These ranged from candles to scented tapers, withered wild flowers, shrivelled oranges, rock hard bread, corn cobs and a live hen! Ding Li added some of his own rice.

An old shepherd who was watching his flock in a corrie below wandered up to see us. We sat huddled together on the tufty grass cushions, buffeted by a strong wind. The shepherd shared his sheepskin cape. Ding Li pulled out some boiled eggs and I offered the men some smokes. There wasn't a patch of snow to be seen. Defiantly, I looked back towards Baoxing: it had been a moderately strenuous hike. Ding Li and I had walked together for five hours.

Rubbing his forehead and temples, Ding Li warned of the head-aching danger of spending too long here on the summit. It reminded me of some advice from by the Xi'an veteran Zhong Ling: "Don't stop on the mountain top, no matter how tired you are." Pressed for time, Ding told me that he would head off for Dawei alone, but before going he gave me typically vague directions for finding my own way down. *"Zhi zou, zhi zou!"* (straight on!) he repeated, waving at the northern horizon. Then off he ran, displaying bravado to the end, charging down a scree like a mountain goat. Once in the grassy corrie below he turned around and yelled *"zai jian!"*, a cry that echoed all around. Soon his dark speck disappeared, merging with other specks, black yaks.

There were two things I wished to do. Despite the chill, I wanted to set up my camera for a self-timer shot of me standing beside a China flag that had been left by a previous summiteer.

Then I picked up a palm-sized rock and using it as a hand axe dug a shallow hole in the tufty grass. I buried my Mao badge there as a tribute to the army's crossing of the mountain. It may still be there.

Cloud now engulfed the summit. I embarked on Ding Li's route, down the scree and into the corrie. Then the heavens opened with a brief downpour.

Three hours later, on the lower part of the trail I walked down a narrow and undulating mule path that hugged the side of a creek. Swollen by the recent deluge, the watercourse rushed down to join the Wori He (River) below. As the confluence came into sight so did the patchwork of fields around Dawei, promising what I was most looking forward to — food. The same viewpoint had given the Central Red Army an even bigger surprise — a glimpse of another army. Stopping, the scouts peered through their field glasses. 'Who are they?' and 'What can you see?' began the burst of questions. 'Tents, field kitchens, smoke and banners ... red banners with a hammer and sickle!' came the answers. A bugle call was sounded to herald the imminent arrival of the Central Red Army.

I stood on the Wori River bridge, which was garlanded in red sashes, imagining the mysterious, incredible, against-all-odds, meeting between the Central and Fourth armies. Not to wonder or ask questions about how it came about, but simply to belatedly share in their delight, and my own. The highest mountain on the Long March was now towering behind us.

34

MEETING POINTS

WHENEVER THE Long March is lauded by the great machine that has promulgated the story over the decades since the Communist takeover in 1949, the four important locations always mentioned are the Golden Sands River, Luding Bridge, the Great Snowy Mountains, and the grasslands. I was now targeting the last of these big four, the most-otherworldly landscape encountered by the Long Marchers on their entire journey. It is a plateau of marshy grasslands in northern Sichuan bordering the Tibetan-Qinghai Plateau. Yet again, for me to simply get there entailed a long approach march through closed areas. And it seemed that even the famous poet Li Bai didn't know the geological instability of his home province well enough. In the poem *The Hardship of the Road to Sichuan*, he'd only described how difficult it was to reach Sichuan, he had failed to mention how difficult it was to travel within the province, from one place to another.

A *fandian laoban* (eatery owner) had told me the latest local news: no buses had come into Dawei from Xiaojin, so that meant that the road was likely blocked by rockfalls, triggered by heavy rain, or more likely an earth tremor.

To avoid blockages or washed-out sections of road, I was advised to take the footpath on the opposite side of the river. I soon learned to follow any path that the peasants walked along. They knew when it was best to cross back and forth, and which

WILD WALL-THE FOUNDATION YEARS

bridges to use to avoid drowning. On my travels, I encountered some very hazardous bridges! While a completely plank-less iron-chained bridge gave a me chillingly vivid impression of what the attackers crossing the Luding Bridge had braved, the deformity of one much-newer bridge aroused in me a great respect for the power of nature. It was a suspension bridge hanging limp and loose, stretched and contorted, twisted along its length like a paper streamer spanning a room, its few remaining planks poised to drop out. I shuddered to think how much the river, some six or seven metres below, had swelled into a torrent so high and powerful that it wrecked such a well-built and anchored suspension bridge in this manner. What was the depth, speed, and turbulence of the churning mass of mud and rocks that had flowed down this valley, I wondered?

Apparently, the chance of the two armies meeting was increased, and came about largely because of Zhang Guotao's strategy of stringing out his 100,000 strong force along the north-south line of two river valleys stretching from the north side of Jiajin Mountain in the south to the south side of Mengbi Mountain in the north. This was my planned connecting route to the grasslands and an appropriate place to ponder the second great leadership and policy challenge that Mao faced on the Long March. Interestingly, Zhang's efforts to ensure his forces met up with Mao's wasn't driven by any respect he had for the Party chief. On the contrary, Zhang felt it was Mao's army, one tenth the size of his own, that should be joining his army, not his army joining Mao's. Based on Mao's own adage, 'Political power grows from the barrel of a gun', Zhang had the balance of firepower in his favour. He had the means to grasp political power, to call the shots, to challenge Mao's paramount leadership, and to decide where the Long March should go from here.

I sat bursting a blister in the rubble of a Tibetan lamasery at

Lianghekou, the site where Mao and Zhang held their second-ever meeting. Zhang wanted to call an end to the Long March and create the new Soviet base in an area to the north, a zone straddling the Sichuan-Gansu-Qinghai regions. Mao rejected his plan because the land there was high, remote and infertile, and there were human threats too. It was a sparsely inhabited Tibetan region, while land to the north was governed by Muslim warlord zealots supported by the Chinese government. Mao favoured an area to the north of Xi'an in Shaanxi Province, which was inhabited entirely by Han Chinese. Rather than the hoped-for unification of Communist forces here, a great schism was developing, one that would see them eventually going their separate ways. Zhang's forces were ultimately defeated by the Muslims; Mao finished his march at the region that he was aiming for, in northern Shaanxi. Later Mao branded Zhang a traitor and a renegade.

Tibetans had reputedly attacked and eaten Red Army stragglers as they crossed the grasslands, but decades later I found them to be friendly and sharing in the beauty of the land, culture and traditions. North of Lianghekou, I passed their blocky fortress-type homes and multi-coloured Buddhist prayer flags flying from trees, bridges and fences while en route to Mengbi Shan, the last mountain of the Great Snowy range. The road here had conquered steep slopes, screes and cliffs with hairpin bends that wound their way upwards, length no object. A road maintenance crew was stationed near the summit, their picks and shovels at the ready to keep the road open, and willing to offer a bed at their depot to travellers in need. Warm though their hospitality was, I later regretted sleeping at that altitude, having suffered in the night with dehydration and a splitting headache.

Early next morning I hurried downhill, and across the

WILD WALL-THE FOUNDATION YEARS

Yangtze River-Yellow River divide, descending into a valley bursting with the fragrance of meadows and flowers, and the heartwarming sight of Tibetan people setting up camp beside the river at Zhuokeji to celebrate their 'summer harvest festival'. Families sat cross-legged on brightly-woven rugs arranged around low wooden tables piled high with the season's harvest and the hamlet's distilling: potatoes in their skins, broad beans, whole roasted piglets, fowls and barley liquor.

Outgoing and animated, the Tibetan people eagerly welcomed me to join in their celebrations. Han Chinese people, in contrast, will observe, say nothing, talk amongst themselves about you on the presumption that a foreigner cannot share their tongue, and then, once spoken to, will exude warmth and friendship. The Tibetans were spontaneous. The difference in their language was an opportunity more than a barrier, circumvented with universally understood gestures, which involved broad rustic smiles, courteous bows, and welcoming, clasped prayerful hands. Ceremony was also their tradition. They offered a communal drinking vessel in both hands — best described as a teapot — to deliver a shot of rice wine, and placed a white scarf around one's neck.

The Red Army never received such a welcome. The Tibetans were the most anti-Han group that they encountered on the Long March. They fled, abandoning their lodges with the surrounding fields unharvested and vegetables left in the earth. Once in Zhuokeji, the Red Army ate well on what they dug up: enormous vegetables mutated to the size of agricultural-show specimens by the rarefied atmosphere. Examples of this gigantic produce graced the barrows of local markets I visited: potatoes like melons, onions like footballs, peas like cherries, and carrots like truncheons.

I was adopted by a family at the festival, and they even offered me a rug for the night in their yurt. However, I was anxious to visit the old village yamen, a fortress-like structure where the *tu si*, Tibetan chieftain had lived. I'd been told to look out for the building by Tan Bing, a Fourth Front Army veteran living in Xi'an. It was, he said, the most impressive landmark he'd seen on his Long March.

The Zhuokeji yamen was within sight of the summer camp and located at the confluence of two rivers, thus it is naturally moated. A young Tibtean showed me where to wade across. Wisps of cloud drifted atop the thickly-wooded hills surrounding the citadel that we neared, and disturbed by our approach, crows squawked. From the outside it appeared to be built entirely of stone, but from the inside no stone at all could be seen; it was wooden at heart.

Mao and Zhou Enlai stayed here for several days, resting before leading the army across the grasslands. The story told is that the entire First Front Army could have lodged in the yamen: that may have been tongue-in-cheek propaganda about the size of Mao's small 'army' compared with Zhang's Fourth Front. I estimated that a couple of hundred might have squeezed in.

A Zhuokeji family was using the ruin as a barn, a place for storing silage and drying bundles of leaves, roots, pods and flowers that were destined for eventual medicinal use. Dust, cobwebs and birds' nests masked the former opulence of its rooms, although fine woodwork remained. It was much in abundance all around, on the facades, balconies, beams, bannisters and window frames. I trod cautiously up a creaking wooden staircase and along a balcony, walking as if on thin ice, braced to react to an imminent collapse. The rooms were dark, because the needle-like fissures in their walls were designed for the release of arrows and barely admitted any light. From the ground floor up were the stables, the larder and servants' quarters, the lamasery, and the chieftain's rooms. The latter were occupied by Mao Zedong because the Tibetan chieftain, like the serfs, had fled. I had planned to sleep with Red Army spirits in the yamen, but the presence of bats and crows and likely much other nocturnal vermin prompted second thoughts. Like the army, I too needed a good night's rest before crossing the grasslands. I headed back towards the festival site with my guide. Its white yurts, adorned with black appliqué, looked like huge lanterns at dusk strung out along the river. Smoke was rising and I could smell meat roasting. It was a good beginning to my last night in the foothills of the Great Snowy Mountains, set to be a long and memorable one spent feasting, drinking black tea, listening to music, and jigging.

My walking companion to Jiaopingdu, the ferry point on the Golden Sands River; Yunnan, November 1990.

Pontoon bridges, like this one in Ganzhou, were built at night and dismantled before dawn to permit the Red Army to vacate its 'Soviet Republic' without enemy detection; Jiangxi, 1990.

Ferryman Zhang Chaoman and his brothers shuttled 30,000 Red Army soldiers across the Golden Sands River in 1935; Jiaopingdu, 1990.

The iron-chain bridge across the Dadu River; (inset), a similar bridge nearby, without wooden planks; Sichuan, 1990.

Luding Bridge, scene of a legendary battle that supposedly saw soldiers crawl along its bare chains after its wooden planks were removed.

Tentatively crossing the swaying bridge, (Qi photo). Luding Bridge was built in 1701 and spans a one hundred metre width gorge.

Summit ridge of Jiajin Mtn. c. 4,100 metres altitude, the highest point of the Long March, which I reached with Ding Li (left inset). After their crossing the mountain, the First Front of the Red Army met the Fourth Front at Dawei, an event marked by a concrete plaque (right inset); July 1991.

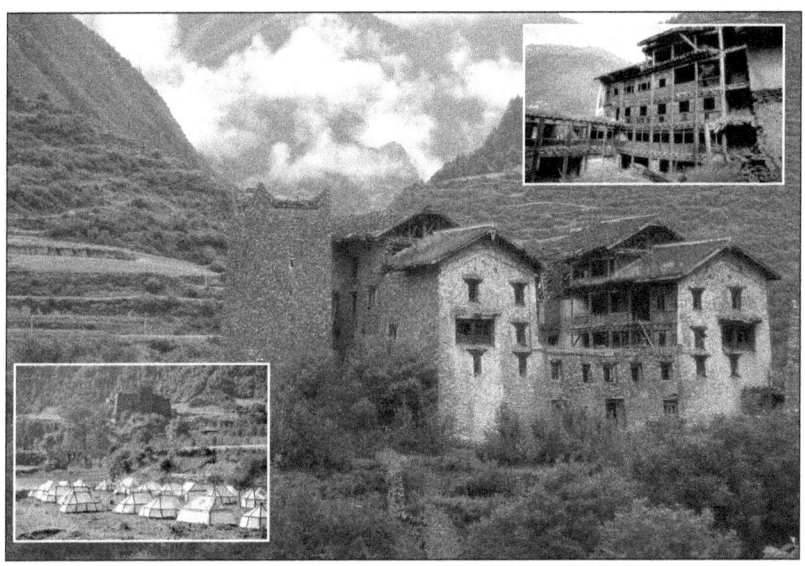

The yamen at Zhuokeji, with its derelict wooden interior (top inset), and the Tibetans' summer camp nearby (lower inset); western Sichuan, August 1991.

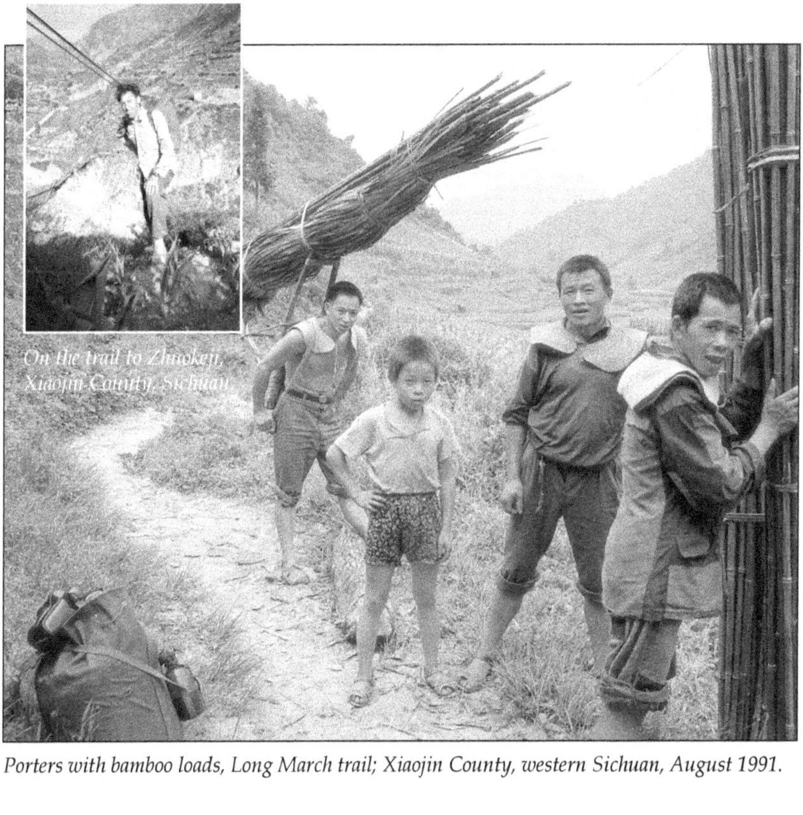

On the trail to Zhuokeji, Xiaojin County, Sichuan

Porters with bamboo loads, Long March trail; Xiaojin County, western Sichuan, August 1991.

Much of the Ruoergai marshland has been reclaimed as grassland. Tibetans herd yak for meat and milk, and use yak wool for yurts (inset) and dung for fires; Zoige, Sichuan, August 1991.

The young road worker Xue Dong and one of the stretches of the road across the grasslands that he is charged to maintain; near Zoige, August 1991. (Insets), Tibetan cowboy and trapper.

Qi and I cycling; South Gate of Xi'an City Wall, 1991.

Home 'English Corner' students, including artist Zhang Da (back, middle), teacher Mike (far right), Helen Wang (front, second right); Xi'an, 1992.

In the cab of the 'Mao Train'; Fengtai Railway Depot, Beijing, 1993

Billboard of Deng Xiaoping, promoting the drive to achieve the 'Four Modernisations'; Xi'an, 1992.

Shooting characters; Chengdu, 1988.

With students at a birthday gathering; Xi'an Mechanical Engineering University, 1992.

Still standing, the largest Mao statue in China, viewed from the top floor of the Sichuan Provincial Exhibition Hall; Chengdu, 1988.

My first view of the Mao statue; Chengdu, 1988.

The statue clad in scaffolding during its annual clean-up for National Day; September 1992.

My face to face meeting with Mao. The statue stands 12.26 metres from head to toe, numbers that correspond to the month and day of his birth.

Wang Anting, the fanatical collector of Mao badges; Chengdu, September 1992.

Flag-raising ceremony at dawn; Tian'anmen Square, Beijing, 1994.

Qi with her father and sister, remembering their historic days in Tian'anmen Square seeing Mao in 1949 and 1966 respectively; Beijing, 1992.

Dr. Ma Yanlong, the cosmetic mortician who prepared Mao's body for lying in state and his mausoleum; Beijing, 1992.

View of Tian'anmen Square from the rostrum where Mao stood to announce the foundation of the People's Republic of China in 1949; Beijing, 1992.

Calendars to mark Mao's centenary in 1993 compete for peoples' attention, money and wall-space alongside those of swimsuited models; street-side market, Xi'an, December 1992.

To the right of Qi and I, Baroness Lynda Chalker, The Rt. Hon. Sir Edward Heath MP and Ambassador Ma Yuzhen; at the launch of Marching with Mao, Chinese Embassy, London, November 1993.

Qi and I with my editor Margaret Body of Hodder & Stoughton Publishers; Chinese Embassy, London, 1993.

Qi and I with our newborn son Jimmy, our 'Wonderful Rice'; Arrowe Park Hospital, Merseyside, 1994.

35

ACROSS TIBETAN MARSHES

THREE DAYS LATER I reached a different world, a town said to be the last one before the *caodi*, or grasslands. Hongyuan was a town of concrete structures, its unimaginative buildings covered in white tiles, and its history was no longer than its name. The town wasn't here in August 1935 when the Red Army travelled through this area: it was built twenty years later during a Han migration. To commemorate the Long March, it was named 'Red Plain'.

Only the pan-flat grasslands surpassed the Great Snowy Mountains for the nightmarish memories they invoked among veterans, and the dramatic gestures they employed to emphasise their recollections. The memories of Tan Bing and Xu Youwan were most vivid. They pointed to their waists. I identified the word *pidai* merely because of its repeated use amid their ramblings. Although the word means leather belt, it seemed impossible to equate it to slurping, until Qi explained that they boiled their leather belts to make a broth to survive. They gestured mud coming up to their waists, even chests, and stressed sheer exhaustion at pulling themselves and others out of the quagmires. From the safe distances of Xi'an and Ruijin, I'd taken these almost-certain exaggerations with a proverbial pinch of salt, dismissing them as dramas introduced to enhance the myth of the Long March. But now that I was in Hongyuan, proximity to the landscape, and a geographical fact, changed everything. The book that I had, *China's Physical Geography* gave 'the grasslands' two names — the Ruoergai Marsh and the Songpan Grassland, implying that both wet and dry terrains existed. Part of the area in question was a number one: the world's largest and highest marsh. In Hongyuan, I began to think seriously about survival.

My PLA standard issue '761' food concentrate biscuits (with a shelf life of a decade) remained unopened, but at only 250 grams each they weren't sufficient. Hongyuan was my last chance to purchase some supplies. I held my breath at the stench of what was on offer at the roadside abattoir, where the butchering of yaks had left the roadside puddles a ruddy mud colour. I rushed into the state-run store in search of my ethnically-preferred Han takeaways. I found two ideal items, peanut brittle and *guoba*, a crunchy and salty deep-fried snack. To bolster my cold weather defences I bought some knitted woollen long-johns. For additional peace of mind I also bought a plastic cycle cape, large enough to use as a shelter to crouch within in the event of a blizzard which were said to occur in any season.

The Fourth Front Army had crossed the grasslands earlier, and assigned scouts to lead the First on their maiden crossing, warning them of the marshy terrain, the absence of food, and the hostility of local Tibetans. The only preparation they could make was in carrying food, and were advised to muster a week's rations for their 8,000 or so, but nowhere near enough could be gathered.

A narrow dirt road was to be my modern way to cross the grasslands, and after a few hours of fast marching I decided it was time to see what I was missing off road. What quagmire conditions had the Red Army really endured in 1935? I was aware that between the 1950s and 1970s there'd been a major push to 'reclaim' the grasslands, to transform them from useless wasteland into a productive area.

Throughout history the Chinese have proven their ability to embark on seemingly impossible large-scale projects and continue them to completion, from generation after generation. This quintessentially Chinese work ethic has been propagated across millennia—reclamation of these marshes included—by the fable 'The foolish man who moved the mountains'. The story features a determined old man who lived in a village that was located between two mountains. He regarded the mountains as annoying obstructions that made it difficult for him and others to come and go, so he began to dig them away. Despite constant ridicule from his neighbours, who scoffed at what they saw as his futile effort to change the nature of things, the old man continued. He declared that his children, and theirs' too, and so on, would all surely carry on and complete the task—and they do! The myth, referred to in Mao's *Little Red Book*, was the one most studied by the masses during the Cultural Revolution for promoting the impact of persistence and willpower, of being able to 'move mountains'. Eventually the marshland became a target for reclamation. The task: to drain the water of the marsh into rivers.

Firstly, they needed access, so they built a road. Then they moved off the road to dig ditches, aiming to excavate thousands of kilometres of them with shovels, criss-crossing the vast marsh. I stepped off the road to see what they had achieved by seeing how far I could get. As a Brit from a wet island who was brought up in the mud as a runner I felt quietly confident to undertake a bog trot.

On first impressions it was bouncy, like a sphagnum-moss bog, a spongey waterbed. When compressed underfoot, the sponge released water, which soon flowed into my footprints. In this way I could how ditch digging would dry out the marsh.

WILD WALL—THE FOUNDATION YEARS

Then, with one foot going under, and my trailing leg also starting to go down further, it triggered an instinctive reaction in me to heave, to release my 'worst' leg. I pulled strongly against the suction and only then appreciated its bog strength, but in doing so my other leg sank deeper. I didn't have a solid spot to stand on. My heart raced. I became increasingly anxious to retrieve my lower calf and foot, and very importantly, with my shoe still on! Heaven forbid! Things would be desperate if I lost a shoe — irreplaceable at a size 14! I pulled more steadily, the right then the left, consciously keeping both feet flat to lessen the chance of my shoes slipping off. After a calm struggle I managed to pull each leg out, caked in a thick, black, odorous slime, with each moment of emergence emitting a deep-toned warning that was reminiscent in sound, but quite the opposite in its smell, of serving the first spoonful of trifle.

Back on the terra firma of the road, I was grateful beyond expression to the teams of workers past who had, over the years, toiled in its building, and also to their successors, the road maintenance crews who are today garrisoned in depots along it to keep it open. Without their road, one could not experience, let alone enjoy, from a safe vantage point that was so close, the one-moment stark — and the next moment astounding — beauty of the grasslands. When the sun shines, its warm golden light transforms an essentially monotone green ocean into a landscape masterpiece specked with the colour of a billion blooms, like a pointillist pastel vista created by the brushes of Seurat.

Inky blue and mauve poppies, miniature orange orchids, giant golden buttercups and dandelions and scores of other unidentifiable flowers presented a pollen feast for bees. Their hives had been carried out here by Hans. For the brief season, the honey people make a home in a rubberised PLA tent, eating little more than wild vegetables and rice. Yak dung is their fuel.

Drinking water is collected from the tent's run off, for it rains almost every day. This dispenses with any need to boil water at 100°C in a pressure cooker, for at this altitude water boils at 85°C. That simple fact accounted for the illnesses that broke out among the Long Marchers as they crossed the grassland drinking 'unboiled' water. But, as the saying goes, a spoonful of honey helps the medicine go down. Honey, spooned on my *al dente* 'hard' rice, made a totally unexpected and very pleasant dessert.

On the unknown road one's fortunes can swing from heaven to hell in a matter of hours, even moments. As I trudged along, three vicious dogs bounded over the grassland from a yurt pitched a few hundred metres from the road. They surrounded me; I continued on my way, turning slowly. First, I snorted a few stern repetitions of *oushi*, but the Mandarin for 'shoo' meant nothing to these Tibetan mastiffs. I picked up stones off the road and tried to act in an unconcerned manner, but it became too scary as the large male darted closer and closer. I suspect they were simply doing their job, protecting the camp when their master was away, and the yurt lay so close to the road that my passing had intruded onto their territory. Certain that I was in danger of great harm, not through rabies (that would be a slow demise), but by being savaged on the spot with nobody close at hand to help, I resorted to all other methods from my book of experience. I feigned madness, exploding with roars and growls to drown their barking, flinging my arms and legs and swinging my stick. It had worked before, but it aggravated them more. I tried silence. Then I feigned throwing. Next, I did throw, only at the male, getting one 'dog's eye' strike hard to its head, sending it away yelping and wincing. But, just a few moments later, it came back to save face, to show it wasn't beaten yet. But it was. Slowly, I must have exited the cordon and, feeling they'd done their job, they just stood their ground, barking, seeing me off,

WILD WALL–THE FOUNDATION YEARS

down the road.

The dogs had done more than see me off: they'd made me realise how dangerous it would be to approach any yurts uninvited, for shelter. I was shaken by the intensity and duration of the struggle. It seemed to have lasted for thirty minutes or so, but was probably only ten. I had no option but to ready myself to literally sleep on the road, or more likely, sleepwalk it, keep moving, because of the mosquitos and the damp cold.

While the reclamation had fallen short of replacing wetlands with wheat fields, it was sufficient to create grasslands, which permitted herding. A horseman rode over to check me out, mounted on a muscular black steed, saddled on a bright wool blanket. Although the handle of a long-bladed knife protruded menacingly from his waistcoat he extended a genuine smile and a practical hand of invitation to mount up and visit his yurt. This was my Trojan Horse past his dogs. However, once inside I was effectively trapped and required an escort even to answer nature's call. This greatly amused my Tibetan hosts, but I took the danger of potentially being 'eunuched' much more seriously.

The yurt of my host family was low—one had to walk stooped within it—and made from woven yak wool, its jet black and greasy surface had the texture of rough sackcloth. The structure was secured by ten or more guy ropes, themselves made of braided yak hair, fixed taut in the turf by yak bone pegs. The inside was illuminated by a shaft of smoke-filled light that beamed down and through the central 'sky light'. Directly underneath it stood a stove fuelled by yak-dung pats. I noted that the whole central chimney area could be sealed off in the event of rain.

We sat on huge yak pelts at the side while the two women, the old mother and grown-up daughter prepared tea. They dropped a chunk of fibrous black matter, brick tea, into a kettle of yak milk, and boiled it. I took out my green mug ready for the pouring. Next came *tsampa*, the staple of the Tibetans on the grassland. The ingredients were kept in a number of similar wooden boxes — chests. There was yak butter, very pale in colour, roasted barley flour that was mixed with a little hot milk, and bones, half roasted but still too hard for my teeth, which gave calcium. A wedge of the dough was placed in my mug, from which point it was DIY: *tsampa* dough is palmed, rolled sausage-like and fed into the mouth, taking care not to break off the dough or to mould a ball- or egg-shape, which appears to be unlucky or offensive.

It was bitterly cold and damp during the night and I was very thankful to be under cover of yak pelts, on top of my sleeping bag and their blankets for insulation from the frigid ground. Next morning, freezing fog blanketed the dawn grassland, dusting the grasses with frost. With a long way to go I left early, to walk northwards along the road. But the memory of my yurt refuge and the family's kindness stayed with me long after I'd finished my lump of *tsampa*, long after the smoky smells had been washed from my clothing.

After a couple of hours' of monotony, some large white objects appeared ahead, looming eerily out of the persistent fog. From their distinctive bell-like shape, I realised that they were large stupas, marking the site of a Buddhist monastery. Close inspection revealed that each stupa bore the portrait of a Buddhist monk, and as expected, even out here in the middle of nowhere, it wasn't the face of Tibetan Buddhism that the whole world recognises, the only one I knew, the exiled Dalai Lama, whose images are banned in China for he is regarded as a 'splittist'. I learned that these images were of the Panchen Lama, supported by the Chinese Government, and the temple village here at the centre of the grasslands was Wu Qie. To arrive here on foot was

WILD WALL-THE FOUNDATION YEARS

both usual and unusual. The most sacred way for pilgrims was literally on all fours, on their hands and knees, bellies and chests, a devout means of progression known as prostration. It begins with a bow, and then hands on the ground, followed by knees, then a thrust forward to be fully prostrate, then rise and repeat. It is said that some pilgrims may take years to travel to a monastery in this most devout manner.

The road was mainly used by Tibetans, although the Hans had built it and still maintained it. Unlike the Tibetans, who lived off the grasslands, Hans had a history of struggling here. The Red Army, the roadbuilding, the reclamation, and now keeping the road open were all struggles in their ways. A new member of the road crew was Xue Dong, a recent middle school graduate of seventeen who spoke a few words of English. I ate pressure-cooked rice and one large pot of stir-fried green peppers with eggs with him that evening, and he kindly shared his room, bed and quilts. As we lay there, top and tail, he told me of his wish to read more books and study. I asked him about the worker's life here. Each person, he said, was responsible for a few different sections of the road, and they worked six days a week, six months a year, from April to October. On Sundays, his day off, he cycled to Ruoergai, known as Zoige in Tibetan, my destination tomorrow, to post a letter to his family.

After breakfast, Xue Dong loaded up his bicycle with a long-handled shovel, pickaxe and wicker basket. He then filled his water bottle and mine with pressure-cooked boiled water before we set off together, towards Zoige. After six kilometres he reached one of his sections, so he parked his bike and began filling a pothole from a pile of stones.

A milepost that showed it was 31 km to Zoige from his depot was perfect for placing my camera upon to take a self-timer photograph of the two of us standing with his bicycle. I asked him to write his address so that I could mail a copy of the photograph to him, which seemed the least I could do in return for his hospitality. An hour later, I could still detect him from four or five kilometres away, a dark speck kicking up dust upon the fawn strand crossing the green grassland. On the four-and-a-half hour long push to Zoige, I was passed by only three vehicles on Xue Dong's road.

Beyond Zoige the straight road began to curve its way down through low hills. After crossing a watershed, it descended, kilometre after kilometre, and didn't flatten out for a long time. Before I realised it, I had completed my crossing of the grasslands.

36

REACHING THE GREAT WALL

WITHOUT EXCEPTION, at every location along the Great Wall that has been repaired and opened to tourism, you will find at its base, around the entrance area, a very large stone set upright in the ground. These stones are inscribed with handsome, deeply carved Chinese characters, written in freehand style, and painted bright red with 不到长城非好汉, *budao changcheng fei haohan*. Chinese tourists almost always take a photograph beside these monuments, but while they can read the column of characters in Chairman Mao's distinctive cursive script, most don't understand the original meaning of it, nor the context, the original purpose, of his now-famous words. Foreigners are even more in the dark. Tour-guide translations give the odd impression that Mao was in some way promoting tourism, while the Chinglish choice of words in the common translation raised amused chuckles. Well, honestly, who wouldn't laugh on hearing 'You are not a real man until you have mounted the Great Wall?'

More than a week after leaving the grasslands of northern Sichuan and travelling through the Minshan Range of Gansu, I entered Ningxia, the eighth provincial region on my own Long March. I was walking to the summit of Liupanshan, a 2,942 metre peak that it is now possible to drive up, even for trucks. In the distance, beside the road, I spotted a shimmering golden-reddish blur that looked almost like a blazing fire, but there was no smoke. As I wound my way back and forth around the hairpin bends, I thought that the mysterious object might be some kind of hoarding, perhaps an advertisement billboard, although I did wonder why they would put such a thing on top of a mountain. I was wrong, though. The words on the hoarding turned out to be the golden calligraphy of a poem mounted against a red background. The poem's title is the name of the mountain, *Liupanshan*, written by Mao Zedong while on the Long March circa late September-early October 1935. Mao, by the way, was an accomplished poet. Arthur Waley, the British lover of classical Chinese poetry, described Mao's work in artistic terms as 'better than Hitler's paintings but not as good as Churchill's (paintings)'.

When I saw this poem, I could neither read Mao's 'grassy' style freehand writing (cursive script), nor understand its meaning. Also, I was unable to appreciate the significance of its location, placed a few hundred kilometres away from Wuqi, the town to the northeast where the Long March was set to conclude in a few weeks' time. In fact, I'd have to wait a lot longer to be enlightened about the poem's true meaning, because it had been subjected to a doubly-damaging fate in recent decades. Its meaning as originally rendered in English had been lost in poor translation; its original purpose had been twisted into what seemed like bland encouragement for tourists, inducing a feeling of self-satisfaction in visiting the Great Wall. Featuring 'true man', 'real man' or 'hero', and the inappropriate verb 'mounted', these inaccurate and unsuitable terms changed Mao's words into drivel.

To reveal what Mao himself, I'm sure, would have deemed a more than 'adequate rendering' in English of his original Chinese, I need to advance a number of years. In 1996, while living in Beijing's Friendship Hotel during my time as a foreign expert, an employee of the Chinese Government, I learned that

WILD WALL—THE FOUNDATION YEARS

I had famous neighbours: Yang Xianyi and Gladys Yang. The Yangs dedicated their lives to crafting accurate and tasteful English translations of classical Chinese works.

In his autobiography *White Tiger*, Yang Xianyi had written that on one of the occasions he'd met Mao, the Chairman expressed scepticism about anyone's ability to adequately render Chinese literature into foreign languages. But Yang was, for me, certainly the translator who managed to explain the meaning of *Liupanshan*. "How might you translate the line *budao changcheng fei haohan* from *Liupanshan*?" I asked him. He thought for a few moments and replied "Who are we if we cannot reach the Great Wall?"

The whole point of the line became clear! It was written to spur on the Red Army. It smacks of 'Come on lads' or 'Are we comrades or not?' and 'We're nearly there, come on, just a little further'. Mao was challenging everyone to pull out the stops, to keep going until they reached the Great Wall—because that is where he wanted to establish his new Soviet base area.

Reaching Wuqi on foot would be the final stage of my own 1,200 km Long March. This relatively brief 'part two' had been intense, focussing on the two most hostile landscape challenges, mountains and grasslands. The ordeal had left me with a thin, harrowed face after going a long way on very few calories. I had a swollen knee, bowel worms resulting from bad water that hadn't boiled to 100°C, a few boil-like mosquito bites, as well as blisters and callouses out of respect for the Red Army. Marching with Mao was a unique way to understand what the Long March was, and where it led to, here in Wuqi. Sadly, despite my blistering method, I was denied the opportunity to take a photograph to record my arrival in the town centre. I was subjected to the irony of ironies—being arrested by the local police on the town's streets. However, it didn't perturb me in the least, for this journey was not about the destination, but the Long March way of getting here. I was tired and hungry, and was no longer amused by these bureaucratic altercations, so simply responded to their questions with ambiguous answers. I expected them to understand nothing, so got the whole predictable procedure over and done with as quickly as possible, without so much as a mention of my own Long March. Fortunately, knowing that Wuqi was in a closed area, I had asked Qi to meet me in the nearby open town of Yan'an, eventually the de facto capital of the 'Shaanxi-Gansu-Ningxia Liberated Area', and Mao's base, for most of the 1940s. There, I'd be assured of a much warmer welcome.

As Qi and I travelled south from Yan'an to Xi'an I reminisced about having taken the same long and winding road across the plateau in May 1987, when I was being deported. A transformative three years had since unfolded and, in a matter of hours, I would be transformed from a foreign trespasser to a 'foreign expert', a teacher at the Shaanxi Institute of Mechanical Engineering. Xi'an, Qi's hometown, was set to be our first home-of-our-own town, and a well-chosen base for me to continue my marching with Mao odyssey to its completion. I'd now covered the first half of Mao's life, from 1893 to 1935. Once settled in, I'd begin my desk jobs: teaching, and writing my book. During vacations and state-holidays I'd continue to travel to the places and events that defined the second half of Mao's life, between 1936 and 1976.

In 1936, Chiang Kai-shek moved his base to Xi'an, relocating there to direct what he envisaged would be the extermination of the Communist forces to the north. I was aware that he was in for the greatest shock of his life: the so-called Xi'an Incident of December 1936. But first things first: Qi and I needed to set up our home and prepare for classes.

'Route of Badges' Key:

(1) Shaoshan – Mao's birthplace (1893); (2) Shanghai/Jiaxing – First CCP Congress (1921); (3) Anyuan – Mao incites miners to rebel (1925); (4) Jinggangshan – Soviet Republic of China (1927); (5) Zunyi – Mao becomes leader of CCP & Red Army (1935); (6) Luding Bridge battle (1935); (7) Great Snowy Mountains crossing (1935); (8) Mount Liupan, Mao's poem (1935); (9) Wuqi – end of Long March (1935); (10) Yan'an – Mao in CCP's new base area; (11) Fengxian – Re-education of youth in the countryside' (1968-71); (12) Foundation of PRC (1949), red guard rally (1966), and Mao's death (1976).

A BIOGRAPHICAL JOURNEY
THROUGH THE LIFE & TIMES OF
CHAIRMAN MAO ZEDONG

Map by Zhang Da; 1993

IV

Feet Under The Table
1991-1993

37

OLD CHINA HAND, NEW CHINA JOB

SMALL IS BEAUTIFUL. Enough is as good as a feast. Happiness has little to do with how much you earn, or how much you own. Cliches they may be, but these are the first thoughts that come to mind as I think back to my teaching years in Xi'an during the early 1990s. Things were simple back then.

I remember that this period began with the dream move, the shortest and easiest move in my life, from Qi's university home at the Xi'an Electronic Sciences University where I was permitted to stay as a family member, to our new university home at the Shaanxi Institute of Mechanical Engineering (SIME). Qi's sister, Xiaoping, who had secured the job for me, came with us in her role as our matchmaker and took us directly to the foreign affairs office (*waishi bangongshe*), just *waiban* for short. In time I would come to learn, as did all foreigners working in China, that this entity was so much more than merely an administrative office. The office was staffed by Mr. Wang, the director, and Mr. Xue, the accountant. My formal qualifications for the job were that I was a native English speaker with a university degree, but being married, and to a Chinese woman, and having an extensive understanding of China were no less important. Qi had prepared all the evidence: my passport to show that I was British; my Bachelor of Science degree certificate from Liverpool University; our marriage certificate and my only copy of *Alone*

WILD WALL–THE FOUNDATION YEARS

on the Great Wall. Mr. Wang flicked through the book, reading the calligraphy at the front 'English friend travelling the Great Wall', and focussed on the colour photographs. "*Zhongguo tong!*" he said cheerfully. I asked Qi what that meant, and she replied "You know everything about China." Both gentlemen appeared to lack one vital skill for their work: neither could speak any English. 'Perfect', I thought, casually retrieving *Alone on the Great Wall* from under their noses, for it contained what were tantamount to blood-boiling foreign affairs stories.

I proceeded to sign my contract with the *waiban*. *Waiban* kept my passport to apply for a work visa and a resident's permit. *Waiban* issued me with a worker's card: "You'll need it to enter the campus gates." *Waiban* issued another card allowing me special 'foreign expert privileges': "You can use Renminbi (RMB), Chinese People's Money, not FEC." (China had dual-track currencies during the early reform period, one for Chinese, one for foreigners – Foreign Exchange Certificates, FEC). *Waiban* also issued me with another card allowing me to pay Chinese prices at tourist sites, where entry to foreigners might be as much as ten times more expensive. *Waiban* also gave me a 'school bicycle', and another card, a bike licence, and a key for its lock. Clutching my pack of cards, *waiban* then walked us over to our assigned accommodation. I was beginning to see how important *waiban* was going to be to us.

Our campus was divided into two parts. On the east side of Jinhua Nanlu (Golden Flower South Road) was the academic area: drab, cookie-cutter teaching blocks that contained classrooms, lecture theatres, laboratories, student dormitories, and administrative offices. On the periphery were basketball courts and the sports ground with a 400-metre cinder track. On the west side of the road were the tenement blocks for housing all teaching and administrative staff, plus a kindergarten and primary school for the families of staff, a clinic, a small coal-fired power station, an outdoor cinema, a few shops, a vegetable market and guest house. Our accommodation wasn't a flat, but an en suite room at the guest house. Three years into matrimony, we began the task of homemaking here, starting from scratch.

Like the exterior of the building, the interior was dull and dusty, largely because of the draughty windows that let in Shaanxi's notorious loess that fills the air at certain times of the year, blocking-out the sun. Qi started to make the interior bright and homely while I set about cleaning the windows that looked out over the main thoroughfare beyond. My work drew a crowd down in the street below. People stopped, stood and talked, pointing up. I waved to them happily, and I asked Qi "Why are they so amused?" She said that Chinese people rarely bothered to clean their windows, so to see the new foreign expert doing such a job in a building that was owned by the university was quite surprising for them.

I wondered whether 'window-cleaning foreigner' might become my moniker, but it turned out that my journeys had preceded me. As soon as the semester began, I heard colleagues and students use that phrase *zhongguo tong* in my presence. I asked Li Jinggang, one of the most-fluent English-speaking teachers, for his version of its meaning, and he translated it as 'an old China Hand'. It was, I learned, a title of respect, an honour almost, bestowed on those foreigners who had not only spent a considerable amount of time in China, but also made an effort to get to know the culture and ways of its people well. I felt that to be anointed with the lofty epithet at the fifteen-month point was somewhat premature. Up until then, most of my time had been concerned with 'extraordinaries', the Great Wall and the Long March. These were faraway places, in China's ancient and recent past, and largely limited to wilderness and rural areas. I had only spent a few months in Beijing but, as with most capital life, that was an exception, a bubble experience. In truth, I remained ignorant of the lives of the masses in the many thousands of large Chinese towns and cities.

For the first time, Xi'an offered me the opportunity to live and work among ordinary urban Chinese, although it was hardly an ordinary Chinese city. Based on the distances to the country's far corners, from the northwest to the southeast, from the northeast to the southwest, it was almost exactly in the geographical centre of today's China. And while Beijing had cumulatively notched up more than 800 years as the capital, Xi'an exceeded that with its impressive 1,200 years as capital. Geographically it had, at certain periods in history, appealed as a strategically safe location, deep inland, far from the northern borders and nomadic attacks — an advantage that partly explained why Qi's family had migrated there. To be distanced from potential American attacks.

In the late 1950s, Chairman Mao ordered strategic industries and important research institutes in the east to be relocated to safer western locations. Xi'an, meaning 'western safe', advertised its advantages in this respect, so it became a centre for translocated military industries and research institutes, one of which was the Xi'an Electronic Sciences University. With this relocation, came the migration of skilled workers and researchers. Thus, Qi's parents, both army teachers based in the military town of Zhangjiakou to the northwest of Beijing, packed up and moved to Xi'an.

Qi had spent most of her life 'at university', and felt very comfortable within the academic environment. Ours was set up to supply Xi'an's heavy industries with engineers. It was built — like all Chinese universities, institutes, factories and companies — in a signature compound style, with an enclosing wall, and gates at which guards were posted. It was self-contained, part of a nationwide network of state-owned work units (*guoying danwei*).

When I first heard that my monthly salary was 700 yuan (US$75) I scoffed, and sarcastically thought about the yawning discrepancy between being titled an 'expert' and being rewarded with peanuts. But compared to Qi's father, for example, a professor in his sixties, it was more than double the local salary. Plus, we had many of the 'iron rice bowl' perks included. Our flat was rent-free, and all our utilities were covered. At the end of each academic year, we would receive a travel allowance, and vacation pay. Everything was convenient: shopping was within arm's reach, classes were just a stone's throw away, a three-minute foot commute across the road.

As a foreigner, this 'village life' was a rather charming environment for me, quite extraordinary. But for the Chinese, it was quite ordinary. Their iron rice bowls guaranteed a fully planned life, a job from assignment to retirement, if you were content to remain within the confines of the work unit, receiving cradle-to-grave care, if you had patience, waiting in the queue, for everything from permission to start a family to getting promoted, to retiring.

I was contracted to teach twelve hours of classes, which meant six sessions per week. That promised me ample time to quietly process my Long March experiences, research the next episodes of the journey, and write *Marching with Mao*, cut off from the rest of the world and all its distractions. It seemed that I'd fallen on my feet, into a Socialist Utopia.

38

BACK TO CLASS

FROM THE YEAR 2000 onwards, my livelihood would be earned by walking and talking. Since childhood, I had always preferred to be on my feet and moving fast, rather than sitting down and taking it easy. But, as the youngest of four children by a long way, I was naturally quite reserved. Interviews and lectures given in the wake of my Great Wall journey and the book's publication enforced my first forays into public speaking. However, thinking back, it was during my teaching years in Xi'an that I gained the confidence to stand up in front of a large crowd, to feel comfortable with an audience, and speak loudly and clearly.

My job was to teach oral English to university students who had already been learning the language for at least seven or eight years. They'd passed the national university entrance exam, which included an English test. They pored over long lists of words that would have any well-educated Brit or American reaching for a dictionary. They had read *David Copperfield*, *Jane Eyre*, *Of Mice and Men*, listened to *Voice of America*, watched the English language teaching TV show *Follow Me* and learned the lyrics of hits by 'The Carpenters', John Denver and 'Boney M'. Despite all this preparation, most of them still didn't have the confidence to say boo to a goose. My aim was to inspire the same transformation that I had made myself. Actually, I wasn't 'teaching' them English at all—and most students would have probably outscored me in a theory of grammar test. What I had to do was simply to encourage them to practice using what they already had in their minds — and move it to their mouths — and speak English!

Waiban telephoned to say that two students would call for me thirty minutes before my first class and escort me to the teaching building and help me by carrying my books. Two neat and nervous students, a girl and a boy, knocked on my door, greeting me with a well-rehearsed "Good morning Teacher William!" With a student outrider on each side of me, we walked across the road, gathering eavesdropping followers as we went. After a pleasant conversation, we duly arrived at a large lecture hall that suddenly fell silent in anticipation. As I reached the front of the room, everyone stood up and broke into loud applause, which I acknowledged with smiles and waves and many a 'thank you'. A large 'Welcome Mr. William' had been beautifully written on the blackboard using coloured chalks. I wrote beside it the words 'Introducing yourself'.

More than a hundred students had packed into the theatre, even sitting on the steps and standing at the back. I had flashbacks to those occasions when I'd faced big crowds in China. A hangar-full of terracotta warriors. Peasants crammed into a Gansu courtyard. That unforgettable and rather intimidating first mass meeting, in Tian'anmen, below the Mao portrait. How hilarious that seemed now, speaking Cantonese, not Mandarin to them, making them laugh.

How different this crowd was! Young, wide-eyed, expectant, focussed, and literally on the edges of their seats, as if they were seeing the moon close-up for the first time. I wasn't staring into the faces of ancient Chinese here, and neither was old China staring at me. I was facing China's bright new future, youngsters with optimism, ideals, hopes and ambitions burning in their

WILD WALL–THE FOUNDATION YEARS

eyes, and to get there they knew they needed to be able to speak English.

I spoke and spoke. There was silence, then rapturous applause and cheers.

I'd spoken not in English, but in Mandarin, to surprise them — and they loved it. And then I said, "I introduced myself in what's a very foreign language for me, to show you that there's no need to feel shy or be bothered about making a few mistakes ... now it's your turn, for five minutes please introduce yourself with as many details as possible to the person sitting next to you."

The hall buzzed, like an English pub on a Saturday night. I eavesdropped. Grammatical gaffs grabbed my attention, phrases like "My mother, he's a worker ... and my father, he's a worker too" and "I go Baoji number three middle school ...."

It was common, even among quite proficient English speakers, to be sloppy with their use of 'he' and 'she', and not differentiate between the genders. A great deal of 'grammar' glue, such as conjunctions, those little words, were left out of sentences. When the Chinese talk about any action, you don't really know whether the event was in the past, present or future.

I realised the need for me to devise simple practice sessions to help students correct their basic mistakes. To conclude my first class, I told a short, true story, to illustrate the importance of stressing the difference between 'he' and 'she'. It went like this.

"We have friends in London. A couple. Hong Fei is Chinese and her husband Alan is British. Alan travels overseas a lot for work. He loves and cares about his wife, and always phones her, most evenings anyway, for a bedtime chat. That night, Alan called Hong Fei from New York. "Hi Fei, I hope you're not too lonely, I'll be home at the weekend," he said. "Thanks Alan ... no need to worry about me ... an old friend has looked me up and he's staying the night with me ...." There was total silence from

Alan. After gulping, a few seconds later he said "What? Could you repeat that ... did you say 'he'?"

Those who understood laughed. Those that didn't, discussed the anecdote in Chinese. And then they laughed.

"So please remember the difference the 's' makes — there's a big difference in English between 'he' and 'she'." But it remained a continuous problem for Chinese speakers, principally because in their spoken language there's no difference between 'he' or 'she', it is just spoken as *ta*.

We rounded off the class with a few minutes of free questions.

"Can you give us English names please?" asked one girl. "Yes," I replied, "I'll sit down and make a long list ... next class."

"Can you sing us a song?" asked another, which generated much excitement and premature clapping. "Mmm ... yes ... but not today ... I'll need to practice!"

"Why did you choose a Chinese girl for your wife? Is she very beautiful?", to which I replied "The most beautiful" to the most rapturous applause.

"Can you use chopsticks?" I answered "very well" and then turned the question around, to which the young man replied, "Of course I can, I am a Chinese!"

"How well? Shall we have a competition?" I asked.

"A ... competition?" he said, looking very puzzled.

"Yes," I said, "a race ... to see how many peanuts you can pick up and eat in one minute ...."

There was a buzz, then chatter in Chinese. "Classmates are looking for the materials now ...."

Ten minutes later they returned from the dining hall with fried peanuts, chopsticks, a vacuum flask of water and two glasses. But nobody volunteered to take up the challenge. Finally, after much coaxing a young man was forced to represent the nation.

We sat down, facing each other across a small table with a

plate of salted fried peanuts placed between us. All the students crowded around, closing in towards the table, the participants like gladiators in an arena. And to the call of *"yibai qi!"* the contest began.

I was pretty skilled with chopsticks because Qi regularly served up a saucer of delicious fried peanuts to accompany my daily Hans Beer. I got off to a good start, while the boy dropped one or two. The students roared. No scooping was allowed, just clean pickups. As we reached 30 seconds, I'd already filled my cheeks with 41 and was so far ahead I slowed down, finally being judged to have eaten 78 within the minute, more than twenty ahead of my competitor. The students went wild, cheering. Once again I heard that phrase *'zhongguo tong'*. I suppose I was an old China Hand with chopsticks.

39

Foreign Affairs

My relationship with China and its people was managed by my wife. Other foreigners were not so fortunate to have such a sensitive and understanding go-between. Instead they came under the control of their *waiban*.

The foreign expert-*waiban* relationship could make or break the outcome of a foreigner's work experience in China. The health of this association determined whether his or her working life was rough or smooth, rewarding or draining, enduring or brief. Reflecting on the importance of this connection, the *waiban* word was used extensively by the foreign expert community without being translated. No translation can convey its wide meaning, nor hint at its true power. So, what is a *waiban*? How can it possibly be described? Perhaps a metaphorical example is a good way to begin to understand part of its function.

A *waiban* is akin to a traffic management mechanism, providing the foreigner with guidance on his journey and advice on avoiding pitfalls. Without the *waiban*, the foreigner would be by himself, facing dangers and inconveniences. He thinks he knows what he's doing. He heads out onto the town's roads, trying to find his own way to his destination, which for example, is a pagoda that lies five km away in the north. The foreigner sets off, confident in his self-guiding ability. He has a compass in hand pointing him in the right direction. It is made in China, as was the very first compass. The Chinese invented it thousands of years ago. But after an hour's cycling he's surprised he hasn't spotted the pagoda. A Chinese student sees the foreigner looking lost, and eager to practice his English, asks him if he needs any help. The student tells him "You are about 10 km away from the pagoda!" and that he needs to make a U-turn and head in the opposite direction. The foreigner was completely unaware that the Chinese compass points south, not north. Next, the foreigner, who is from Britain, is not so sure which side of the road they drive on in China. He was told it was the right, but he sees they drive down the middle of the road. "I'm glad that I'm cycling and not driving," he thinks to himself, happily going with the flow, until he nearly has a head on collision with another cyclist speeding contra flow. Shaken by the near miss, he decides to walk, but even on the pavement he's not safe. A cyclist from behind nearly hits him. Finally, he reaches the pagoda, much later than expected and with frayed nerves. It's been an interesting morning for our foreign friend, and he's learned one very important thing: they do many things very differently in China. One of the *waiban's* roles is to make sure differences don't cause mishaps or trouble that may harm either side.

The expert-*waiban* relationship was best conducted in a diplomatic way, the name of the game being to gently persuade the other party to see things your way, and then to do things your way, for your benefit. Qi told me that Zhou Enlai, who was Minister of Foreign Affairs for China throughout the 1950s, had once stressed that 'nothing in the sphere of foreign affairs should be considered a small matter'.

And it never has been. China has a long history of cautiously tolerating foreigners living in the country in return for what knowledge and practices that they might divulge, introduce or import. Eventually official government programs were developed to invite the outsiders in to reside, work and contribute to state development.

I think the concept of the foreign expert dates back to the 16th Century, when the first Europeans, Jesuit missionaries, arrived in South China. Initially they were restricted to staying on the peninsula of Macau and were prohibited from learning the Chinese language. At the beginning of the 17th Century, the most prominent Jesuit, Matteo Ricci, was permitted to travel to Beijing and allowed to reside in the imperial city. He became highly respected for his knowledge. Some Jesuits were given official ministerial positions, for example Adam Schall in the Board of Astronomy. Brilliant scholarship was at the cutting edge of the Jesuit's conversion plan. They were specifically trained to attract Chinese interest in their outstanding Western scientific knowledge and promote the premise that it was principally a gift from God. This was in an age when traditional wisdom was being challenged, even overtaken, by the discoveries and facts of scientific endeavour. By the early 18th Century Jesuit skills in scientific cartography won the trust of the Kangxi Emperor to the extent that he allowed a team of French surveyors to travel freely to conduct a geographical survey of the entire Qing empire. However, they brought not only new scientific skills, but an alien belief, rituals and teachings, practices that were seen by most as threatening. Thus, they aroused controversy and suspicion, for their primary motive was to Christianise China.

From the late 18th Century onwards, merchant and diplomatic missions followed Jesuits to China and it is in response to their exploitations, and most of all their occupation of Chinese territory that deep animosity and hatred for foreigners arose. The refusal of the Qing to open their empire to Western trade prompted the British to resort to force. Aware of Chinese use of opium the British shipped-in large quantities of the drug from India, which increased its use. This iniquitous practice created a cycle that precipitated an 'opium war'. Unable to settle payments for the drug in silver, China was forced to pay in lieu, by signing so-called 'unequal treaties' that ceded territory and forced them to open up to foreign trade. Hong Kong was handed over to British sovereignty. Many other foreign powers also gained sizeable footholds in China during the 19th Century. So called 'concessions' were established in Beijing, Tianjin, Shanghai and Canton, in port cities along the south China coast, and along the navigable parts of the Yangtze River. Some of the most enduring 'international settlements' were administered by foreign powers until as late as the mid-1940s. The end to this era of humiliation was announced by Mao during his address to establish the People's Republic of China in October 1949. Arguably his most poignant line was 'The Chinese people have stood up!' — meaning that all foreign powers had finally been evicted from Chinese land. Ever since that moment, the presence and actions of foreigners in China, and the existence of foreign things in China, have been considered 'sensitive' and requiring of observation and control. Against this background history, the special sphere of *waishi*, or foreign affairs, a system of managing invited-only foreign experts was established post-1949.

Foreign experts from the Soviet Union were the first to enter the People's Republic, in the 1950s. However, a fundamental divergence of political opinion soon divided Russia and China with the so-called Sino-Soviet Split after 1956, and the experts were withdrawn by Moscow.

The next wave of foreign expertise came early in Deng Xiaoping's reform period. After decades of economic dereliction and consequent decline, foreign expertise in all sectors of the Chinese economy was needed to spearhead the planned rejuvenation programmes. Thus, Westerners were invited in, to see what they could do, bring in and teach. But although China needed foreigners, they wanted them on their own terms. They came only as invited foreign experts. China was careful to avoid the possibility that the invitees would begin to change their position from merely being present to establishing significant footholds. Local managers would wear kid gloves, and always smile. Westerners were welcomed as friends, but watched to make sure that they were not enemies, doing things against the public good, against China. But the benefits that were possible obviously outweighed the risks. Many foreign experts have stayed for decades.

Deng Xiaoping said: "When you open the window to let in the fresh air some flies will come in." Our *waiban* managed four foreign experts, and it was their job to make sure there were no flies among us. In this way, the *waiban* acted as a net on the window. They saw us as a single kind of ethnic minority, even though we were from different countries and cultures: the UK, the US, Ukraine and Japan. The languages we taught, the numbers attending our classes, essentially reflected the ups and downs of our respective bilateral histories, but more so the current climate of political and economic relations between China and our countries of origin. In the early 1990s, China was striving to achieve 'Four Modernisations' in agriculture, industry, defence, science and technology. Learning from the West was seen as a short-cut to that end, and that demanded speaking the world language, English. Marx said "a foreign language is a weapon in the struggle of life", but in Deng's China, foreign languages were needed to discuss trade and thrash out deals. The numbers of students enrolling for each expert's classes were falling and rising barometers in this landscape. Russian had been on the wane since the Sino-Soviet Split. It was seen as old-fashioned, its day had past: Halida had just a handful of students. Yoko had many more. The Japanese were in the ascendancy. They entered China in force when the reforms began, investing heavily, setting up joint venture companies, and exchange programmes. They filled stores with their advanced electronics: Panasonic TVs, Hitachi air-conditioners, and Canon cameras. Japanese was the language of business. But the language that was most in-demand to facilitate China's open-door policy and economic reform drive was English. The path had been well paved by the enormously successful BBC programme *Follow Me*, an English teaching course, broadcast on CCTV and published as readers that would fill an entire bookshelf. Tom and I taught classes that were crammed full.

Surprisingly, we experts didn't get together that often, but when we did, especially with Tom and Debbie, the Americans, there were several recurrent talking points. These included our *waiban*, getting paid on time, what travel allowances were due, as well as holiday pay, accommodation problems, and shopping advice, especially where sought-after essentials like bread, cakes, biscuits and cooking ingredients could be purchased.

Tom and Debbie had made their own novel reinterpretation of the concept of 'family of five good practices' (*wuhao jiating*), an award granted by the local neighbourhood committee, a grass-roots group typically made up of grannies of the work unit that proposed recognition of 'ideal families' to the internal Communist Party committee. Shown by a small red plate bearing four golden characters, the award was proudly displayed on, above or beside the recipient's door. It recognised five family and household achievements and good habits selected from among a host of possibilities. These included marital harmony, respect for the elderly, love of the young, thrift and frugality, female equality, love of learning, good neighbourliness, rejection of superstition and feudalism, and so on. Tom and Debbie's 'five goods' were their five children. They were known on campus and across Xi'an as *wugewa*, or 'those with five children'. Debbie made no secret of the family's plans, to emulate the von Trapp family in *The Sound of Music* and have seven.

Concerning allocation of accommodation, neither I, with only a wife, nor either of the other experts, who were alone, could possibly compete with them, bearing in mind that the character for good (好) by its components regards a good man as having a woman and a child. Tom had a woman and five children. Consequently, he was allocated a palatial flat in the most exclusive block that the university possessed. He was neighbour to eminent professors and the university president, much to the envy of the rest of us who didn't even have kitchens in our guesthouse quarters. In the eyes of the Chinese, who were at the time restricted by the one child per family policy, Tom and Debbie were looked upon with wonder and curiosity, and doubtless by some with a degree of jealously, highlighting America as the land of the free. But among the pragmatic Chinese, the large size of their family prompted questions about how the couple could afford to feed five children, to clothe and educate them. Debbie was a magical cook, improvising ingredients if the necessary ones were unobtainable. She succeeded in producing a wide range of American meals and recipes, from burgers to brownies. Quality was one thing, and quantity another; Debbie got our *waiban* to employ a handyman to fit a padlock on the family's fridge! She was also an accomplished seamstress and knitter. Both parents were rigidly strict with their timetabling of home-schooling classes across seven grades. Yet Tom and I received the same 700 yuan salary, an amount far from sufficient to maintain a family of seven. How they did it remained a mystery to the Chinese, but we gathered that Tom and Debbie were missionaries and suspected that a church in the US funded their work.

WILD WALL-THE FOUNDATION YEARS

In fact, as time went on, it became clear that almost all the foreign experts working in China fell into one of three broad groups. They either had an aim, a direction, or an ulterior motive, or they were escapists, completely lost. By far the largest group were the missionaries, and during my own final year of teaching in Xi'an, some twenty-four teachers were deported for carrying out illegal missionary work. Another large group were the seniors, people in their late fifties or even sixties who had retired back home, in some cases divorced, seeking rejuvenation, a new sense of purpose. Yet another distinct group were the freshers, usually in their mid-twenties, lacking a little in direction, usually men, who were soon to be captivated by the beauty of Chinese women. We witnessed all manner of these foreign affairs, which were virtually impossible for their participants to keep discrete because they themselves were so obtrusive. In addition, any *waiban* was always on the alert for these relationships. The experts at my university were demographically all 'low risk' and well behaved in this respect, being married with wives and children, while few foreign women cultivated close relations with Chinese men at the time. But in the wider city circle of other foreign experts, especially those at neighbouring universities, we became privy to, and entertained by, some fascinating foreign affairs.

David McCulloch was a teacher from Glasgow. He had grown up in Argentina and went on to spend most of his adult life in Africa as a missionary, raising a large family of his own. But in his late fifties his return to the UK had brought hard times, and the only work he could obtain was at McDonald's serving burgers and fries—until he heard about teaching in China. David was softly-spoken, diligent, well-groomed, gentlemanly and sensitive, and had a popular asset in China: a very good singing voice. A middle-aged female colleague, unmarried in her forties—known as a *lao guniang* in Chinese, which literally means 'old girl' but actually describes a spinster who's been overlooked—took persistent interest in David. Being happily married, and due to be joined in Xi'an by his wife Sue and their youngest daughter Stephanie, David confided in Qi and I, making his 'concerns' on the spinster known to us.

"Maybe you gave her the wrong idea, letting her teach you a Chinese love song," I told him.

"Maybe I did," said David in his Scottish accent, "And now she keeps asking me to go dancing with her … she's heard me talk about Scottish dancing you know."

David couldn't be direct and bold to her and say 'no'. He eventually said "Okay, just once then, before my wife arrives next week." Reluctantly he agreed to go dancing with her, at seven-thirty one Saturday.

The day arrived, and there was a knock at his door early in the morning. David scurried to answer it, dressed in his pyjamas, and was astounded to see the lady teacher standing there, already wearing a chiffon evening dress! Both had got the wrong end of the stick. In China, dancing was primarily considered an exercise, and was done at dawn, outdoors, in the park, while David thought they had set a dance-hall date, in the evening of course.

Another foreign expert, a young American, Mike, worked at the adjacent Xi'an College of Fashion Design. He was a little overweight, a problem exacerbated by his residence in China because he fell in love with Chinese food, and needed to run—as I did too, but for a different reason. I was always on the lookout for someone who was keen to run a few miles with me. My new year's resolution for 1992, as it had been the previous year, was to run every day of the year, a minimum of 5 km each day, come hell or high water, fatigue or illness. One Wednesday afternoon,

WILD WALL—THE FOUNDATION YEARS

Mike and I enjoyed a run of about 18 km around the foot of Xi'an's Ming Dynasty city wall, a route that became a regular weekly outing thereafter. Wednesday afternoons were always free of classes for we foreigners while all the Chinese studied their politics—nationwide, in every work unit. Mike's ambition was to be a gynaecologist, and he loved virtually every Chinese woman he saw. One morning he called unexpectedly on us, in a mad rage. He'd chatted-up a female student in one of his classes, then, late the previous night, had been caught by the patrolling college guards while 'making out in the bushes'. This turned out to be his *waiban's* worst nightmare. *Waibans* viewed any sexual relationship with local women as illegal and forbade all such liaisons, in fact it was one of their main jobs to ensure such things never happened. The only safe and acceptable international relationship was achieved by getting married, and no 'pre-school' was allowed. But Mike's debacle was about the worst one could imagine: even student-to-student liaisons were not permitted because the authorities considered that students were at university to learn, not to date. But Mike didn't see things the Chinese way. Enraged, he shouted at his *waiban* director, telling them they had no right to interfere with his personal affairs. The *waiban* sent him to explain his behaviour to the university president. Mike upped the ante, telling the president "Wake up … smell the coffee … the Cultural Revolution is over, it's 1992!"

Mike and I didn't run around the city wall again. He was sacked, and the unfortunate student expelled.

By great fortune, Mike's replacement, Ian, was another keen runner, ex-army, from the UK. And if Mike was the brash American playboy boat-rocker, Ian was quite the opposite, softly spoken and staunchly religious who also rocked the boat, but not so publicly. He fell madly in love with Miss Feng, the very attractive head of English teaching at his university, and a Party member. The two soon talked about marriage, but there was one stumbling block: Ian wanted Miss Feng to 'accept Jesus Christ as her saviour' and quit membership of the Communist Party, which contravenes Party rules. After months of secret courting, with Ian having heart to heart conversations with me, and Miss Feng confiding in Qi, Ian could not simply marry Miss Feng for love; he insisted that she believed what he believed in. Because she couldn't, they parted, and Ian left after a year of teaching and religious zealotry. With her unique personal experience of foreign affairs, Miss Feng soon became the *waiban* director of her university!

40

Xi'an Incidents

Marching with Mao: A Biographical Journey, as I was now inclined to title the book, was to be my second, and last, handwritten book—all my subsequent books would be written on computers. Handwriting, or typing, was not considered a hardship at all at that time, it was merely part and parcel of the author's graft. But the real science-fiction-come-true part of modern writing is the universe of information that is available at one's fingertips. This makes background research—which I consider to be the 'glue' to stick the 'guts' of my stories together—immediate, accessible, cheap and easy. My feet-on experiences of *Marching with Mao* were yielding the guts, but the glue was harder to come by, and without it my writing often ground to a frustrating halt. Xi'an in 1991 was a veritable desert for English books. The university library had none. While Karl Marx had chosen the optimum place to sit and write his books, in the reading room of the British Library, I'd chosen the worst.

Come what may, I simply had to acquire copies of certain reference books. The only previous recent foreign work on the Long March by an author who had spent any significant time in China was *The Long March* written in 1984 by US journalist Harrison Salisbury. Although he'd gained official permission and support for his journey, the censors clearly didn't like everything he'd written, so the title wasn't imported into China: I needed to request a copy from the UK. It was the age of letter writing and I particularly liked to affix commemorative, rather than drab utilitarian stamps, on to my envelopes. I'd buy attractive stamps at face value from the 'stamp market'. This was simply an enthusiastic crowd of dealers who gathered to tout their collections, black PVC despatch cases in hand, outside every town and city post office in the land. I became known to the Xi'an vendors: I often mingled among them, looking for 'Mao stamps'. These were highly sought-after by locals for their skyrocketing prices, and by me for the unusual insight they revealed into his cult status. One dealer showed me some twenty-four 'red' stamps issued over a three-month period in 1967 to wish Mao *wansui*, or '10,000 years'. He showed me old envelopes to demonstrate how carefully Mao stamps were affixed, and how the frankings never soiled Mao's face or body, for fear that the offending post office clerk was criticised, or quite possibly beaten-up, or even lynched (communicated by an interesting mime).

No foreign expert, me included, was without their own fund of stories about shady Chinese post office experiences. All had numerous — and I, countless — experiences of parcels 'lost-in-the-post'. There was widespread paranoia that incoming mail was systematically opened and scrutinised by some secret department reporting to the powers-that-be — a claim I personally, perhaps naively, always doubted and disputed by sarcastically asking, 'D'you honestly think they're really that interested in what you're doing?' Many were, perfectly understandably, seriously concerned because they were doing 'undercover' missionary work. I endured a unique Post Office encounter, one that was new to us all, a collector's item.

Because the post office clerks were extremely fastidious in the application of the rules, they wouldn't turn a blind eye to a letter being a few grams overweight. Therefore, it was absolutely

WILD WALL-THE FOUNDATION YEARS

necessary to have one's letters weighed to ensure that they would go by airmail and not be demoted to the sea mail bag. As usual, I handed my envelope to the clerk, with more than sufficient stamps affixed. She snatched the letter, snarled at its weight, and its cost, and then growled *"buxing! youpiao tiede buxing!,"* (unacceptable, the stamps affixed are unacceptable).

"You mean the rate is higher?" I asked.

"No!" she snarled, "the stamps have a 'problem'."

I took the letter back and looked at the stamps, thinking that surely I could not have been so careless as to affix fake stamps. Indeed, I had not been. They were new PRC stamps, affixed with glue, and 1.5 yuan in value more than was required.

"Sorry ... I still don't understand what you mean by a 'problem with the stamps' ...."

"You didn't buy them here!" she snarled, holding up a sheet of her own stamps that bore special franks on the back, presumably to signify their origin.

The penny dropped. It was obviously in her interest, financially, for some reason to sell the stamps she had in her ledger, and not to accept my letter bearing stamps from a different vendor.

A conversation like this could never take place without drawing a gawping audience—for several reasons. First, any dialogue at a significant volume attracts observers. Foreigners always attract observers. Foreigners speaking Chinese especially attract a large crowd of listeners.

"So," I said, "let me just get this right. Is this city called the 'People's Republic of Xi'an'? Tell me, is Xi'an still part of the People's Republic of China?"

The crowd howled with laughter. I surprised even myself that in this very annoying situation I'd managed to keep my Chinese at such a succinct, lucid—even witty—standard. The clerk snorted *"zhege ren you maobing"* (this person has an illness), a term that insinuates someone has a mental problem. Then she slammed a 'position closed' block of wood on the counter and strutted away.

I'd proved my point. She had completely 'lost face' in front of a foreigner, and a large crowd. But I still hadn't managed to post my letter. I took it to an adjacent counter, where it was snatched from my hand, not even weighed, and tossed into a sack.

The letter apparently never arrived. I wrote another, and the addressee received it, and eventually posted the book. And it is not necessary to state what happened to it.

I could manage without Salisbury's Long March book, but I couldn't do without Edgar Snow's *Red Star Over China*. Funnily enough, it seemed a good bet, even certain, that I'd find one there in Xi'an. After all, what better comment on the dust-jacket could there be than 'Originally banned in the United States …' to promote sales?

I found a batch of sanitised Mao biographies in Xi'an's Foreign Language Bookstore (FLB), but surprisingly no sign of *Red Star Over China*, which is considered a classic. Qi had told me about Edgar Snow's adventurous exploits when we were in Yan'an, because that's where he went in 1936 to interview Mao Zedong. And it was Snow who'd famously photographed Mao, aged 43, wearing a red-starred cap and looking thoughtful, confident, slim, and honed by war. But where was Snow's book? Only then did I notice a sign (in Chinese) indicating 'Imported Books Second Floor'. Halfway up the stairs an assistant yelled at me to stop. Apparently, it was a 'forbidden area' to foreigners!

Qi immediately clarified the mystery; she was an avid reader and a regular browser at the Beijing branch of the FLB. "The second floor sells foreign books that have been illegally photocopied," she explained. "You know, maybe the foreign edition costs 80 yuan or something, that's too expensive for Chinese people, so they just photocopy it and sell it without a cover to avoid the copyright problems." Qi duly went to the store and bought me a pirated copy of *Red Star Over China,* for a few yuan.

I soon became riveted by *Red Star.* The book is history, journalism and adventure, and if ever there was a right time and place to read it, it was now, in Xi'an at the end of my Long March, the ideal prelude to the 'Xi'an Incident'.

Red Star first prompted me to visit Xi'an's 'Eighth Route Army Office Museum' where I learned of a 'Snow Studies Center' established by a Mr. An Wei, whom, it turned out, we knew already. When Qi and I were married, we needed a government-authorised translation of my English-language documents, and An Wei was the man who did that job. Set up in early 1992, the prized exhibits of the Study Center were Edgar's Snow's belongings used on his journey to Xi'an and Yan'an: his khaki uniform and knapsack. I was particularly fascinated to see 'his' grass sandals displayed, which, I thought, like my own, had surely been acquired for their Long March curiosity value rather than wearing.

Snow's *Red Star* story began when he left Yenching University in Peking, where he was a visiting scholar teaching journalism. He wanted to find the 'red bandits', as the Communists were called in the West, and secure an interview with Mao. Inoculated against smallpox, cholera, plague and typhoid, and armed with a letter of introduction written in invisible ink (later revealed as having been written by Madam Soong Chingling, the younger sister of Chiang Kai-Shek's wife) attesting his credentials as a trustworthy journalist, Snow boarded the night train to Xi'an via Zhengzhou. Xi'an was the headquarters of two KMT-allied warlord divisions commanded by generals Yang Hucheng and Zhang Xueliang. They were supposedly ready to implement the final suppression of all surviving red bandits of the Long March—once Chiang arrived to direct the operation.

As instructed, Snow lodged at the Xijing Hotel outside Xi'an Railway Station and waited patiently to be intercepted by a man named Wang. A few days later, a pastor of that name, fluent in English thanks to his missionary education in Shanghai, came to the hotel and organised Snow's onward travel to the Communist 'capital' at Bao'an, 350 km to the north. Escorted by troops of Zhang Xueliang's army, Snow passed through the wooden gates of the walled city in the half light of dawn. After crossing the Wei River by ferry, he was in no-man's land, then in red territory. There he was met by Zhou Enlai and taken to meet Mao.

What happened in the ensuing few months is the stuff of journalistic history. Snow interviewed Mao over many nights, taking notes that totalled 20,000 words. These he would use to write the first eyewitness account of life and conditions in the communist enclave, a biographical sketch of Mao's revolutionary struggles, and a summary of the fundamental policies of the People's Soviet Republic.

In mid-October 1936, Snow bade farewell to his hosts and a week later crossed Nationalist lines to reach Xianyang, just northwest of Xi'an. From there he rode to Xi'an in the back of a truck, disembarking at the Drum Tower. To his absolute horror, his kitbag, containing a dozen diaries and notebooks, 30 rolls of film and many propaganda magazines and newspapers collected during his stay in Bao'an, had mysteriously disappeared. A nerve-wracking few hours ensued before Snow was reunited with his bag, which had been mistakenly offloaded 30 km back. The very next day, Xi'an came to standstill. Chiang had arrived to personally command the extermination campaign against the Communist base area.

I was fascinated by Edgar Snow's immediacy, his adventurous

spirit, gruelling journey and considerable bravery. To this day, whenever I'm asked to recommend reading on 20th Century China, *Red Star Over China* is always on my list. And if people ask me why, I reply: 'Because he found out by going to see for himself, and not writing about China or things Chinese from the other side of the world ... that's just 'viewing flowers from horseback'.

Everyone visiting China knows of Xi'an's terracotta warriors, but few know that on the way to the mausoleum complex of the First Emperor one passes the site of hot springs, Huaqingchi, which has been a resort health since the Tang Dynasty (618-907AD). The therapeutic qualities of the waters have attracted an impressive patronage throughout history, from the 'ruling' Empress Wu Zetian to, of all people, Generalissimo Chiang Kai-shek, who made the spa his base for the final crackdown on the Reds, an assault that never materialised.

The wavering loyalty of Chiang's warlord allies, Zhang Xueliang and Yang Hucheng, was signalled by their willingness to let Edgar Snow pass through the city wall en route to meet the Communists. The patriotically-minded generals were concerned that as Chiang focussed on the civil war, the Japanese were helping themselves to Chinese territory, as Zhang knew only too well. His father, the de facto ruler of Manchuria (comprising the northeastern provinces, the so-called 'rooster's head' on the map of China) during the warlord period that followed the fall of the Qing Dynasty in 1911, was assassinated by the Japanese prior to their annexation of the region on September 18th, 1931. The Japanese established Manchukuo, a puppet state of their empire shortly after, installing Puyi—of Manchu nationality—who had abdicated as the 'Last Emperor' of China, as the 'puppet emperor' of his ancestral homeland. Zhang Xueliang wanted the Nationalists to stop fighting the Communists and form a united front of Chinese armies that could mount a joint-military effort against the Japanese. What he did to this make happen was one of the most extraordinary events in modern Chinese history. He arrested and kidnapped the Generalissimo from the hot springs resort of Huaqingchi, and forced him to sign a ceasefire pact, thus suspending the civil war and initiating the Anti-Japanese War.

That war raged from 1937 until it was abruptly terminated in 1945 when the US bombed Hiroshima and Nagasaki, events that finally persuaded the Japanese Emperor Hirohito to surrender unconditionally. Following the withdrawal of the occupying Japanese forces, the Chinese resumed their domestic war, which ended when Mao founded his 'New China' in 1949 after the retreat of the remaining Nationalist forces to the island of Taiwan.

41

Hypothetical Questions

My sister-in-law Xiaoping had a fairly relaxed job in her university, employed as a technician looking after her department's computer system. Upon hearing me speak about how our room was submerged under reams of paper, she offered to type my book for me. I was delighted to learn of her willingness, but doubted whether someone who could hardly speak a word of English would be able to read even my neatest handwriting, and then type it without hundreds of errors. But the sisters assured me that it would be no problem. "You know how good Chinese are at copying things," said Qi.

She was absolutely right! A couple of weeks later I was amazed to be presented with the first few chapters of my book, neatly typed, double-spaced, with hardly an error in sight. Her diligence proved to be an enormous help, allowing me to separate the proverbial wood from the trees. The very conversion of handwritten text into a typed manuscript made it look more like a book, and also helped me to critically read the work, not as the author but as a purchaser of the book. Moreover, the text had not merely been typed, it had been typed on a word processor and the content memorised on a gizmo called a floppy disk. This allowed the text to be 'saved', brought back onto the screen at any time, and to be amended. At the time, we considered this technology to be cutting edge.

As the weeks flew by, small talk among the experts changed with the weather. Just a few weeks before, the gripes had been about the tepid central heating system and lukewarm 'hot' showers. Now, all of a sudden, everyone was complaining about their air conditioning, which seemed to heat the room rather than cool it, and holes in their mosquito nets. Xi'an was certainly a contender alongside the likes of Shanghai, Nanjing, Wuhan and Chongqing to be one of the great furnaces of China. Temperatures towards the end of term in mid-June began to soar, with days of 39°C becoming quite the norm. With typical Chinese indomitable humour, colleagues and students told me that the 'official temperature' could never reach 40°C—because if it did, according to government regulations, everyone was entitled to stop working. And they were right, it never did, not once. Despite the heat, I was determined not to break my resolution of running every day of the year—and certainly not with the lame excuse that the road was melting and the tar was sticking to my training shoes like black treacle.

Air conditioning was not the only thing struggling to deal with the heat—the students were too. They looked drained and soporific. Teaching was especially hard work at this time because language classes were mainly scheduled for early evening, after dinner. To jolt the dozing students to speak, I came up with, on the spur of the moment, my most successful class ever, if that can be judged by volume of chatter and stirred emotions. It was such a hit that it became the format for a once every now and then class called 'hypothetical questions'. In retrospect I should have called them 'controversial hypothetical' questions, because the more controversial the questions were, the more they were able to stir emotions.

The premiere and most successful in this series was prompted by the hottest pop song release of 1992, and one of our

WILD WALL-THE FOUNDATION YEARS

favourites, *My 1997* composed and sung by Ai Jing. In the semi-autobiographical ballad, Ai Jing sings and strums her frustration as a mainlander not being allowed to Hong Kong to visit her boyfriend there, whom she met in Guangzhou.

As the students were nodding off, I started to sing the closing lines of *My 1997*, in Chinese: *"Take me to that wonderful world ... Give me a big red stamp ... Come on 1997 so I can go to Hong Kong!"* They woke up. The song resonated with all students. They yearned for their own freedoms, to date who they fancied and visit the glamorous city. They, too, were impatient for 1997, the agreed handover date when Hong Kong would be returned to Chinese sovereignty and all mainlanders would be free to go there. Now I had their attention, I introduced the controversy.

"Okay students ... this is a *hypothetical* question. As we all know, the British Prime Minister, Mrs. Thatcher, the 'Iron Lady', signed an accord with Deng Xiaoping to return Hong Kong to Chinese sovereignty in July 1997 — in five years' time. But what would you do, and how would you feel, if you listened to tomorrow's news and heard it reported that, due to a change of mind on the British side, the deal was cancelled?"

There was silence. Deadly silence.

"Discuss it, among yourselves," I said.

There was uproar! The sleeping lecture theatre was suddenly transformed into a scene reminiscent of one of the most boisterous exchanges in the House of Commons, but with one major difference. There was unanimous agreement that the British should be forced to honour the agreement. Students cited historical events, back to the mid-1800s, accusing the British of inhumanity in dumping opium on Chinese markets. Students said that they would take to the streets and protest, would call on the government to act firmly to take Hong Kong back immediately. 'An agreement cannot be changed!' they repeated.

'We should send the PLA to seize Hong Kong now!' declared one student.

I learned much from their cries. There was blanket condemnation of the British actions. It was clear how humiliating the issue of Hong Kong's cessation to the British was for the Chinese, and how it had remained so.

If any of my students asked for a jolt that the hypothetical questions exercise triggered, it was likely to be the most outstanding student of the class, Xiao Peng, from Hangzhou. Most of these questions concerned sensitive international relations issues, but I did have other themes, very personal ones, to probe morality and encourage soul searching.

"So, you'll be taking end of term exams next week, right? You're scratching your head, chewing the end of your pencil to think clearly, but then, in the corner of your eye, you see your best friend appearing to peep at something they're holding under their desk. You realise that he's cheating. What would you do?"

It was another silencer. Then Xiao Peng stood up again and said, "Mr. William, this isn't a hypothetical question, it is a real question. I've seen classmates cheating at middle school and here at university." He turned around and added, "I think we all know that there are many cheats, it makes me feel really bad."

Students told me that cheating wasn't a modern problem. It had been commonplace in the old imperial examination system, too. Candidates aspiring to work as officials were seated in tiny cubicles at examination halls around the country, effectively taking the exam in private and therefore away from any exam monitors, so they were quite free to copy out answers in seclusion. The consensus was that nearly all officials had cheated their way through examinations, and so it became an accepted practice. I told the students that I'd much rather get zero in an exam than cheat. They said that in China failure was a shameful thing, cheating was less shameful, so they had perfected clever ways to avoid being caught.

During the following term, I actually caught two students cheating during an unimportant spelling test of new vocabulary. Rather than turning a blind eye, I warned them and explained my standing on the matter. But their shame proved too much of a burden to bear. They didn't turn up for the next class. I never saw them again.

Years later, while living and working in Beijing, I was sought by the National Museum of China to check the English-language labels of 4,000-plus antiquities that make up the stunning *Ancient China* permanent exhibit. In the late Qing collection, the curator and I stood in front of a soiled-looking robe, greyish in colour, labelled 'Robe of Malpractice'.

"What exactly d'you mean by that term?" I asked her, chuckling.

"Well, look closely at the textile," she replied, "and perhaps you can see tiny Chinese characters … it's an undergarment, a robe used by a dishonest imperial examinations candidate … covered with the entire text of a Chinese classic that they needed to write down, character by character, to pass … of course few could do that, so most had to cheat … in the examination cubicle the candidate could just take off their robe and cheat."

Once university examinations were over, the students took group photographs, invited classmates to write messages and addresses in their exercise books, then boarded buses heading for the railway station. They all travelled home, to the distant corners of China, to be with their families for the long, hot summer.

Qi and I also headed to the railway station, with her father and sister. The four of us were going to Beijing to remember two historical days that they had personally experienced – witnessing the foundation of Mao's New China in 1949, and attending a massive red guard rally in 1966.

42

HISTORIC DAYS REMEMBERED

CHINA SEEMS a whole lot smaller since its ultra-high speed rail network was constructed. As I proofread this in 2022, Xi'an is just four hours away by bullet train from Beijing. Thirty years earlier in 1992, long-distance train journeys were always overnighters, opportunities for appreciating the vastness of the country. Tens of hours' long, they were punctuated by frequent stops, long enough to allow passengers to climb down onto the platform, to stretch, stride, snack and smoke, until the sounding of the two-minute bell to usher 'platformers' back aboard. It was while Qi and I were out for dawn exercises on the platform of Shijiazhuang Station in Hebei that she mentioned how the city — the last stop on our 22-hour ride from Xi'an to Beijing — earned itself the nickname of being 'Mao's last stop before Beiping'.

As the fine focus of the civil war shifted, so did Mao's base: in 1948 he relocated his revolutionary HQ eastwards, from Yan'an to Xibaipo, a village north of Shijiazhuang. During his stay there, over a fifteen-month period, the map of China turned largely red after a succession of decisive Communist victories that took him to within reach of his greatest achievement. To seize it, Mao made a final move, into newly-captured Beiping, for it was almost time to claim victory by renaming the country, redesigning its flag, relocating its capital from Nanjing, and replacing its government. 'New China' (*xin zhongguo*) was about to be born.

WILLIAM LINDESAY

My father-in-law Wu Wanchun was a student of Peking University from 1947 to 1950. In October 1949 he was immersed within the masses crowding Tian'anmen Square for the 'founding of the nation ceremony'. The key moment, featuring the victorious revolutionary cast standing on the rostrum overlooking the Square, is commemorated in a painting titled 'The Foundation of the Nation' (*kaiguo didian*) by artist Dong Xiwen. I'd seen a copy of the work hanging inside the empty railway-station waiting room at Shaoshan, Mao's birthplace. It showed Mao, no longer in war-torn clothing as depicted in Edgar Snow's photographs, but wearing a tailored worsted-wool suit, holding a paper containing a prepared speech, and standing in front of a microphone. This was his finest hour, his victory parade. It was Wu Wanchun's one-and-only look at Mao, although his daughter would get the next family viewing, in 1966. Wu Xiaoping attended a red guard rally that year. She was 'wedged in' by a much larger crowd, for the Square had been expanded since 1949. Holding *The Quotations of Mao Zedong*, dubbed 'The Little Red Book' by foreigners, she was one of the 1.25 million teenagers there on the day. They all cried hysterically and chanted 'Long Life to Chairman Mao!'

These two events, those two days, the two family members, brings to mind two questions that I once asked a colleague. The first was "What makes you feel proud to be Chinese?" Her immediate response was "Our history!" My second question was "As a Chinese, what makes you feel ashamed?" She paused for a few seconds, and then gave the same answer, but in a different lower tone of voice. "Our history."

Both occasions were joyous for all those who were there, memorable days in themselves. October 1st 1949—a new beginning, a day of nationwide hope for unity and stability after so many years of war and chaos; October 18th 1966, a day of fever-pitch idolatry that ushered in a decade of chaos and killing after so much hard work and progress to bring stability. But how times have changed once again! The pendulum had just swung back, returning from the grim past to a stable and prosperous present. China in 1992 was buzzing with talk of new opportunities, going places, and optimism. My graduating students spoke of personal ambitions instead of job assignments from the state, of 'going to Shenzhen' to do business, and of making money. A few brave colleagues had left their iron-rice-bowl employment as teachers to *xiahai*, to 'jump into the sea', to sink or swim, and work as private entrepreneurs. Many more were 'preparing to go abroad' to study. For Chinese participants and foreign observers alike, these were unprecedented times. Enjoyment was no longer bourgeois, banqueting was acceptable, Western street culture was growing in popularity.

"According to tourist administrations, they say when in Beijing you must eat roast duck, otherwise, they say, you'll regret it." Thus spoke my father-in-law, before adding wryly "and if you do eat duck you'll also regret it."

His tongue-in-cheek comment had many nuances, but one interpretation was that Beijing duck, though delicious, was pure fat. Having tasted the high culinary life, how could we possible keep up our good life standards? By eating a 'healthy' meal, at the newly-opened, and world's largest McDonalds, at the intersection of Wangfujing Street and Chang'an Avenue. The Chinese, I discovered, my in-laws included, had no trouble eating Big Macs.

We were all up in the early hours so that we could make it on time for the contemporary edition of the grand ceremony, the dawn raising of the national flag. As we approached the edge of Tian'anmen Square, just as the sky started to lighten in the northeast sky, the street lights went out, leaving us in the semi darkness. My senses were sharpened. Outlines struggled to emerge from the midsummer night's haze. I heard a tune — its musical-box-like pitch and chimes not loud but just about identifiable above our shuffles and breathing and the occasional chirping of cicadas. Faint, yet half-recognisable. Yes! It was *The East is Red* drifting across the rooftops of the sleeping city, all the way from Beijing Railway Station, or was it the Xidan Telecommunications Building? Wherever it came from, it was 4.30 a.m.. We still had fifteen minutes or so before the ceremony.

An historic, heavy and humbling panorama was emerging. The curved eaves of the Gate of Heavenly Peace at the northern edge of Tian'anmen Square were silouetted ahead. Nobody spoke a word, for it, like the imperial palace to its immediate north, had joined the ranks of the forbidden. Across the avenue and its empty sea of flagstones, neo-classical columns of granite stood like cliffs at the front of the Great Hall of the People, where the fate of so many was decided by so few. Deep and alone at the far end of the Square, like a blocky island levitating above still grey water loomed the mausoleum of Mao Zedong. As I surveyed this dim and silent stage a slew of archive images flashed through my mind before my thoughts were distracted by a metronomic, piston-like sound — pounding and puffing — which was getting closer, growing louder. A glance behind revealed the approach of a cloud-like phalanx of men, soldiers in white singlets and army-green drill shorts that breezed past us on 'its' dawn run. I say 'its' because they were all the same height and weight, and had the same haircuts, the same cadence, footfall, the same gait and rhythm, like one long engine, drilled to perfection.

Swallows were darting, diving and twittering above the gate and around the Chairman's face. 'Yanjing', meaning

WILD WALL-THE FOUNDATION YEARS

'The City of Swallows' came to mind, for that was the name of the first capital here, dating back a thousand years to the Liao Dynasty. Then, the birds were was drowned out by the echoing, amplified sound of machine-like smacks of soles on stone, signalling the approach of the flag-raising sentry. Out of the tunnel which pierces the centre of the gate they emerged, under the portrait of Mao, marching immediately in front of us, across the bridge spanning the Golden Stream to the edge of Chang'an Avenue. A few buses gave way; cyclists freewheeled, dismounted, for it wasn't advisable to cycle across the path of the Sentry of the Motherland. As *The March of the Volunteers* played loudly across the Square to the raising of the flag, we looked at the closest loudspeakers. Forty-three years before, in 1949, a quarter of a million cheered. Today there were no more than a hundred.

Sixty-eight years old now, Wu Wanchun was a twenty-six-year-old physics student back then. In late September 1949, he and other students in his department were given an unusual 'lab work' task: to overhaul a US-made public-address system, which consisted of nine loudspeakers. They completed the job in an afternoon, nicknaming it the 'nine-headed bird' — and thought no more of it. The city was buzzing with talk of a forthcoming grand ceremony to be staged in front of Tian'anmen. Wu Wanchun took a rickshaw there and found the Square, which was much smaller in those days, already packed.

"I was so far away that I couldn't see who was on the balcony (Mao, Zhou Enlai and others), but then as soon as the first person spoke (it was Zhu De), my ears pricked up. I looked around to see where the sound was coming from—then I saw the 'nine headed bird' that our department had been given to fix!"

He felt a surge of excitement and pride, but then he was overcome with a terrible thought. "I just hoped that the speaker system kept on working and didn't go wrong," he said.

Mao spoke next. His most famous line 'The Chinese People have stood up!' came over loud and clear. The People's Republic of China came into being.

43

THOUGHTS ABOUT CHAIRMAN MAO

BACK ON CAMPUS in Xi'an, a new academic year was starting. Students from all over China were arriving, carrying quilts and army great coats, preparing to embark on or continue with their four-year-long degree courses. Banners of welcome were hung throughout the campus, as well as others to wish resounding success to the forthcoming 14th Communist Party Congress in Beijing.

A summer's travels had left us hard-up, so it came as a great relief when two young men from the university's newly-established adult education department paid us a call telling us of plans to set up evening courses in oral English. With three two-hour classes per week for four months, paying at the handsome rate of 40 yuan (US$4) per hour, the teaching would more than double my basic monthly salary. I replied with an emphatic yes!

The course was advertised and soon attracted a group of about twenty-five students, ambitious graduates in their early-to-mid twenties. As usual at the first class of a course I tried to get to know everyone by name. Although many students already had English names, many were open to improving them, especially to being named by their foreign teacher. One student introduced himself as Winston. "That's a great name, very British," I commented. Then he asked me if I smoked, which I considered a strange turn in the conversation when I was expecting to discuss grander things, like Churchill's speech making. He then surprised me even more by saying it was 'Winston' cigarettes that he liked. This led to other smokers of American Kent and Marlboro cigarettes to introduce themselves. Girls were very enthusiastic about being given names that better suited their maturing personalities and appearances since they had left college. Agnes for one was unhappy with her name. I'll never forget the smile on her face when I suggested Nefertiti.

Another element of the introductions was the rather complex Chinese question, 'Where are you from?' One place was rarely enough, and there were often three. Everyone had an ancestral home (place of roots), a birthplace, and place where they grew up. So the question actually explored whether these were one and the same (rarely), or all different. Mention of places gave me the chance to show-off my geographical and historical knowledge, where I'd been, why I'd gone there, and what I'd seen. My revelations drew comments like 'You've been to more places than even we Chinese' and 'You know more Chinese history than we do', and of course 'You're an old China Hand'. One such place name dialogue with a chirpy young teacher, Helen, originally from Chengdu, prompted a comment from me about the large Mao statue there. I'd heard that it was cleaned annually, so asked her if she knew if that was the case because I thought it would make for an interesting photograph. "I don't know, but I can ask my friend about it," was her answer.

At the next class, Helen told me that her friend Peng had responded, naming a date, just before National Day, and inviting me to go there—and he would arrange for me to climb the scaffolding with the workers to take good photographs. It provided a chance beyond my wildest hope, so I asked her how she'd done it. "*Guanxi*," she replied (connections).

This unbelievable opportunity now made it imperative for

me to visit Chengdu, for two reasons. I'd seen a *China Daily* brief reporting that an 'ordinary citizen' named Wang Anting had collected more than 20,000 Mao badges. Peng found him, and his 'museum' was our first destination in Chengdu.

Wufu Jie was a grey street with low-rise buildings until we saw its splash of red, at number 23. Wang Anting told me that he'd wanted to call his home 'Museum of the Cultural Revolution', but the authorities wouldn't let him. "They were embarrassed," he said, "accusing me of holding an exhibition with the nation's dirty underwear."

His home was a mere twenty square metres in area, but it reeked of revolution with red badges everywhere: in home-made cases, pinned on to sheets, glued on walls, suspended from the ceiling, stuffed into gunny sacks, and filling water butts. "I have more than 20,000, but only 10,039 different ones," he said, "enough to wear a different badge every day."

Ranging in size from one centimetre to a plate-like thirty-eight cm, they came in porcelain and plastic, but mainly in alloy that would normally have been used in the aviation industry. This alternative use was authorised by Lin Biao who, pre-liberation, was Mao's top marshal and in 1966 became his chosen successor and 'close comrade in arms'. I'd first learned of him via Mao stamps, outside the main Xi'an Post Office. There was one stamp issue in May 1967, called 'Long Live Chairman Mao', that featured two stamps showing Mao and Lin Biao side by side. When I pointed out to the dealer that those stamps were damaged, he replied, "That's correct. To be damaged is correct." The defacing of Lin Biao was done post-1973 during the 'Criticise Lin Biao and Confucius Campaign'. Lin had tried to assassinate Mao in 1971 by blowing up his train, but the plot was foiled. Lin escaped, fleeing towards the Soviet Union, but Chinese fighters shot his plane down over Mongolia. (The crash site is now a tourist attraction, appealing solely to dedicated Chinese tourists!). Why Lin tried to kill Mao remains a mystery. Was he impatient to succeed him? Did he regard Mao as a monster running wild, or as a senile old man? He knew that Mao was losing control to his scheming wife Jiang Qing and her gang accomplices.

I felt mixed emotions seeing Wang Anting's badge collection. I have always admired eccentricity, but felt immense sadness for the hundreds of millions of people who'd pinned their badges on, every day for years, out of loyalty and out of fear. Each one of them had been used, abused, misled, let down. After Mao died they took their badges off, not knowing quite what to do with them. Most remained respectful to their cruel patriarch. They could not bring themselves to throw their badges away, so they just hid them, out of sight and out of mind. Sixteen years on, people had no qualms about distancing themselves from the haunting reminder of the national tragedy, selling their badges to the junk man for scrap value, who then sells them on to Wang Anting for 2 yuan per *jin* (US$ 25 cents) per half kilo.

We took a break for lunch, but not from revolution. Sichuan arguably boasts China's best food and we headed to Chengdu's most famous restaurant, the birthplace of *mapo doufu*, or 'pockmarked old woman's (face) bean curd' — which tastes much better that it translates. If you want to experience one dish — a small rice-bowl-sized serving is standard — that encapsulates the charisma of Chinese cuisine, it's *mapo doufu*. The offering is colourful, piquantly fragrant, intensely fiery and numbingly peppery, both a treat and a terror for the tongue and tastebuds. A second mouthful triggers the fire alarm in your brain, which then messages your sprinkler system — salivary glands — telling them to extinguish the fire. Mao is said to have made fun of the German Comintern advisor Otto Braun for the weakness of his throat and guts in tolerating fiery food, saying that a person's revolutionary spirit could be judged by their liking of hot and spicy food. It was, therefore, the perfect meal to have prior to my face-to-face meeting with Mao himself.

Mao had been gazing down on the people of Chengdu for 25 years. He'd been covered in scaffolding that many times, for his annual baths. He'd become so much a part of the scenery that he hardly drew a passing glance from locals. Few looked up to him anymore, until now. Seeing a foreigner donning a hard hat and harness though was enough to start heads turning.

I'd been briefed on the vital statistics of Chengdu's Mao and the height of the plinth and steps on which it stands—12.26 and 7.1 and 8.1—outside the quarry where the statute was made in Baoxing. A sculptor there told me that these measurements corresponded to his date of birth, and the dates when the Party and the army were founded.

A quick sum made me realise that the real climb up, by ladder and scaffolding, would be about 20 metres. The first stage, from the top of the steps to the top of the plinth, where Mao's feet are planted, was by ladder. That was the easy part. I joked with the cleaning team, a bunch of five young men, about the size of his feet. I reckoned he was about an 80, compared to my 14. Finally, I'd met someone in China with feet bigger than me. In the shadow of his overhanging overcoat I felt like an ant about to be crushed by a dinosaur. Then, as we started to clamber up the scaffolding, I had a strange sense of *deja vu*. The lines of my favourite Chinese poem, *On Climbing the Big Wild Goose Pagoda in Chang'an*, came to mind. The pagoda was a regular sight for me in Xi'an, and I loved to climb it while reciting Du Fu (712-770). As I mouthed the poem, I swapped two of his original words, pagoda and Buddha, for new ones, statue and Mao, which created some food for thought:

WILLIAM LINDESAY

At the top of the statue one feels
To have truly entered the sky
Wind drums incessantly,
I'm not one free of care
Here my worry increases
This statue
Representing the power of Mao
Makes one wish to understand
And penetrate the depths of his powers.

Twenty-five metres above the ground I was face to face with Chairman Mao Zedong, truly looking him in the eye.

From his birthplace Shaoshan, in 1893, I'd traced the rise of a man. But by the time this statue was erected in 1968 Mao wasn't the man he used to be. This colossus showed his heightened status. I'd seen mega-statues elsewhere in China, of giant Buddhas, at Datong, and in Leshan. Presented out of proportion, pedestaled like this, put Mao up there, somewhere, alongside the likes of Egyptian pharaohs, god kings. They commissioned colossal images of themselves, in their quests for eternity. Being large meant being remembered — or despised — forever.

Seeing Mao now on high, made me, in Du Fu's words, 'wish to understand ... to penetrate the depths of his powers'. This point of view of his put the scale of the scam, his deification, his so-called Cultural Revolution, into perspective as I looked down along an avenue filled with the ant-like masses. How incredulous, I thought, that in the mid-late 20th century, just 25 years ago, so many people were hoodwinked by one man and his ideology. How could the Chinese, seven hundred million of them, a people with a pedigree of five thousand years of civilisation, who for countless generations had nurtured so much culture, crafted philosophical and literary wisdom, who had kept so many traditions, practiced filial piety, benevolence and promoted the love of knowledge, be misled, and remain benighted, for so long, for ten years? How could they fobbed off by the issue a shiny new Mao badge every few weeks? How could learning be confined to parroting passages from little red books? How could they endure struggle sessions, at meals times, three times a day, around half-empty tables, with pangs of hunger, sitting beneath posters of their plump savior, their great teacher and great this, that and the other? But still, this mob adulation went on for a decade. They went out, smashing the 'four olds', criticizing teachers (even Confucius, who died in 479 BC), beating and killing anyone landlord related, 'capitalist roaders' and 'counter revolutionaries'. At the same time, others celebrated the beauty of it all; groups of cute young women performed loyalty dances; masses paraded with portable statues of Mao and oversized portraits of Stalin, and happily pulled floats laden with oversized harvest produce made of papier-mâche, with the venerated (but unobtainable) mango placed aloft. Up until now on my biographical journey I had nurtured some respect for Mao's leadership and military acumen, but here above Chengdu the absurdity of the Cultural Revolution truly hit me. I was well into the 'bad 30%' that Deng Xiaoping had talked about in his assessment of Mao's life. With 700 million participants the Cultural Revolution was the largest mass display of nonsense in history.

Not even the tallest mango juice could stop the old man from withering. In his seventies, Mao found himself facing the problem of getting old, looking podgy and being seen as physically and mentally unfit to rule. The age-old problem was nothing new to the experienced Egyptian pharaohs — and they had a solution to it. They took part in what were tantamount to fitness tests, by participating in 'festivals of revival' called Heb-Sed, traditionally convened thirty years into their reigns. The results of course were always emphatic passes. A pharaoh demonstrated his vigour by completing a long run at a respectable speed. (Archaeologists have found a purpose-built 'revival of youthful vigour' courtyard beside King Zoser's pyramid).

It's inconceivable that Mao's advisors learned anything from the ancient Egyptian practices. However, his spin-doctor, Lin Biao, who we can regard as the 'Minister of the Mao Cult', did conceive a propaganda stunt in July 1966 that was remarkably similar: at the age of 73 (31 years after taking control of the Party) Mao went marathon swimming in the Yangtze River at Wuhan, reportedly covering a distance of twelve km. According to my sister-in-law's 'Cultural Revolution' diary, this achievement left a strong impression. She wrote:

> *'Swimming is a sport that pits you against nature. However, I am always in a swimming pool. A thousand-mile horse can't be trained in a small courtyard, and ten thousand year old trees cannot be cultivated in small pots. So, you cannot develop your fighting ability in a calm pool. After Chairman Mao's swim he called upon us to temper our minds and bodies in wild rivers and the open seas. We can only be distinguished as good or bad in those waters. I am eager to rush into big rivers and seas and go forward facing the waves, exercising my body and reddening my heart's loyalty to Chairman Mao. Armed with Mao Zedong Thought, the revolutionary weapon, the huge waves are symphonic music on a voyage.'*

Mao's Wuhan swim was inspirational, showing him as no ordinary old man, bathing to ease stiff joints, but a superhuman, capable of swimming a long distance, and leaving hundreds trailing in his wake.

WILD WALL–THE FOUNDATION YEARS

In reality, Mao's body fat helped him float like a cork, while a strong current took him with the flow. Much skinnier people needed to work hard to swim and stay afloat, and at the same time grapple with floating gantries that displayed larger-than-life images of the 'Great Helmsman'.

And so, the Cultural Revolution began. It lasted ten years, and even now that it is long over, it never ends. The nightmare continues to haunt, to be a headache, to persist as a national embarrassment.

First of all, a thought about its name: the Great Cultural Revolution. Didn't anyone ever criticise that choice of titles? I've always regarded it a complete misnomer. During the Industrial Revolution, industry proliferated. Similarly, during the Scientific Revolution and the Digital Revolution it was these fields of endeavour that progressed. But during the Cultural Revolution, culture was decimated. Rule number one in trying to understand the Cultural Revolution begins by realising that its very name makes no sense. So what on earth was it all about?

First, the prelude. By 1962 Mao had lost face. He had shown himself to be unwilling to govern pragmatically, and had failed hopelessly to develop China's poor agrarian economy. In desperation he launched the Great Leap Forward, which unfolded as a great economic and human disaster. He had conceived the scheme in 1958. Its aim was to accelerate all sectors of the economy, in double-quick time. But without expertise, economic foundations or a capable workforce the campaign produced a procession of hideous production drives, a barrage of empty slogans and widespread publication of fudged figures to meet targets. According to reports, aims to produce more grain were 'gloriously over-fulfilled'. In reality, harvests failed, causing mass starvation, poverty and cannibalism. Qi was born on the eve of the disaster, in 1957. There were acute food shortages, so her parents put her in the care of relatives, deep in the countryside of Anhui Province, where they grew their own food. After four years of the nation pretending that all was well, the only way Mao could hold on to his power amidst hardships, suffering and whispered criticism was to unleash a new diversionary policy, of chaos, by naming his critics and blaming the past — the Cultural Revolution. Mao was good at fighting and war, not good at governing in peace time.

Mao began by purging the Communist Party of revisionists. He exploited the energy of gullible youth as his battering rams, authorising them to launch class warfare against everyone, including their parents and teachers and leaders—to ferret-out the so-called pretenders. The safest activities at the time were to study 'Mao Zedong Thought' and show loyalty to him by wearing a badge. Teenagers went wild with revolutionary enthusiasm, which would soon become violent and murderous. Schools were closed. Clever students were sent down to the countryside to do manual work, poor students were admitted to 'university' without the need to sit an entrance examination. Nowadays, China's education system is a world beater, receiving top marks. Fear induced by so-called tiger mothers is one of the reasons, because they harangue or even beat their children if they score under 90%. During the Cultural Revolution, things were quite the opposite. One student, Zhang Tiesheng, famously scored zero by refusing to write a single character, because writing anything that made conventional sense would expose him as a good for nothing who'd buried his head in useless books, instead of being a real asset to the country who had increased national production.

Three months after Mao's swim, in the autumn of 1966, Wu Xiaoping boarded a train from Xi'an to Beijing with thousands of other teenagers, to see the 'Great Helmsman' in the flesh.

WILD WALL-THE FOUNDATION YEARS

A quarter of a century later in 1992, she chuckled at my questioning, giving the distinct impression that she regarded her Cultural Revolution activities as a bit of a joke, certainly an embarrassment. Her reaction was similar to age 70+ Westerners who squirm when they see photographs of themselves from the 1960s, taken during their hippy days wearing long hair and flowery shirts. She could laugh at photographs of red guards carrying statues of Mao, carrying billboard-sized embroideries of his portrait, because she had a clear conscience.

"I didn't do anything that bad, I didn't even spit on anyone, let alone vilify or kick them, beat or smash any of the 'four olds'. Generally speaking, the worst students made the 'best' red guards, so I was a 'bad' one," Xiaoping said laughing. "But I loved Chairman Mao dearly, and he gave us the opportunity to taste revolution, although I and the whole country paid for it."

Indeed, after her trip to Beijing 'the honeymoon' was definitely over.

Later in the autumn term, Xiaoping, Qi and I travelled into the countryside, to a solitary farm in a valley just south of the Shaanxi-Sichuan provincial boundary. Its mud-walled rooms were like many I'd slept and eaten in on my Great Wall and Long March journeys, but with one major difference. In the standard frame of treasured images was a family that I recognised: the Wu family. This is where Xiaoping stayed for four years under a directive from Chairman Mao that called upon intellectual youth to work as farm labourers with poor peasants. That was the personal price she paid, cheap by comparison to most others. It was her taste of revolution, her misfortune for being born into an intellectual family. Xiaoping's stay in Fengxian ended in 1971. Her peasant-re-education qualified her to attend a Worker-Peasant-Soldier 'university' in Baoji to study farm machinery from 1973-1975, 'majoring' in 'the tractor'. As a little girl she wanted to be a doctor.

Qi was the lucky one among her sisters, the youngest, for by dint of her age she narrowly avoided a dark red childhood. In 1977, when national university entrance examinations were reintroduced, she competed with students who'd missed the opportunity of taking the exam for the last ten years. Despite the intense competition she passed, winning a place in the esteemed 'class of '77' to study history at Xi'an's Northwest University.

"As one of the very youngest students, I was immature. Everyone was better than me at everything, but I was determined to be the best at something—so I chose English and studied it hard, by myself."

I'm so glad that she did.

44

Centennial Timing

Since the '14th Big' Chinese Communist Party Congress ('*shisida*'), had convened just weeks before in October 1992, all of China, from the media to the masses, was buzzing with talk of doing business, in observance of the meeting's defining slogan: to accelerate the implementation of a 'Socialist Market Economy'. What had been happening for years, but in a rather covert and cautious way — making individual wealth — was now officially approved and encouraged. Preferential policies to expand and accelerate it were being promulgated.

In response to the Tian'anmen Square protests of 1989, the government answered student demands for democracy with a violent clearance of the space, a loud 'no' that reverberated across China and around the world. In the aftermath, ringleaders were hunted, political scapegoats were sought, and officials, including Party chief Zhao Ziyang arrested. University students were branded culprits of the upheaval. To prevent any reoccurrence of dissent a course of political indoctrination was prescribed for all existing and future university students.

In September 1991 my campus athletics track became a military training arena. Uniformed and regimented, the 18-year-old freshers were drilled 12/7, marching, flag bearing and chanting patriotic slogans. Their parade practice was interspersed with skill and study sessions, such as marksmanship (with unloaded rifles) and 'correct political thinking', all conducted in the field-events area inside the track. As I ran my laps I watched them training, day after day for 28 days. Most of my students admitted to dreading this induction marathon prior to their arrival on campus, for most of them, being only-children, were somewhat mollycoddled by their families. Few of them were sporty. This became blatantly clear on annual sports days when I, the greying 'middle aged' teacher, romped across the finishing lines to win the 5,000 metres track event and the winter 5 K road race, leaving scores of students in my wake.

Apparently, the officers and squaddies assigned by local garrisons to run the student boot camps ended up making them slipper camps, primarily because everyone had to pass. They were pretty easygoing and lenient on the physical side of things. The training month concluded just before National Day on October 1st, culminating with a 'Long March' of 30 kilometres on roads encircling Xi'an, followed by a graduation ceremony, a passing out parade, on the track watched over by the local top brass and teaching staff seated in the stand.

My students said that their experiences had been 'quite fun' and 'significant'. Now, in 1992, three years after having their political inductions, doses of bitter medicine for most of them, the same students were set to receive a bonus graduation gift, an unexpected sweetener—unprecedented private business freedoms and official encouragement from the CCP for all individuals to make money.

Students couldn't wait to graduate, and were not afraid to display their head starts. They were proud of their new entrepreneurial status, some willing to show it off, at least by hanging a pager on their belt. This device was the beginners' alternative to the as-yet unaffordable *dageda,* or mobile phone. It

WILD WALL–THE FOUNDATION YEARS

bleeped loudly, and indicated the phone number of the caller. The pager-owner then proceeded to a nearby public-use telephone – almost all shops and stalls had one – to return the call. These businesses were one- or two-man operations with no premises, dubbed 'briefcase companies' (*pibao gongsi*) with only a service or a few items to sell. Face and connections were everything. One hour business-card design and printing services sprouted on every corner. Teaching staff set up side businesses of their own. Mr. Wang, our *waiban* director, was the boldest entrepreneur that I knew. He opened a restaurant. China's start-up era was dawning.

I came home after class one evening to find Qi crying: her problem was quite the opposite to mine. She didn't have enough to do, so I suggested that she could help by assisting in acting-out dialogues at the front of classes with me. These demonstrations worked very well, and Qi soon made a new circle of friends from among the female students in the classes. Not long afterwards, we decided to hold by-invitation only 'English corners' in our tiny apartment for the best of our student friends. Among these were Sam and Joy, Nora, Rebecca, Jane, Simon, Steven, and Ben – and also Helen, who had arranged my ascent of the Mao statue in Chengdu.

Speaking one evening about my book, I mentioned that it was progressing well into the editorial phase, with little more than a year to go before scheduled publication in November 1993. I was beginning to think about which illustrations and maps to include, in addition to my own colour photographs. I'd decided against using any archive photographs, primarily because of their grey and blurry quality. Helen made an interesting suggestion that her husband, Zhang Da, a fashion-design teacher, could help me if I needed any drawings.

I hadn't thought of drawings because I was unable to draw, except maps. Qi and I visited Helen and Zhang Da in their apartment (which made our guesthouse suite seem large) in the campus of the neighbouring institute. We developed an instant rapport with Zhang Da. He was softly spoken, with a shock of thick, longish hair, wore self-designed *avant garde* clothing, was a rock-music fan, and appeared totally unconventional—a really cool guy! With Cui Jian's album, *Rock and Roll on the New Long March* playing in the background while we drank Nescafé—always a treat and never refused in those days—I summarised the highlights of my journey.

The following weekend, Zhang Da presented a 'Route of Badges' map that featured excellent pencil drawings, with principal place names on my biographical journey marked, and his title calligraphy and name-chop. This map is now framed as a journey-treasure and hangs in the study where I write. Its design appealed instantly, so we discussed how we could use more artwork in the book. I'd been toying with the idea of placing quotations beside chapter titles, but was conscious that such inclusions had become too common in recent publications. Also, I was becoming a little weary of Mao's red wisdom. We came up with the fresh idea of fronting each chapter with a small drawing. I envisaged that each drawing might be reproduced at the size of a name card. Thus, with eighteen or so possible chapters, plus a prologue, foreword and chronology, I would require more than twenty illustrations.

To convince Margaret Body to agree to the idea, I felt it necessary to provide some persuasive examples. Qi and I shuttled back and forth to talk to Zhang Da, describing how I envisaged some of the most dramatic Long March events never captured by photographers might have appeared—such as the Red Army's crossing of the Golden Sands River, the Great Snowy Mountains and the grasslands. Working with charcoal, his resulting sketches of the ferry and marsh crossings were stunning, and I confidently faxed them to Hodders in London. Margaret agreed that, even

WILD WALL-THE FOUNDATION YEARS

on a grainy fax, the artwork was excellent and would add a stylish 'archive' dimension to the book. However, she explained the difficulty of satisfactorily reproducing charcoal originals on the type of paper used for printing text — any shading was lost. Instead, she advocated the use of an ink pen to produce line drawings. Zhang Da made the change, and the results were still outstanding, and to our relief were accepted.

Meanwhile, my manuscript editor, David Blomfield, had been doing an excellent job getting my chapters into shape. Margaret was a specialist adventure-book editor. She'd handled *Alone on the Great Wall* quite comfortably, but decided to delegate the editing of *Marching* because it had evolved into a different genre — history and journalism as well as adventure. David had conceived and spearheaded condensed book sales at *Readers Digest*, and he proved to be an excellent choice, being a brilliantly brutal editor to introduce brevity, and he was a history specialist.

We were into the final stages of the book's production, a time of both relief and regret. Margaret asked me for a succinct book description and author's biography — those bits that go on the dust-jacket flaps — which were also urgently needed for Hodder's Autumn 1993 sales catalogue. But when I received their draft jacket design my heart sank. I was bitterly disappointed. It didn't appeal at all. I disliked the cover picture of myself, crossing Luding Bridge, and hated their choice of red trim, the classic stereotypical colour of all books on the Chinese revolution.

Desperate to present an alternative cover idea I rushed over to see Zhang Da. We worked for a whole day and produced a totally new design concept — photographs, colour, font and feel — that he sketched in ink and I faxed to Hodders. I was preparing to fight in defence of my views but was pleasantly surprised to receive a return fax saying that they liked our draft design a lot. We were so delighted that Qi and I organised an impromptu dinner party as our home students class that week, an opportunity to toast Zhang Da's new role as a book designer.

Last minute invitations were quite the norm in the university. On Christmas Eve we received one from students who were organising a party 'in my honour', starting at six o'clock (in the evening!). To prevent us from dodging the obligation, two students called for us and accompanied us to the venue, the campus gymnasium. It was a large, cold, dimly lit building. About 150 students were sitting along each side, all clad in heavy coats and headgear. The central area for the 'disco party' was as yet empty, apart from slow-moving strobe lights emitting fruit-drop coloured beams that gyrated across the boards to the distorted sound of 'Boney M's' *By the Rivers of Babylon*.

"Good evening. Now the special party for Teacher William and Mrs. Lindesay is beginning," said the MC. Nothing happened next, except for the students clapping.

"Let's invite Teacher William to give us an interesting performance."

At the end of the applause, and after a few seconds of deadly silence, I did my bit. I gave a ten-minute speech about Christmas in Britain.

"Next, let's invite anyone to give a wonderful performance."

After an embarrassing silence of twenty seconds or so, a brave young man stepped forward to save the evening. "My performance is called 'Mechanical agriculture in America's Midwest,'" he announced.

For fifteen minutes, the student praised the scientific level of American farming and its economic benefits in a speech sprinkled with rising production figures. What an extraordinary Christmas gathering!

Two days later came December 26th, the 99th anniversary of Mao's birth. The countdown to the centenary had begun, now just one year away. I'd intentionally left one important part of my journey until this late, in 1993. The concluding act of my pilgrimage was to visit the final stop on his journey, his death in 1976 and his subsequent legacy. Obviously, this would entail a walk through his mausoleum, and as the time approached, I continued to search — so far in vain — for a suitable person to accompany me. I was looking for someone special, a witness to the event in one way or another.

Two traditions, one Chinese and one Western, consumed New Year's Eve. Qi and I went to the South Gate in Xi'an's City Wall where scores of calendar sellers hung their 1993 design offerings. In those days, they were huge publications — in both popularity and size — about twice the size of a broadsheet newspaper. Just as a newspaper was once a daily standard in every household, so was a 'big poster calendar' to adorn the walls of every Chinese home and office from the mid-1980s to the late-1990s. The contrasting assortment offered was a photographer's dream, that words could not describe. As Qi made our choice, I photographed them, editions dedicated to Chairman Mao, Zhou Enlai, and Zhu De, heroic individuals hung beside others depicting luxury foreign cars, Harley Davidson motorbikes, tropical beaches, beauties in bikinis, and dream mansions. That same afternoon, I went for my last run of the year down on the campus track with Xiao Ning, a student who'd become a regular training partner. After thirty minutes of warm up I managed 6 x 400 metre repetitions, all of them sub-60 seconds. Thus, 1992 became the second successive year that I'd run every day. My New Year's resolution for 1993, a very Western convention at the time, was to keep running without missing a day, offering no excuses, to make it a hat trick. It promised to be a big year, but we didn't know where our near future would lie beyond that, after the book, post-1994, whether in Xi'an or elsewhere.

45

FAMILY PLANNING

ONE DAY in March 1993 I returned home from class and, completely out of the blue, Qi announced, "I want to have a baby."

We hadn't talked about starting a family for several years. It was something we planned to do 'when we can afford it'. We certainly didn't have sufficient income from teaching, and wouldn't become well-off in the near future—unless *Marching with Mao* became a bestseller. We were going back to Britain for the book's publication anyway, and planned to stay there a short while before returning. I'd be receiving a handy £2,500 on arrival in London, the second half of my advance from Hodders, and our airfares were being covered by the university, a perk of our two and a half years' service. But, most significantly, if we could time the birth of our baby to coincide with our stay in Britain, Qi would be fulfilling a dream and I keeping a promise. Qi had mentioned a baby in 1989, while in Arrowe Park Hospital on the Wirral. She'd imported a stomach ulcer from China in 1988 and needed to have it investigated. I was at her bedside in the ward when she came out of the anaesthetic. I vividly recalled her opening her eyes, smiling and mumbling "This hospital so beautiful ... I want to have my baby here."

"Yes dear, I promise you, we'll do it!" was my bold reply.

Now was the time to do it: Qi's idea made perfect sense. If we were fortunate, we could have a productive winter in Britain and return to China in the spring with a new baby and a new book.

Qi was also busy language-training two of our students, Helen and Nora, who were working part-time as waitresses in Mr. Wang's newly-opened restaurant, '*Shiwexian*'. By employing Debbie's home-cooking skills, he was offering a Western café menu alongside a Chinese one, much to the delight of the local foreign teacher community. To compensate Qi for her efforts, we were given free lunches every day of the week, quite a treat to look forward to at the end of a morning of teaching. *Shiweixian* took just three minutes to reach by bike. There I was waited on hand and foot, being served chicken fajitas and French fries, with chocolate-covered coconut macaroons and coffee for dessert.

Before long, Qi raised her eyebrows, grinned and said, "No riding the red horse yet," suspecting that she might already be pregnant. We waited a few days more before visiting a tiny women's clinic. I waited outside, nervously pacing back and forth on the street. Ten minutes later Qi came out beaming. We would be having a baby in January 1994!

With our trip to England all organised, I began to think about how I would make a living in 1994. I'd seen advertisements in *China Daily*, reposted from time to time, recruiting foreign experts to work as copy editors for the newspaper in Beijing. Their basic requirements were a university degree and a minimum twelve months' experience in journalism, which I didn't have. However, I was the author of two books published by a reputable London publishing house. I was becoming physically tired of teaching; my voice was exhausted by having to talk so loudly for so long. With my extra classes scheduled over six days each week, I was talking for around four hours a day. I not only felt that I needed a change, and a move, but I desperately wanted to return to the Great Wall. If we lived in Beijing, I mused, I'd have the classic sections of the Wall on our front doorstep.

I sent my CV and a covering letter to Mr. Wang Yanping, head of the *waiban* at *China Daily*. He telephoned me, asking me to travel to Beijing to take an examination. At the time, that was easier said than done; return rail tickets to Beijing were the hardest to obtain. They were generally only available on the black market at almost double the price. I told Mr. Wang that the earliest time that I could possibly visit Beijing would be the summer — when I had planned to visit Mao's mausoleum. Then he took me completely by surprise, saying "we can post the examination to you."

A large package from *China Daily* duly arrived. Inside was a sealed envelope with the examination instructions that read: 'Here is a typical morning's work of 2.5 hours for an experienced foreign expert at *China Daily*. Use an HB pencil to make editorial corrections and amendments on the papers inside. When you have finished editing, please write the time spent working on the envelope and post all materials back to *China Daily*'.

Remembering the golden rule of examinations, I first looked over all the papers so that I could allocate my time most efficiently. There was a main feature, comprising about five A4 pages. The article was about an 'ordinary worker' at an iron and steel works in Baotou who had an eccentric interest: collecting matchbox covers. There were also a few medium-length news reports to edit. One was about a Chinese leader meeting a visiting foreign head of state, another on the rosiness of bilateral relations between China and somewhere, and another on increasingly favourable national economic figures, all of it classic *China Daily* front-page news. Then there were about twenty briefs, including some sports reports and general news items.

I looked at the clock, made a determined start, and ground to an immediate standstill. The feature had no structure, was full of grammatical mistakes and typographical errors. After an hour, I began to develop an initial understanding of the content. Then I re-wrote it. In all, I spent an exhausting six hours editing. I bundled everything back in the envelope, wrote '2.5 hours plus a little bit extra' on the flap and posted it back to Beijing, certain that I wouldn't be offered the job.

A few days later, Mr. Wang telephoned to inform me that *China Daily* would like to invite me to work as a foreign expert, on three months' probation for RMB 2,500 yuan per month, increasing to 3,500 for the remainder of the year-long contract. In addition, I would receive housing benefits, namely a three-roomed apartment, one month's fully paid leave and return air fares to the UK for the whole family. We were delighted. Everything was now in place for us to return to China with a new baby and new book to start a new job. I would have a change of occupation, and a different life in a comfortable home.

46

EIGHTY-THREE, FORTY-ONE

IN THE SUMMER of 1949, Mao was told enigmatically that 83 and 41 would prove to be the most important numbers in his life. Soon afterwards, he named his personal guard the '8341 detachment', but nobody really knew the significance of the numbers—until he died. Only then did his followers realise that he had lived for 83 years, and led the Communist Party for 41 years. Meanwhile, plans were being made to ensure that Mao would live on.

I'd decided that the best way to add personality to the final, as yet unwritten chapter, of my book was to ask a handful of people to recall their memories of the day that Mao died: September 9th, 1976. How did you hear the news? Where were you? How did you feel? These are the questions that I would ask.

However, after I read a short report in the magazine *China Today* about a Dr. Ma Yanlong, that became plan B. The doctor worked at 'Beijing Hospital' and he was the country's leading cosmetic mortician. Whenever a VIPP (very important Party person) died, Dr. Ma was called upon to prepare the body for the 'last viewing' by mourners before the cremation ceremony. When Mao died, his task was quite different. He was required to prepare the Chairman's body for everlasting viewing.

The chance of the doctor agreeing to speak to me, even if I could track him down in 'Beijing Hospital', was surely rather remote. Most city hospitals were differentiated by numbers, and

WILD WALL-THE FOUNDATION YEARS

I suspected that it had been omitted by the reporter to protect the doctor's anonymity. Not necessarily so, according to Qi. She said Beijing Hospital was renowned for treating China's leaders, and was in the city centre, near Chongwenmen. After managing to accomplish what was surely the first foreign ascent of the Mao statue in Chengdu, I tasked myself with a another mission impossible, to try to track-down Dr. Ma and invite him to tell me his story.

Qi and I walked into the hospital building and were directed to an annexe, the mortuary department. There we met a student doctor clad in a white lab coat. "Dr. Ma is resting, he'll be along in a moment," he told us.

After a few minutes, a jovial man entered the room, bowing, clasping his hands prayer-like, and repeating a warm welcome. Qi introduced me and my project. Dr. Ma nodded appreciatively, giving a thumbs up sign to show his approval of my journey through Mao's life. He confessed to Qi that he had never wanted to answer a foreigner's prying, and possibly disrespectful, questions on such a solemn subject. Luckily, he viewed me as a special case. Presenting me with his name card, he invited us to his home that evening, saying: "If Mr. William has walked over one thousand kilometres of the Long March then he must respect Chairman Mao very much."

That evening in his home it seemed disrespectful to flick through Dr. Ma's remarkable photograph albums while eating watermelon. But he seemed very down-to-earth about his profession and the public's view of it. "Some people won't shake hands with me despite the fact that I've prepared all the Motherland's leaders," he explained. "They think my job is terrible. It is of course neither easy nor pleasant, as there's always the risk of infection," he admitted.

Dr. Ma had fourteen photograph albums, with his most

treasured one showing Chairman Mao and Premier Zhou Enlai sharing the same page. "Although I've provided services to many powerful people, I've never asked for anything from their relatives, apart from a photograph of their loved ones to keep as records in my albums for study. The most expensive gift he was given was a domestically manufactured Qingdao camera, which he uses to take his photographs.

Dr. Ma passed me his 'process album', full of before-and-after photographs illustrating the procedures of his profession.

"In general, my job is to beautify. The pallid appearance of a deceased person's face bears little resemblance to that person when they're alive."

Firstly, Dr. Ma places the corpse in an appropriate position, lifting the head and posing the chin. He then spreads the legs to facilitate dressing. Antiseptic measures come next, followed by the most difficult and rewarding process, the cosmetics. These are 'actually a combination of make-up and plastic surgery'. His workbox contains scalpels, scissors, gauze and cotton wool, ethyl alcohol, razors, clippers, combs, greasepaint, lipstick and brushes.

"I usually request a good picture of the deceased taken ten to twenty years before," he said. "But when I worked on Chairman Mao, they provided a picture taken in 1972 during his meeting with Nixon."

"The final and most pleasant stage is what I've now become famous for — the flowers and flag formula," said Dr. Ma proudly.

"Lighting is important too, a couple of 500-watt spotlights meet on the dead person's breast ... I did that at first to provide light for television and press photographers, but then realised that the lighting actually made the corpse appear to be breathing."

Dr. Ma told me that he graduated from a one-year army medical school in 1951, doing his first make-up job on a general

WILD WALL-THE FOUNDATION YEARS

"simply by painting his face and draping a flag over his corpse laid out in a pool of flowers."

Initially he disliked his job, but with the advancing age of the leadership he became busier and eventually accepting of his role as providing a service to the Motherland. Then he sought to improve his results by studying plastics, painting, aesthetics and psychology.

Born into a 'reasonably well-off family' and brought up as a Catholic — he had since converted to Buddhism — he was branded a bourgeois reactionary and intellectual, the latter because of the many research hours spent in the mortuary. Ironically, it was during his Cultural Revolution exile at a 'May 7th Cadre School' that his most important assignment occurred.

"I was working in the fields of a commune in Changping County about fifty km north of Beijing when a Red Flag limousine, the state car of China, arrived. I thought it must be from Zhongnanhai (the compound in Beijing where the state leaders live)," recalled Dr. Ma. The bearer of the news was in tears as he told Dr. Ma that he'd been listed as member of a group to prepare Mao's corpse for the state funeral.

Once in Zhongnanhai, Dr. Ma waited in a large house with other medical specialists. "I was shaking and sweating like never before," he recalled. A group of seven, headed by Xu Jinbing, who became director of the mausoleum, performed their task. "Despite Chairman Mao having signed a pledge in 1956 to be cremated in order to set an example to the masses who were consuming too much farmland with burials, we knew from our orders that we were preparing his remains for permanent viewing."

The work took more than one hour. In addition to the group of seven there were more than thirty supporting medical assistants. The entire procedure was watched over by Jiang Qing, Zhang

Qunqiao, Yao Wenyuan and Wang Hongwen (later dubbed the Gang of Four) — but not Hua Guofeng, Mao's anointed successor.

"Were they sobbing?" I asked.

"Someone was ... but I dared not look behind," he replied. Once the work was completed, Mao's wife and her colleagues shook each mortician's hand in turn before the corpse was transferred to the Great Hall of the People to lie in state for thirty days. Dr. Ma stayed by the body, on hand for two days, in case any finishing touches were required.

The funeral rally was held in Tian'anmen Square at 3.00 p.m. on September 18th. An estimated 250,000 mourners, clad in white shirts and wearing black armbands, faced north towards the gate where Mao had stood in 1949. A three-minute silence began. China had surely never been so still. Dr. Ma listened to Hua Guofeng's eulogy on the radio at his commune, where he was back in the fields, farming again. Qi attended a memorial rally on Xi'an's East Street. It was raining heavily, but neither umbrellas nor raincoats were permitted. Her mother had hastily made alterations to rain capes for the family to wear under their white shirts.

One calendar year after Mao's death, his corpse went on public display. It was enclosed in a crystal coffin housed in a huge 'memorial hall' sited on the central axis of Tian'anmen Square. We joined the long queue to visit the mausoleum with Dr. Ma. "To many people, the respect and fulfilment they receive at death is what they've strived for all their lives ... it's my pleasure to help them realise their last dreams."

47

Foreword and Forward

THE UNIVERSITY KINDLY gave me a short-term contract until mid-November, which meant that we could stay in Xi'an over the hot summer. The final chapter of *Marching with Mao* was soon completed where the rest of it had been written, on campus. Xiaoping typed it for me, and I faxed it to Hodders so that they had everything necessary for producing the page proofs. Then Margaret Body contacted me to ask, "Do you have any thoughts on who might write a foreword?"

Two names came to mind. One was Ji Chaozhu, the Chinese Ambassador in London who in 1988 had welcomed me back from the Great Wall with a press reception. As a former interpreter for Zhou Enlai, Mao Zedong and Deng Xiaoping in succession, he seemed the perfect choice, if I was able to contact him. Another possibility was Sir Edward Heath. I hadn't met him personally, but he was the only British Prime Minister who had ever met Chairman Mao, in Beijing in May 1974.

It transpired that Ji Chaozhu had left London, retiring to Beijing. Lacking any foreign ministry connections, we decided that he was too difficult to contact. Turning to the tracing of Sir Edward, my brother Nick suggested that our former Wallasey MP, Baroness Chalker, a fellow Conservative now sitting in the House of Lords, would be a suitable go-between to ask if 'Ted' would agree. She did contact him, and he replied that he would be willing to look at the book. Margaret was delighted and faxed, "We can hardly send Sir Edward a ream of printed pages, can we? We're producing a proper bound book proof." And so they did. Sir Edward wrote this:

> 'I first visited China in 1974. The warmth of the welcome that I received from the Chinese people, on this and many subsequent occasions, made a powerful and lasting impression on me.
>
> During my visit in '74 and again in '76, I had long discussions with Chairman Mao Zedong. I was the first and only British Prime Minister ever to do so. I found in him many of the qualities I had seen in Churchill, Adenauer, de Gaulle and Tito. They all possessed the ability to go to the heart of the matter, to sort out the important from the insignificant, and to see their policies through to the end.
>
> I remember asking Mao what motivated the Chinese people today. "Ah," he replied, "that's a long story. There's no point going back over the past. You must look towards the future, that's what you've got to do." I have always believed, however, that China's past is as fascinating as her future and itself offers insight into a remarkable country and people.
>
> 'Marching with Mao' recounts William Lindesay's experiences while retracing the route of the Long March of 1934. His account of the six-thousand-mile journey, from the south to the north of China, provides an intriguing history of the Long March and its impact on modern Chinese society.
>
> China is a huge country with over one billion inhabitants. However, it is a land little understood by those outside it. As this true giant among nations looks ever-

WILD WALL–THE FOUNDATION YEARS

increasingly outwards, so we must endeavour to improve our understanding of China, its history, its people and its future. 'Marching with Mao' is an interesting personal introduction to China and I am delighted to contribute this foreword to it'.

Edward Heath

With the book now completed, for the first time in years I had virtually nothing to do. Qi had a medical check-up, and we were delighted to learn that our baby was going to be a boy. Thinking of him as a little lad, and experiencing withdrawal symptoms from having no writing tasks, I began to think about a Great Wall story for him.

I based it on my own story, but set it within a magical framework. One summer, 'Little' William is taken to Hadrian's Wall by his parents. While they are laying-out a picnic, William and his dog go off to play, and unearth a Roman coin. That evening William thanks Mum and Dad for taking him to 'the greatest wall in the world', but Dad says he didn't, because that is in China—the Great Wall. William looks for it on his globe, finds it, and before going to sleep places his Roman coin under his pillow. That night he dreams of a journey along the Great Wall, and as a token of friendship he offers his coin to an army commander at the gates of the Jiayuguan fortress, who in exchange gives little William a Chinese coin, to serve as his pass during his journey along the Wall. Next morning, William is woken up by his mother to discover it was all a dream, but one that he wants to describe to his parents. He looks for the Roman coin under his pillow, but it's not there. There is only a Chinese coin.

Once it was perfected, I read it for the first time, to Qi and our baby boy. "It's a very good story," said Qi, "but to be a real children's book it needs illustrations."

"Yes, you're right, and we know who could do those, don't we?!"

We were asking Zhang Da to make a rather dramatic shift in style, but he had the talent and only needed the materials, paint and paper. His initial drafts were amazing. Even at this early stage, I was thinking that the book deserved to be published. To increase the appeal, I thought that we should follow the market trends, which at the time meant a pop-up book. I borrowed an example from a friend who had children. Zhang Da looked at it for a few seconds, then smiled and said confidently "I'll have a try." Over the next few months he became a master of paper engineering in producing a series of twelve folding colour plates, each with a few interactive features of doors to open and tabs to rotate. Placed alongside my manuscript, the components of our baby's first book were ready.

After three years of teaching in Xi'an, we were sad to leave the university, the place where we had made our first small and simple, but very happy home. The next stage of our life, back at the Great Wall, was about to begin. Surprisingly though, it came before we even returned to Beijing the following the year. It began soon after arriving in the UK.

48

Introducing Dr William Edgar Geil

Nick had been active on the diplomatic front after Sir Edward Heath had written the foreword. He viewed the publication of the book as an opportunity for furthering cultural relations between the UK and China. To that end he approached the Chinese Embassy in London to solicit their interest in staging a launch event. According to the Secretary for Culture the idea 'would be presented to Ambassador Ma Yuzhen for consideration'.

Our most pressing family concern was to register Qi with our local GP and to book her into hospital for the birth, for the happy event, scheduled for the end of January. To our great relief, our wish was granted, and we were assigned to Arrowe Park Hospital. Part of their antenatal programme was 'future-parent talks and training', with 'expectant fathers' encouraged to attend. I had always thought of babies as mini-people, who needed to be clean, amused, fed and suckled, but the classes presented parenthood as a complicated science and recommended the purchase of all manner of mother and baby 'essentials'. As soon as my cheque from Hodders arrived, Qi and I went shopping in Liverpool. We debated, doubted and delayed most items on the list, apart from two things. An Italian-made stroller, capable of handling 'off road' conditions, because of the state of sidewalks in China, and a beautiful maternity outfit for Qi. The embassy event was confirmed, with Sir Edward Heath agreeing to attend as well. The family group photograph on the day promised to be one destined for the top of the piano for years to come.

The pile of correspondence that had accumulated for me over three years was enormous, filling a large sports holdall with scores of envelopes. Most of it was junk mail, particularly the repeated demands for 'poll tax' for both Qi and I. This hideous scheme dated back to 1990 and was soon abolished in response to mass opposition. Despite my air-mailed protestations to the poll tax office, stating that we had been employed in temporary and part-time capacities before leaving the country, I received the unbelievable reply that we should nevertheless pay the sum demanded, and then claim it back. Absurd, I thought, and easier said than done from the other side of the world! Equally annoying was a statement from the Public Libraries Lending Authority detailing how many book loans I had accrued at a remuneration of one penny for each. They enclosed a pitiful cheque for less than £80, which represented almost 8,000 loans. Oddly, time has made that payment decent and generous. Who would ever have believed that one of the world's wealthiest companies would, without permission or compensation, place my works in a public space on the internet, as Google Books did for several years?

There was but one genuine treasure in the capacious holdall, a packet that had been preceded by a letter, already opened, addressed to me care of Hodder & Stoughton. Dated November 1991, the gist of it read:

> 'Dear Mr. Lindesay, I have just been reading your book, 'Alone on the Great Wall', with much interest and admiration. Perhaps it is too late to be of use, I have in my possession 'The Great Wall of China' by an American, William Edgar Geil, published in 1909 by John Murray. It is an impressive account, about 350 pages long, with more

WILD WALL-THE FOUNDATION YEARS

than 100 photographic illustrations ... I would be glad to give it to you. Sincerely, Marjorie Hessel-Tiltman.

Nick had told me of this marvellous letter and had responded on my behalf, and Mrs. Hessel-Tiltman had kindly sent the book. I'd seen references to it during my superficial research in 1986, and discovered why it was not obtainable from local libraries — its high-price tag. It was not only way out of my price range but, I unwisely consoled myself, unlikely to be of any real use, being almost a century out of date. Now, here it was, *The Great Wall of China*, effectively 'two years in the post'. I had been handed a valuable gift, worth £275 at the time. A dragon motif adorned the front board, the character for Qin was embossed on its spine. At the top of each of its pages were well-translated Chinese proverbs. I can't remember now which impressed me the most, but every time I re-open the book they remain as powerfully attractive as they were when I first encountered them: absolute nuggets of wisdom. I digress, but what truisms they are: 'Soldiers may not be needed for one hundred years, but cannot be dispensed with for a single day' or 'An inch of time is more precious than an inch of gold'.

Speaking of time, I hadn't been back to the Great Wall since the summer of 1992 when Qi and I travelled to Jiayuguan to research a Silk Road guidebook. Our forthcoming move to Beijing would enable frequent visits to the Wall. In anticipation of that return, it was, for the time being at least, therapeutic to delve into Geil's book and enjoy his various viewpoints. I found myself pausing at every one, challenging myself to identify the location of each photograph.

Forget about who was on foot (me), and who rode on horseback much of the way, making forays on foot up to the Wall (him). The panoramas that William Geil was presenting before me in *The Great Wall of China* convincingly documented his travels from Shanhaiguan to Jiayuguan. So, I was not William the Conqueror after all, I was William the Second. Our chosen means of locomotion did not make any difference, in my mind, as to who was the first to complete the journey. He was the first, in 1908. All right, I could argue that by travelling on foot I had seen more of the Wall, because in mountainous areas it is inaccessible by any other means. However, even though I could claim a first transect on foot, I was second overall and, as a consequence my ego was a little deflated. As a competitive athlete, I'd always told myself that 'first is first and second is nowhere'. This latest discovery was hard to accept.

But once I'd accepted the facts, I began to think much more constructively about our parallels. Two Williams fascinated by the Great Wall, Chinese history and culture. Fellow authors detailing our experiences in books on both sides of the Atlantic. We also shared a common starting point, both directed to our explorations of the great monument by maps. I found that the opening lines of his book read: *'There is a Great Wall of China. So much the geographies tell everybody; but they do not make it clear whether it is built of china, or why it is, or long it is, or long it has been'*. Only a Great Wall genius could write anything so pithy and thought-provoking. My respect for this man grew.

Our relationship strengthened still further when I discovered a remarkable coincidence. It began with my scrutiny of his photograph captioned 'East of Mule Horse Pass'. I vaguely recognised the location, but was unable to quite place it. I tried jogging my memory by glancing away and then looking back, but it still eluded me. If I had ever been there, it was already six years ago now. Then I noticed that someone was sitting on the Wall in the foreground, Geil himself. Had I not also photographed myself in almost the identical spot, plus or minus ten metres?

Yes, I had, during the final stage of my journey. At Luowenyu, I had clambered up a steep stretch of Wall in deep snow and, even though the condition of the Wall was not terribly photogenic, took a shot using the self-timer. It turned out to be a one-shot wonder and was chosen from among hundreds for inclusion in my book.

It was almost as if our meeting had been scheduled by William Geil as long ago as 1908, and my going there in 1987 was my acceptance to become acquainted. Our respective publishers had taken the next essential steps. They chose to publish the photographs we'd taken for the same reason: both included the Great Wall and the traveller. I placed the two open books side by side with his photograph and my photograph of the same location adjacent to each other. His photograph told his story. My photograph told my story. The two together told a different story, the Great Wall's story, of changes. There was as much stark juxtaposition as striking similarity. It was a sight to both behold and bemoan, rejoice and regret. Geil was sitting and I was walking, so we met here, and that was fortuitous. But the forces that spoke the loudest and clearest here were the ravages of time. A large watchtower behind him had been reduced to a mound of rubble behind me.

Without maintenance, old buildings eventually collapse, that is inevitable. William Geil's watchtower appeared to have been in near pristine condition in 1908, so what event might have happened in the intervening seventy-nine years to bring it down? I'd asked myself a similar question at Old Dragon's Head years before, as I surveyed the pitiful sight of the monument lying with its head injuries, as broken blocks on the beach. Right there, back then, I had suspected the Japanese, and their dastardly doings could not be ruled out at Luowenyu. Local villagers in search of free and convenient building materials would always be on the list of suspects, especially if their homes were not too far away. It was also unlikely that nature was free of guilt. From time to time it vented its wrath in a sudden rage, with earthquakes being the most destructive weapons of its arsenal. Within days of walking the Luowenyu section, I had lodged at Tangshan. The city is renowned as the epicentre of the Great Tangshan Earthquake of 1976 which measured 7.8 on the Richter Scale.

When offering me the book, Mrs. Hessel-Tiltman had written that her gift was 'perhaps too late to be of use,' but on the contrary I was optimistic about the timeliness of the book's arrival in my hands. One photograph was enough to bring home the fact that the Wall that Geil had seen was greater than the Wall that I had seen. His views preserved an 'out-of-date' Great Wall in print, a record of the condition of the Wall in 1908. At the very least, I thought, Geil's archive would be worthwhile exhibiting in 2008 to show what the Great Wall had looked like a century earlier.

49

Diplomats, Politicians and Journalists

Two days before the Chinese embassy event, Qi and I went down to London to see the printed book and dust jacket for the first time. Exactly as Zhang Da had designed it, the iron-chained Luding Bridge was the full-bleed cover shot, while the back showed a full facial of the Mao statue being cleaned, with his poem *The Long March* beneath. It looked stunning, my best cover yet.

Reading snippets of text, I saw what a superb job the Hodders' specialist-editor David Blomfield had done. I had achieved what I'd set out to do, to tell the Mao Zedong story from the places where it happened. At its core on the route of the Long March I had broken free where and when it really mattered, maintaining my ability as an escapist and exhibiting at least in place the fighting and survivalist spirit of the Marchers themselves. At the start and end of the journey I'd been fortunate enough to meet participants, all of them ordinary people, hearing snippets of the peoples' history, meeting Mao face to face literally at the height of his monumental power, high above Chengdu and then brought down to earth, six feet above, prepared for his afterlife. I'd done my absolute best, travelling, researching and writing. I had no regrets. It was all very worthwhile.

For a second time in my life, I stood in front of the large painting of the Great Wall of China in the function room of the Chinese Embassy, London. Around the sides of the room, Hodders' PR team had placed large images of the book cover, and we had arranged Zhang Da's original ink-pen artwork of chapter-header drawings.

The line-up of speakers and audience had changed completely from almost six years before. At the front now were Ambassador Ma Yuzhen, Sir Edward Heath, Baroness Chalker of Wallasey, Qi and I. In the audience there were family members, the team from Hodders, and embassy staff.

There were no sponsors.

During my planning for Mao Zedong's Long March, I had failed to interest any outdoor equipment brands, despite my best efforts to present it as an epic military odyssey, in the same league as the exploits of Alexander the Great, Hannibal, Genghis Khan, Tamerlane and Napoleon. None of these men had clean swords, but the difference was that their actions were cushioned from living generations by the passing of many centuries. Those disappointing 'It's not for us' replies that I received in response to my Mao's Long March proposal underscored what he was most remembered for — the second half of his life and its resultant human catastrophes. These events were too close for comfort, within living memory, just a few decades before.

Members of the press were not invited. Western media was buzzing with the reviews of another book published for the centenary date, *The Private Life of Chairman Mao* by his personal doctor, Li Zhisui. Our embassy gathering was designed to be a diplomatic event to further cultural understanding on the eve of an important historical occasion. Neither side, the embassy nor I, wanted any embarrassing or politically insensitive headlines to be released by the media.

Ambassador Ma Yuzhen spoke first, saying that he'd read my book with great interest, and commended my 'innovative research approach' of going to 'so many revolutionary places' to see and learn for myself. He also paid tribute to Wu Qi's supporting role of finding 'participants of what are now legendary events'.

"There is much even we Chinese can learn from Mr. Lindesay's book and I would like to extend an invitation to him to come to the embassy to give my staff a report on his 'new' Long March experiences," the Ambassador said.

I'd heard the phrase 'even we Chinese' used more than a few times over the years to acknowledge that it was just possible for a foreigner to amass more knowledge or experience about a Chinese subject than the Chinese themselves. Nevertheless, I did not really expect there to be a follow-up request for a talk.

Sir Edward was given hearty applause and was clearly highly respected by the Chinese. "After meeting Chairman Mao in 1974, I've continued to visit China regularly. I've lost count of how many times I've been there. Each time I've been astounded at the great progress of the great country which has a great past and I believe an even greater future," he said.

Baroness Chalker received an enthusiastic welcome from the many Wallaseyans in the audience, telling a little about the town, a tale that emphasised that a journey of a thousand miles begins with a single step. It was a nostalgic reminder of my hometown beginnings and the importance of family support and encouragement.

Hodders had kindly provided books for everyone. These were much appreciated by the younger members of the Lindesay family, who, on seeing a queue lining up for me to sign, decided to ask in turn the Ambassador, Sir Edward and then Baroness Chalker to sign as well, much to the amusement of everyone present. Those copies have become the most treasured examples of *Marching with Mao*.

Margaret asked "What's next, William?" I replied that the

baby boy was our priority, and then told her about the children's book I'd written.

"If you have any aim to publish it, one of my best friends is Gina Pollinger. She's the leading literary agent in town for children's books," said Margaret.

I hadn't had much success with literary agents before. One big-name agency, Curtis Brown, had contacted me after the good PR coverage on *Alone of the Great Wall*, so I went down to London to talk about my future writing plans, specifically *Marching*, which was then in its early stages. But in the end, they rejected me. I was disillusioned by their attempt to fit me into their winning-formula mould, a square peg, in their round, formatted, successful author hole, telling me that the book should be like this and avoid being like that. But since Qi and I were in London anyway, we had nothing to lose by taking up Margaret's offer to see what Gina Pollinger thought about the pop-up book.

Gina loved Qi, our story, and the idea of giving our baby boy a Great Wall story to listen to. She had a soft spot for China, and Chinese design, and was just as I imagined a promoter of children's books to be: bright, energetic, super enthusiastic, radiant and charged with positive youthful energy. She was astounded at the colour of Zhang Da's artwork and enthralled by *The Dream of the Great Wall* storyline.

"I only deal with the top children's publishers in London and New York. Give me six weeks to present this to them and good luck with the baby!" said Gina.

Considering the prejudices that I was facing with *Marching with Mao*, the media coverage and book reviews I received were quite reasonable. I was given whole page space for excerpts in the *Singapore Straits Times* and *De Volkskrant* (Netherlands), and eventually a five-page feature fronted by a stunning 'route of badges' map in Hong Kong's *Sunday South China Morning*

WILD WALL–THE FOUNDATION YEARS

Post colour magazine. My approach to the Long March was, according to *New Statesman & Society*, ' ... in the great tradition of British travel writing ... a delight to read and highly informative on village China'. In the *Western Morning News* I was described as 'an eccentric genius without whom the world would be a duller place'.

In addition to a few more reviews that were eminently forgettable, one unforgivable review is worth mentioning, headed 'Marching Orders' which included four travel books. 'If you want long, then Map's Long March (sic) probably beats the lot and William Lindesay retraces it in his *Marching with Map* (sic). This is an oddity', wrote Nicholas Lezard in *The Sunday Times*, December 19th, 1993. There I was, having spent all my life telling people how to spell my surname correctly, and here was a 'reviewer' who actually spelt my name right, but got Mao's name wrong, and so got the book title wrong! This was an unprecedented comedy of errors! Was this 'writer' a careless intern, or what? Whether it was the Anglocentric spellchecker that was to blame, the adjacency of the 'o' and 'p' keys on qwerty, sloppy proofreading, a few too many pints on Saturday night, or the writer's fatigue covering four journeys at once, I never found out, and I didn't receive an apology. I note as I write that Mr. Lezard's error did nothing to jeopardise his career reviewing books: in 2019 he published his recollections in *It Gets Worse* — of all appropriate titles! But for me it didn't get much worse than Lezard's attempted review.

The difference, they say, between a good haircut and a bad one is ten days. I hadn't so much as opened *Marching with Mao* since 1994 until I came to incorporate the story in these recollections. A quarter of a century had elapsed. Veterans of the Long March had passed away. Ordinary China, poor and backward that it was, has become relatively well off and advanced. The book has become more of an historical document with the passage of time. It was a detour away from the Wall that was well worth taking.

50

Wonderful Rice

Qi gave birth in her dream hospital, Arrowe Park. Baby Lindesay, a bouncing boy and a healthy weight, was born without complications on January 22nd 1994 after a normal labour. Qi had been working on another baby project in the final weeks of her pregnancy, a needlepoint tapestry to mark the occasion, and now the only missing information was his name. I had named hundreds of students before as a teacher, but never my own flesh and blood. Qi became increasingly frustrated with some of the names I had shortlisted. As soon as she heard them, she translated them phonetically, to see how they sounded in Chinese and thought about which characters would be most suited. A good name had to sound right, write well, and have an auspicious meaning. We decided on James for his first name; it was traditionally a popular Lindesay name, and we'd shorten it to Jimmy, which translated well into Chinese characters as *jie mi* or 'Wonderful Rice'. For his middle name I chose Alistair to reflect the Lindesay's Scottish roots.

After being discharged from hospital, we broke our first old wives' rule. On a blustery day we took Jimmy out in his stroller along the Wallasey promenade from where we could see ships leaving Liverpool to cross the Irish Sea. Slowly, like explorers getting to know a foreign land called parenthood, Qi and I worked out Jimmy's feeding, sleeping and bathing habits.

WILLIAM LINDESAY

Meanwhile, I did receive a letter of invitation to deliver a report on my 'New Long March' to members of staff at the Chinese Embassy. I hadn't really expected them to follow this up, but was interested and honoured to make a presentation. I scheduled the visit close to another London appointment, also at the Chinese Embassy, to mark the publication of Han Suyin's book *Eldest Son*, her biography of Zhou Enlai.

Nick accompanied me to the Embassy's Cultural Section, a large mansion house on the edge of Hampstead Heath — a familiar cross-country racing venue of times past. The talk was hosted by Major Kong, a young suited man with a confident presence, disciplined stature and excellent English. He presented his name card to me: 'Kong Jining, Assistant to the Defence Attaché'. The small audience of about twenty officials was highly attentive, and a cordial and respectful atmosphere prevailed throughout my presentation. At the conclusion, there was genuine applause and comments of 'a commendable achievement' and the honourable epithet '*zhongguo tong*', old China Hand.

We had earned our Embassy lunch! Nick was very hungry, and quite unfamiliar with the rollout of a large Chinese lunch. He made the mistake of thinking that the table set with the cold dishes at the start was the whole deal, and he ate far too much, and too ambitiously. Seating as always reflected rank and importance, with Nick and I sitting beside Major Kong. During one conversation, I was distracted by a strange crunching sound. A glance to my left revealed Nick, grimacing and distressed. He was chewing, and trying to swallow, half a preserved egg, the shell included. Nick's complexion had turned green, the colour of the eggs. I picked up my beer glass and called out '*ganbei*', cheers, to encourage him to wash it down! Thankfully he didn't choke.

The following evening I attended Dr. Han Suyin's book launch at the embassy, meeting Ambassador Ma Yuzhen and Major Kong and other officials again. It was my third meeting with the elegant, eloquent and brilliantly-minded Han Suyin, whom I loved, admired and respected immensely for her simplicity, friendship, humanity and diplomacy. We exchanged books, Mao for Zhou, took photographs together and chatted. Putting her arm on my shoulder she whispered, "Dearest William, we have an important and difficult job to do. We must help China explain herself to the world, help the world understand China, and help China understand the world. Only people like us can do this. You're still young. You must continue to do this work ...."

I mentioned delivering my 'Long March report' the day before. "Major Kong told me about that, they were genuinely impressed. That's not easy," she said. "It's exactly what I'm talking about. You know that he's the grandson of Chairman Mao, don't you?"

I didn't. Apparently, the Major's mother was Lin Min (b. 1936), a daughter of Mao Zedong from his marriage to He Zichen, who was forced to go to Moscow when Jiang Qing appeared on the scene at the end of the Long March.

Before leaving London, I telephoned Gina Pollinger, hopeful of hearing favourable news from a publisher.

"William," she strained, "I'm afraid it's not very good news. I don't think it's quite good enough for my very demanding clients. I'll give you a more considered report in a letter."

I was disappointed, but not enormously so because it hadn't been conceived as a book for publication, it was done for fun, and it would be fun in a few years' time to read to little Jimmy.

Gina kept her word, and I did receive a letter from her with the plates returned. To be kind, she tried to explain why none of the six publishers she'd approached didn't snap it up, and that was simply because 'the market's so competitive that any book must promise dazzling fulfilment'. She then went on to assess the story and the art. 'The subject's terrific, the story needs attention, in the main, to be pared down to a max of two or three sentences per double-page spread, the language must be graphic, elegant and spare; the artwork is, at its best, splendid, but it is erratic in scale, use of colour and execution, things which put the fear of God into publishers, more especially when the artist is overseas and difficult to deal with on a one-to-one basis. If you are interested in bearing these points in mind to produce a new dummy, I would gladly take it to the Bologna Children's Book Fair in April'.

Qi and I were too busy with little Jimmy, and preparing to go back to China, so we were not able to pursue Gina's offer at the time. We had so much baby stuff to carry back that we left the artwork and manuscript in Wallasey, and completely forgot about the project for years — until 2015.

Our arrival in Beijing in March 1994 was to herald the dawn of a new era in my fascination for the Great Wall. From then on there would be no more detours away from the monument that had lured me to China in the first place. I was returning to China for the Wall, more of the Wall, and soon after, for nothing but the Wall.

ACKNOWLEDGEMENTS

MOST OF THE people I have mentioned in this book helped me in one way or another, from lesser degrees to greater ways or immeasurable extents. To those of you who are still living, please consider the inclusion a heartfelt expression of my thanks for the part you have played in my Great Wall life story. To those departed, I will never forget what you taught me. Your lessons certainly helped me set worthwhile goals and guided me towards achieving them. I am also thankful to those persons who have tried to hinder me. They served as barriers along the way that I was determined to overcome. I could leave my acknowledgements there, full stop, but I feel it is only right to select a few individuals from certain stages of my story who remain deserving of mention in name again.

First my mother and father, brothers David and Nicholas and sister Dorothy Jane, for a happy childhood of enduring love and support. I cannot express enough thanks to Nicholas, my most loyal supporter and guiding mentor, for the idea at Hadrian's Wall, your advice to me in China, and for your PR and diplomatic work in the UK. To David, thanks for never letting me win and showing me what real training is like. To my inspirational teacher, 'Maccie', at St. Aidan's in Wallasey, thanks for imparting a lifelong fascination for geography and history in me, and for making learning so interesting at my most formative age. To my sponsors at Thomas Cook, Neil Pirie, and Lance Browne of the Midland Bank office in Beijing, and his helpful local staff, especially Stephanie and Jennifer, thank you for your funding, immense patience and friendship. To my generous equipment sponsors, Asics Tiger and Mountain Equipment, thanks for the Gel cushioning and Ultrafleece warmth. To my editors at Hodder & Stoughton in London, Margaret Body and David Blomley thanks for their work on *Alone* and *Marching*.

The reason for the Great Wall evolving from a long journey to a life in China is my wife. To highlight her love, friendship, support and selflessness, I have titled a chapter 'Beautiful Jade', the translation of her given name. Traversing 4,000 km across China in finding and following the lines of the Great Wall and Long March, I drank the water, ate the rice and slept in the homes of many incredibly kind strangers, who refused to accept anything in return from me. They are also beauties of China.

On the flip side, I will never underestimate the inspiration that Sir Chris Brasher and David Griffiths kindly provided before I went to China and before I got to the Wall. Along the eventual way, the police frequently intercepted me for trespass in closed areas. They were my essential foils. I took every escape chance that I was given, making a way over walls, through the night and under the veil of a sandstorm.

I wrote this book fast and furiously during the grim days of the Covid-19 pandemic in 2020. I then sent it chapter by chapter to the diligent Dr. Raynor Shaw in Cumbria for his initial round of editing to ready it for presentation to a publisher. The manuscript found its way to Earnshaw Books. I have had good editors before, but this is the first time I've had an editor who has spent more time in China than me (34 years at the time of writing this page in December 2021), and who knows more about China than me. Sincere thanks to Graham Earnshaw, publisher and editor, for his personal work on my manuscript which he has turned into this reader-friendly version for presentation to you.

WILD WALL–THE FOUNDATION YEARS

I hope that you are ready for the rest of my story, to date, published as *Wild Wall–The Jiankou Years*.

About The Author

William Lindesay OBE is a British geographer, a research fellow at his alma mater, Liverpool University, and a recipient of The Special Award of the Royal Society for Asian Affairs. After a milestone journey of 2,500 km on foot along the Great Wall in 1987, Lindesay returned to China in 1990 to retrace sections of the Long March. Since 2000, he has dedicated himself to the Great Wall in a myriad ways. He lives beside a section of Wild Wall at Jiankou, and has published six books on the subject, including *Alone on the Great Wall*, *The Great Wall Explained* and *The Great Wall in 50 Objects*. Lindesay received the Friendship Award of China in 1998, was made an Officer, Order of the British Empire by HM Queen Elizabeth II in 2006, and was awarded the Great Wall Friendship Medal of Beijing in 2008. Recently he has been named as a luminary member of 'The Explorers Club 50, Class of 2022'. William Lindesay is married to Wu Qi, and they have two children, James and Thomas.